14.50

Personal Development

Personal Development

Theory and Practice in Management Training

Bert Juch
Shell International

JOHN WILEY & SONS

Chichester · New York · Brisbane · Toronto · Singapore

Library of Congress Cataloging in Publication Data:
Juch, Bert.
   Personal development: theory and practice in management
training.
   Includes index.
   1. Learning, Psychology of.   I. Title.
BF318.J83   153.1′5   82-7062
                         AACR2
ISBN 0 471 10458 2

British Library Cataloguing in Publication Data:
Juch, Bert
   Personal development.
   1. Learning, Psychology of   1. Management.
   I. Title
   153.1′5   BF318

   ISBN 0 471 10458 2

Phototypeset by Dobbie Typesetting Service, Plymouth.
Printed at The Pitman Press, Bath.

Acknowledgements

To HESTER   who made it all possible
                with more than a smile,
                who shared the agonizing process
                of shaping thoughts into proper form,

to HAN   who challenged and helped
                to found my praxis,

to GEOFFREY   who guided
                whilst giving free rein,

to GEORGE   who taught me this level of language
                most conveniently,

to BOB   who provided a firm base
                at the right moment,

to ALL   who encouraged me to persevere.

Contents

PART III THE INTERLUDE

x

Introduction

After twenty-five years of varied assignments in a number of countries, I have taken the opportunity and time to sit back, reflect, re-think, and digest the accumulated experience in a comprehensive manner. I had started as an engineer and petroleum-production specialist in a multinational company. Through computer work I had become a systems analyst and later a management trainer and organization consultant.

Having joined the education profession somewhat later in life as a second career, I had to build my knowledge and experience mainly on the job through a number of courses and constant reference to the latest publications on organization and management. Whilst overseas there are, however, fewer opportunities for in-depth discussions and rubbing shoulders with professional colleagues.

Responsibility for the training and development of people in developing countries confronted me with the moral and professional questions: Do I really know what I am doing? Can I accept responsibility for accelerating their development and for the changes in their views and culture? How well-grounded are my ideas and how well-founded is my praxis? What principles should be observed? Can one think of better and more indigenous methods of preparing adult persons in such countries for management positions?

These issues made me decide to take a sabbatical for two years at a university to broaden my insight with the latest state of the art in the fields of education and culture. I wanted critical tutors and peers to refresh my thinking and be instrumental in reassessing the level and process of my own development. This book is an account of what actually emerged from a fundamental review of my experience combined with studies on human development. Its purpose is fourfold:

First. As an internal consultant I had become increasingly concerned about the gap between industry and university. Managers are too busy to take note of, to reflect on, or to apply the findings of science; an unabating stream of problems demand their continuous attention; what counts are the tangible achievements; getting-things-done produces the satisfaction. At the university I became fully aware that the primary purpose of scientists is understanding;

curiosity drives them; their loyalty is often more to their particular (world-wide) profession than to the local academic organization or to the education of the students.

It is unfortunate that these worlds of industry and university are so far apart. Their languages, opinions and values can become mutually incomprehensible. One needs to be broad-minded in order to appreciate both groups and be exceptionally good to be held in high esteem with influence in both environments.

Initially, I was ambiguous about my loyalty; as a doer, I cannot abstain long from being busy in a practical way, but I also wanted to clarify the above-mentioned issues and follow my curiosity. I have always wished to try out things *and* to understand what makes people tick. This sabbatical period would require me to deal personally with the dialectic tension between theory and practice. It would provide ample opportunity for cross-fertilization and for bridging the gap between science and management. This book is written with the specific purpose of reconciling 'grounded theory and founded practice' in personal development.

Second. The many 'respectable' schools of thought on human development have to be taken seriously. However, authors do not always relate their ideas about learning to those of others; some are rather one-sided and a few are even in outright conflict and/or ignored.

I do acknowledge the usefulness of differentiation in life, and that progress is often one-sided and takes place in spurts. (Brakel: as alternating leg movements in skating). I very much felt the need for a more comprehensive theory that emanates from a sense-making integration, for a theory on diversity that helps the educator to choose an effective approach in all sorts of situations for many kinds of people and (sub)cultures.

I found that professional and personal development could best be understood and striven for with the help of a cyclic process model and three levels of awareness of learning. The learning and development models presented in this book were derived and founded on experience through the participation of a few hundred managers, supervisors and staff of different cultures and educational levels in the Netherlands, in the UK and in the Sultanate of Oman. The two process models cover a wide variety of operational practices and span a wide range of cognitive abstraction.

The models are also grounded theoretically, they show that many theories and practices can indeed be integrated, much more so than the propounding authors and practitioners themselves have been suggesting. The models relate the psychology of learning cross-functionally with the biological aspects of the brain and the social and philosophical aspects of human development.

Third. In my training function I started to question the appropriateness of our methods of education and teaching. The front-loaded education imposed on the new generation grows heavier every year, yet it does not appear to prepare the students adequately for the jobs that are becoming available, or to enable them to cope on their own with the many imminent changes. An ever-increasing number of adults have to be retrained owing to obsolescence of jobs and need regular updating of their knowledge and skills. *'Education-permanente'* is quickly becoming the rule rather than the exception.

The principal features of the Personal Development models presented in this book, learning-to-learn and self-managed development, may greatly help to satisfy this increasing demand and improve the effectiveness of methods and resources. If the educational institutes would invest more time and effort in teaching our youngsters *how to learn on their own*, students and school-leavers would be able to cope (better) with changes in work, family, and society throughout their adult lives. If many people acquired the skills of organizing their own *'education-permanente'*, there would be less psychosomatic stress and more people would manage their own careers successfully.

This is true particularly for managers, who must of increasing necessity be competent in coping with new developments. They have to interact with many individuals and groups of people in a turbulent environment of unpredicted changes. In addition to knowing specific techniques they must acquire the ability to deal realistically with novel situations all the time. Managers for whom learning and development is a way of life will cope best.

Fourth. Last but not least, the principles of learning-to-learn and self-managed development are of immense importance in developing nations. Young adults are impatient and wish to catch up quickly. Imitation, emulation, and import of technology from the West is not the only, nor the best, way. They have to learn to manage their own situation in the appropriate way, that is: formulating realistic objectives and setting priorities of development based on the preferences, strengths, and sociocultural circumstances of themselves and of their own country. This should not take a generation. Is it possible to accelerate the learning process in a responsible way?

The structure of the book follows a natural, mainly chronological line. It starts straight away with my original 'learning-to-learn' experiments (Chapters 1 and 2), which lead to the design of a cyclic learning model (Chapters 3 and 4). After taking time to explore some theories on human development, I try to reconcile them with my experience (Chapters 5–9). I was fortunate that I could apply these fresh insights to a new training assignment (Chapters 10 and 11). The book ends (Chapter 12) with a few thoughts arising from this new experience.

I hope that many of the logically inclined (left-brain) readers will note that the book itself exemplifies the model: the chapters follow closely the stages of the cyclic learning process: Doing—Sensing—Thinking—Planning—followed by a second round of the model: Application—Evaluation—Rethinking—New ideas—etc. It will be just as pleasurable, though somewhat unusual, to appreciate the book's content with one's artistic (right) brain, for instance as pieces of music. I hope that the light touch of my (musical!) tutor at Bath University comes through the titles of the Parts I–V.

My intention is, for once, to practise what I preach: composing this book in congruence with the principles and practices it advocates. But whether the chapters constitute *Stages of Learning* on successively higher *Levels of Awareness* leading to *Personal Development*, and whether the views and practices are complementary, holistic, interactive, liberating, and challenging, that I must leave to the judgement of the reader.

PART I

The Prelude

This prelude serves to acquaint the reader with the original basic experiments carried out in my practice of trainer/consultant from which the subjects and issues of this book emerged. It tries to picture the reality of the learning situations and the actual experiences of facilitator *and* learners. These form the practical background on which the conceptual considerations of Parts II and III are based.

Chapter 1 gives an account of my experience with trying to foster the principle of 'learning-to-learn' in managers, supervisors, and specialists through encouraging them to develop themselves more consciously; the focus is mainly on the learning *process*. Chapter 2 describes why I was interested in, but gradually less happy with, an early and simple *model* that I was using for this 'learning-to-learn' purpose. Through experimental adaptations its usefulness continued to grow in meaning and significance. This led me to review the fundamental learning process in order to combine this insight with practical experience, resulting in a new comprehensive model for personal development.

1

Experiments with the Learning *Process*

From the popular saying that it is better to teach people 'how to fish' than to give them food repeatedly, it would follow that it is also better to teach people 'how to learn' than to continue to run courses for practically everything. Indeed, it seems a sound principle that a consultant/trainer/facilitator should be rather reluctant to operate in the pure instructional mode, teaching the dos and don'ts. He should rather help people to learn for themselves how to develop their talents and use their skills. However, this may not be easy, for example when 'learning to fish' is not appreciated by the persons concerned. Quite often people prefer donations, or straightforward instruction.

This chapter summarizes my early experience with applying the 'learning-to-learn' principle in the training of managers and supervisors. I first define what it means and argue why its importance is increasing (Section 1.1). Secondly, I describe some ways and means of building this principle into various learning situations (Sections 1.2, 1.3, and 1.4), and more specifically how to use a learning model as a self-reflective, diagnostic tool (Section 1.5). This is followed by a free-style account of how managers and engineers are reacting to ideas of accepting responsibility for their own learning and development (Sections 1.6, 1.7, and 1.8).

1.1 'Learning-to-learn' is fundamental

The term 'learning-to-learn' (LTL) is a fashionable catchphrase nowadays, an overused slogan in many articles on education and adult training. Its meaning suffers from inflation while the real social *need* for LTL has become more pressing during recent years, not least for managers.

Rapid developments in technology and constraints in resources are shaking the established patterns of jobs and careers. Societies are growing more complex through the information explosion and international dependencies. For years to come the industrialized countries will be faced with high levels of unemployment *and* unfillable demands for the 'latest' skills. Developing countries are realizing, often the hard way, that modern technology and products can be imported relatively quickly but that acquiring the human skills to operate, maintain, and develop them locally is a long-term process. Learning remains the bottleneck everywhere.

3

How are we to educate and prepare the young and the adult, not for yester-year's and tomorrow's situation but for the turbulent future? Is it at all possible to define abilities and skills.that are likely to be required say ten to twenty years ahead? No assets are more valuable than developed human assets. Yet little more than lipservice is paid to the principle of LTL. Few people really know what it means. Even in management-development programmes it is seldom included as a subject in its own right. *Un*consciously, yes, people are (slowly) learning how to learn; in that sense animals can learn to learn. But LTL means (in the sense of this book) the *conscious* ability of a human being to *continue* to learn by *himself* in many situations. The criteria are: self-awareness, initiative, self-direction, and self-control.

LTL has been defined and illustrated by various writers. Watzlawick *et al.* (1974) emphasize the need to break out to the next higher (meta-) level of abstraction; Argyris (1977) names it 'double-loop learning'; and Bateson (1978) 'deutero learning'. Freire and Negt (1975) have worked hard to prove that LTL is a fundamental, useful principle for community programmes in developing countries. However, the 'freedom to learn' (Rogers, 1969), that is an equal opportunity for all peoples of all races and both sexes, is still a long, long way off.

LTL does *not* result automatically from greater efforts in education and training, nor from reschooling, sabbaticals, or open universities. LTL is *not* the same as personality education, it is not teaching people how to remedy particular weaknesses. Even 'human resource development', to mention another fashionable phrase, can be counter to LTL when it is 'outer-directed', that is, done by others and by organizations *to* someone. The person himself should be in the driver's seat, he has to determine the purpose and manage the resources. In short: LTL is development of Self by Self (Juch, 1979:38).

1.2   No facilitator can be neutral

(F stands for facilitator in the terms of Rogers (1969): it loosely encompasses all types of educators, tutors, teachers, trainers, consultants, etc.; and L stands for learner, pupil, student, course participant, client, etc.) Applying the LTL principle raises a few issues for the F. First the ethical question: has any F the right and/or duty to induce development-of-self in the L? Secondly, the professional issue: should all Fs be able to build it into their educational practice? It surely requires energy, skill, psychological health, and maturity.

A fact is that any F always conveys, willy-nilly, some of his values. He shows *un*consciously his basic assumptions about learning. His attitude permeates his consultancy and training activities in a great number of explicit and/or subtle implicit ways, unless he acts as a robot or tries to deceive. Even then, his selection of method and process is based on how he sees his clients/ students as human beings. The F's non-verbal behaviour in dealing with his position, power, motivation, approval, and the way in which he handles questions, procedures, objections, etc., are often more 'informative' about his values in life than his espoused opinions. Even if he tries to remain neutral, that is a message in itself.

Boot and Boxer propound that even the technology of education is never neutral: 'We have frequently been struck by the fact that different trainers can use an identical technique and claim to be involved in the same process and yet seem to provide quite different experiences for the learner' (1980:232). Both the design of the programme and its execution have their origin in ideological standpoints. They quote (1980:232) Cooper and Levine: 'It is terribly important for trainers to be aware that their behaviour reflects, communicates and in many cases models certain values which can influence immediate learning and subsequent behaviour of participants'. F's ideology is of prime importance, his influence on the learning of his pupils is incalculable.

One can imagine how confusing and irritating it is to Ls when F behaves differently from what he preaches and if the message *content* is not congruent with the *process* or technology that he is using. It is my experience that Ls despise any *in*authentic behaviour of F. Learning is then minimal. This means that it is always important that F's words and actions are consistent with his values, that his development principles and his interactions with L are authentic.

1.3 Building in 'learning-to-learn'

Of course, there are consulting situations and courses with very technical or rigidly defined learning tasks (say in economics, engineering, drilling, banking, electronics, computer programming, etc.). In these cases it may be considered inappropriate to talk about the learning process itself. Sometimes the clients/participants object when F deviates from straightforward instruction and starts to raise 'psychological' issues. Indeed, there are teaching situations that would become counter-productive if an 'enlightened' F were reluctant to be directive. What to do in those cases?

I consider it important that my approach should be clear and agreed at the beginning of any working relationship. Establishing a contact means exchanging and agreeing on expectations and objectives (a more or less explicit 'contract'). As a minimum, F should check *from the start* whether L knows/agrees with the objectives and whether he is prepared to review at a later date how effective the work relationship has been.

In specific terms: I cannot imagine any situation where it is not legitimate and appropriate to clarify in some way that I:

(i) feel responsible for the content *and* for the process;
(ii) intend to monitor and evaluate at certain times 'how it is going';
(iii) hope the L accepts some responsibility as well;
(iv) appreciate his (their) comment on what he/they got out of the activity and invite suggestions to improve its effectiveness (next time).

It is my experience that this is completely acceptable even in the most hard-nosed situations. When at an appropriate moment F says something about the process and suggests how L could become more competent and confident, it always appears natural that L should give his views as well. In roughly 80 per cent of such 'technical' cases the discussion about learning principles was very much appreciated, 25 per cent of which led to further exploration of ways and means of improving their learning capabilities.

In conclusion, I acknowledge the rights of clients, students/participants to limit the purpose of the relationship to specific information/assistance on a particular subject. At the same time I consider it equally legitimate and advisable for the F to offer more: jointly raising the awareness of and improving the process of learning. F's satisfaction lies in the scope for advancing self-development, in creating 'eye-openers' for initially uninterested clients/students.

1.4 Explicit encouragement of self-development

Improving the learning style/ability of the learner should be made an explicit objective in many educational and training situations (in schools, universities, courses, etc.). But it is relatively seldom specifically acknowledged to be the main task of F to assist L in increasing his competence in learning itself. In the early 1970s I could not find much guidance in the literature for actual application of the LTL principle *throughout* courses. In fact, I was experimenting with the process *un*consciously until an American consultant gave me Rogers' *Freedom to learn* (1969) and *Encounter Groups* (1970).

My experience is that misunderstanding or uneasiness with objectives and methods remain suppressed for too long, until they are actually blocking the learning. Then I try *not* to limit consultancy or training to the 'problem' or subject matter itself but to introduce explicit *process objectives* right from the start. Gradually I found quite a number of ways to work jointly on the learning process at a much earlier stage in the working relationship. But I continued to struggle with finding natural interventions and with how much time to allocate to LTL.

The following is drawn from experience with some thirty groups of managers and supervisors. Participants were of mixed nationality: about a third of each of Arabians, Dutch, and English. They were not (particularly) familiar with principles of human behaviour or self-development. I was pleasantly surprised that it seemed quite natural and relatively easy for the participants of all three nationalities to advance to a fairly high level of accepting joint responsibility for the process of the course, perhaps less so for their own learning (see below and Section 12.2).

The first experiment with content and process objectives was too ambitious. Being open and honest about the rights and duties of course participants can be somewhat frightening. Appendix 1 is an example of such an experiment. It was sent out together with the programme, list of participants, etc., in the usual way (not to be called joining *instructions*, please!) to the participants' superiors with a suggestion that they should discuss them with the prospective participant(s). In general, bosses find this too difficult to do well. And pressure of time and work is always a ready excuse for no meaningful discussion to take place between boss and subordinate.

Much more successful were the activities designed to build up the joint responsibility for the process of learning *during* the courses. The *first* day included some or all of the following activities:

(1) Each participant's expectation of the course was elicited, if not voiced spontaneously, during the round of personal introduction. To be noted on a flip chart in L's *own* words, whatever these may be (for example the 'neutral': 'Don't know, I was sent by my boss').

(2) F presented some dilemmas: the likely difference in needs and appreciation of methods in such a diverse group of personalities; the choices that had to be made from the available resources; when to cut off discussions, etc. I usually say that I prefer not to make all these decisions by myself, because of the very personal nature of relevance and effectiveness for the participants.

(3) After (1) and (2), participants were normally more forthcoming and had more thoughts and ideas for an open discussion on the process objectives (see Appendix 1), which could be amended and prioritized in line with their wishes and opinions.

(4) Depending on the evolving 'climate', *un*published objectives, for example better appreciation of other cultures could also be discussed.

The following activities were included at appropriate times during the *week*. :

(5) A learning-style-inventory test and discussion of a four-stage cyclic learning model. As this became one of the most prominent experimental parts of the programme, it will be described in detail in Section 1.5.

(6) Visiting speakers (say on safety, industrial relations, finance, etc.) provided rich opportunities for learning how to use human resources and how to arrange joint responsibility with the speakers for content *and* process. Also very successful were *Panel* discussions with *management* (the ideas behind such panel discussions are specified in Appendix 2). These sessions can constitute intensive experiential learning, not least for the speaker and managers, in particular for those who are not accustomed to *sharing* responsibility for the usefulness of such encounters!

(7) 'How realistic is this training course?' This question came up most of the time and therefore it had better be utilized as an explicit topic. It usually leads to the recognition that a course can be made real enough, for instance with respect to communication, interpersonal relations, contributing to group discussions, formulating proposals, challenging others, daring to say that one is lost or does not understand, etc.

(8) Every day one participant presided over a short evaluation session, leading up to a preview and adaptation of the next day's programme. These sessions helped them to assume responsibility for integrating personal learning in the constraints of a group.

(9) Participants were encouraged to keep a *personal diary* of 'points I learned' as a practical application of the notion that 'learning is the awareness of the personal meaning of experiences'. This turned out to be one of the self-directed learning activities that seemed hard for the participants to do (to be discussed in Section 12.2).

The design, organization, and guidance of the above events are not particularly difficult in themselves. However, these types of activities may not be so flattering for the ego of the trainer/facilitator since they are often not so smoothly under control or polished as some trainers and participants would like them. It is unfortunate that training events are judged too often on how slick F's performance is and not on the amount of learning that has been generated.

Before discussing in more detail the reactions of managers and supervisors to the challenge of accepting responsibility for their own learning style and personal development, let me testify that the nine activities listed above with these mixed multinational groups are equally effective with respect to raising awareness, questioning attitudes, building cross-cultural relations, and practising co-operative behaviour.

1.5 Reflective diagnosis of one's learning style

The most direct method of raising L's awareness about his strengths and preferences in learning was applying Kolb's 'Learning-Style-Inventory' test and discussing the underlying principles. Compared with the many other models and instruments that I have tried out over the years, this subject earned high evaluation marks: 'useful', 'enjoyed it', 'learned from it', etc. The exercise is easy, short, self-scoring, and has a pictorial presentation (see Figure 1) which is much appreciated by technically oriented persons. The test is objective in that it does not give a value judgement about a person's style or about his levels of skill or knowledge. There is thus no reason at all for participants to deceive themselves by trying to produce a socially acceptable picture, as with some other instruments, for example those on motivation or leadership style.

If the reader is curious about his own learning style, I suggest that he fills out Kolb's simple questionnaire now, which is Appendix 3. The test is self-explanatory and takes only a few minutes. To find out how your scores fit in with those of others a pictorial presentation can be drawn by transferring your scores into Figure 1. This profile may be readily recognized by you, or it may be a surprise, but it is very likely that you will want to know more about its meaning. The kite-type diagram (as in Figure 1) is generally seen as indicating disposition and abilities, though sometimes perceived as a direct, comparable measure of strengths and weaknesses. I noted that a skewed profile is often more meaningful to the 'owner' than a balanced one.

This learning-style-inventory test can be applied individually and in courses to different degrees of intensity:

(i) a quick exercise to make L think about factors in learning;
(ii) inducing L to reflect on what his individual style means for the course, his job, and his private life;
(iii) diagnosing personal strengths, weaknesses, and barriers;
(iv) creating motivation and ideas for self-development;
(v) individual counselling by F.

In courses, I usually stress dutifully the confidentiality of such tests, but in the majority of cases pressure was exerted on me *not* to leave the exercise as a completely individual and private matter. Quite a number of people liked to talk about what they had just 'found out about themselves'; they wanted to verbalize evidence or reason, seek confirmation, or share their learning profile with others and get at least some comment from the facilitator.

In fact, I was often struck by the many non-verbal signs of recognition and by the students' keenness to get more insight into the meaning of their profiles. This is an indication that 'reflection-on-self' is indeed, as Boot and Boxer suggest (1980: 231–51), a rather neglected mode of learning in the life of many

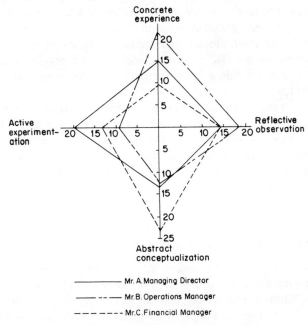

Figure 1   Some actual learning style profiles

managers, supervisors, and engineers. In order to stimulate these reflective thoughts further and to encourage the sharing of their meaning with others, I often proceed with observations and questions of the type shown in Appendix 4 (the reader may apply these to his own profile).

If not arising naturally during discussions, the *dynamics* of a person's profile can easily be brought in more systematically by doing the style-inventory test twice, the first time by ranking one's *present* strengths and abilities and the second time by marking those activities from which one *learns* most. The beauty of the cyclic process is that it shows the multitude of opportunities that the individual gets throughout his lifetime, by trying things out, creating all sorts of new experiences for himself. It conveys the notion that learning patterns are *not* fixed forever, that Man is never too old to become wiser or to appreciate other things than hitherto.

Initially, I tried to avoid becoming too deeply involved in discussing internal personality factors with individuals. But the need to advance LTL by explaining the whys and hows of the learning profiles of students captured my curiosity. It forced me to adapt and extend the model by introducing the global concept of Inner Self and its psychological projections in the form of mental barriers. This is described fully in Chapters 2 and 3.

Let me relate first a few other reactions of managers and supervisors to the challenge of accepting responsibility for their own development. These can roughly be divided into the following categories:

(1) Those who see no need for any (further) learning or development. When there is little latent energy or motivation to latch on to, I seem to have little zest for energizing such uphill struggles.
(2) People who continuously and habitually blame others; the 'I-am-OK' and 'they-are-not-OK' attitude. Since this is a relatively large group (I had to explore this a little further, with some success (see the next section).
(3) People caught in the perennial 'nature-nurture' argument. The comments I heard from many managers/supervisors often challenged me to help them break out of this trap (see Sections 1.7 and 1.8).
(4) Persons who are in real difficulties. This requires the art of gracefully drawing the line when the discussion threatens to become too confidential or too intimate. It may call for private therapeutic counselling (by a specialist).

1.6 External forces. Scapegoat or opportunity?

As might be expected, reflections on personal learning styles frequently trigger second thoughts about the (mis)match between one's present job/situation in life and one's innate abilities or personal ambitions. When it comes to serious discussions it is rather striking that so many managers and supervisors have frustrated aspirations and that environmental situations and social constraints figure so prominently in their thinking. They 'blame' mostly: (a) a dominating boss—he seems to be the single most important source of stress in work situations (confirmed by Cooper in Beck and Cox (eds), 1980: 9–20); (b) lack of prospects in their present job and/or threat of unemployment (less serious in the overseas oil industry); (c) some feel that they were thwarted in their youth by circumstances, parents, and educators, were denied opportunities or compelled to take up particular jobs which were not in line with their best or favourite talents. Middle-aged, middle-class managers especially can feel stagnated in their careers. They say that they would welcome and benefit greatly from a stimulative horizontal move and/or from training their hitherto untried abilities.

It can easily become a depressing experience listening to all sorts of cynical complaints about people's demands and constraints. How does one break out of this? Convinced by practical need and the importance of individual counselling in these matters I drew heavily on my five years' experience with consultants of the Netherlands Pedagogical Institute, Zeist, Netherlands.* Their special method of *in*direct counselling, through creating insights into the client's own personal growth (bio-psychologically, socially, and culturally) when passing through different periods of life, is widely appreciated. It is particularly successful in helping middle-aged managers and supervisors to explore and accept their needs (and crises) for reassessing their personal ambitions and possibilities for further development. Recently a number of excellent books have become available for the layman about the natural passages and crises in life: see Sheehy (1976), Vaillant (1977), Lievegoed (1979), and Evans (1980). In my experience this can be a surprisingly useful subject in the practice of management and supervisory training. (I feel that this is another underused model for reflective diagnosis.)

It is useful and often rewarding to help clients/students explore not only their own psychological make up and history but also their situation in life: external factors, circumstances, resources, persons, etc. Once we get an eye for opportunities, almost any situation, encounter, problem, or conflict can be turned into a learning opportunity. There are always experienced people around to consult, jobs can be enriched and rotated, volunteers are required for ad hoc projects, information from libraries and professional organizations is plentiful, etc.

I often challenged those who felt blocked in their organizational situation to sit down with me to explore the possibilities still open to them. In many cases this resulted in a substantial list of 'learning resources and opportunities in my organization', often more than they could handle! We tend to overlook resources that lie under our feet. It is amazing how a bogged-down situation can turn into another problem: that of determining priorities. Rosemary

*NPI's sister organization in the UK is Emerson College, a Centre for social development in Sharpthorne, Sussex. Affiliated Consultants are organized in 'Social Ecology Associates' in Gloucester, UK (see *Leadership & OD journal*, 1, no. 1, 1980, centre section (MCB Publication).

Stewart (1978) is currently researching a systematic method for helping managers to realize the many choices that exist in their jobs. 'The scope of discretion becomes visible and proves to be greater when someone else takes over the job.'

From this practice of encouraging and assisting managers and engineers to explore existing opportunities and to take initiatives themselves instead of relying in vain on someone else, I collected a number of ideas which were published in an article called 'Self-development within the organization' (Juch, 1979). 'Liberating reading' and 'repowering discoveries' reported some managers.

1.7 Self-profiling. Myopia or expertise?

Man is a *Homo Discriminator* (see Section 8.7) who senses (sees, hears, feels) only what he wants or needs to perceive. This biased behaviour favours maturation of those abilities that come easily, making these manifest while leaving dormant or even atrophying those which require more (initial) effort. I have given this human inclination the name of 'self-profiling'. It is the tendency to reinforce one's own innate or initial preferences, while neglecting those abilities which are harder to develop. Outside pressure may compel a person to 'diversify' or to minimize his risk and fall back on his strength. Freedom may motivate him to develop alternative abilities or it may make him lazy. There is no uniform reaction to external restraining or encouraging factors. This self-profiling principle can be for the better, say specialization to a high degree of excellence, or for the worse, say when it leads to one-sidedness, for example job *de*formation.

The research done by Kolb *et al.* with students reveals a similar selection effect. They comment (1974:37):

> What these data show is that one's undergraduate education is a major factor in the development of one's style. Whether the individuals' learning styles are shaped by the field they enter or whether there is a natural selection process that puts people into and out of disciplines is an open question at this point. Most probably both factors are operating — people choose fields of study that are consistent with their learning styles and are further shaped to fit the learning norms of their fields once they are in. When there is a mismatch between the fields and one's individual learning style, one will either change or leave the field.

(see also Figure 3 in Section 2.1.)

A number of managers were concerned that their idiosyncratic style had become strengthened irreversibly *after* their studies, that is when options started to diminish rapidly as the result of choosing a job, a marriage partner, a place to live, etc. They were not referring to external factors or to a dominant boss or spouse, but to cases with established division of work. 'If I am good at something I am obliged to continue to do it' and vice versa. Utilizing complementarity in skills can be very efficient but also disturbingly oppressive. Women's lib movements have been condemning this bias with some success. The negative attitudes towards self-profiling are (a) accepting it as something unavoidable, and (b) letting it happen unintentionally and unconsciously, by default rather than by design. Self-profiling is then the euphemism for professional deformation and for myopia, which Schein called the prime source of obstinate communication problems in organizations (in Kolb, *et al.* (eds), 1974).

Since people are inclined to accept such self-promoted specializations as if personalities were a for-ever-fixed bag of characteristics, I found that I had to discourage managers and students from stereotyping themselves or each other with results of 'tests'. For the sake of development we must resist the temptation of addressing people with simple labels. Stereotyping is the danger of all psychological tests and questionnaires from the 'personality traits' school, for example those by Briggs–Myers, Blake and Mouton, Reddin, the 16PF of ITRU, etc., including those used by Kolb in his matrix shown in Figure 3.

Some persons who did Kolb's LSI test voiced their concern that they were seemingly displaying *two* different styles, one at home and the other at work. Although such cases may be rather complicated, the person himself can often give a fairly plausible explanation for such behaviour. For instance, the freedom to act may be very different in those situations or the 'significant Other' (boss, wife, etc.) may demand different complementary skills. This has led me to advocate a 'contingency-learning' style in analogy with the contingency-leadership style, that is not applying one fixed behaviour pattern for all occasions but adopting the style that best suits the particular objective and situation and other persons involved. This contingency principle (see Section 4.8) will keep managers and specialists (including facilitators) from profiling themselves too rigidly.

Incidentally, educators, teachers, trainers, consultants, etc. are just as susceptible to this self-profiling principle as many other experts. A recent experience brought this home quite sharply: a number of management teachers/consultants were asked to prepare individually a short lecture for a given audience on a given subject. It was a somewhat unpleasant surprise to them when subsequent analyses proved that each had organized and structured his talk according to the personally preferred style of the presenter (inductive or deductive, verbal or visual, practical or conceptual, etc.). This 'test' was a clear warning signal that many teachers/consultants are far less prepared (and less able?) to adapt to the 'needs of the client/audience' than, with the best of intentions, they think themselves.

Of course, educators/facilitators may follow their individual preferences, and are free to specialize themselves 'by design', but let us hope not through ignorance. And I consider them well advised to train themselves beyond the confines of their own dispositions in all types of learning styles so that they can truly be relaxed and competent enough in whatever mode appears appropriate for the client.

1.8   Birds of a feather . . . Nature or nurture?

There is nothing wrong with a person who lets his learning style determine the choices he makes, for his study, his career, his partner in life, as long as he realizes that this can be stimulating as well as stultifying. Like Rosemary Stewart, I have reason to believe (see Section 1.6 above) that there is more personal freedom within organizations, and within limits imposed by nature, than people generally think they have. It is however not always possible, in such short sessions, to clarify and agree on the relative importance of and the interaction between innate and external learning forces, especially when there are so many plausible and supportive arguments for the predominance of either nurture or nature, as espoused for instance by the behaviourist schools (for example, Skinner, 1971) and the humanistic schools (for example, Rogers, 1969). I myself experience this issue as chameleonic: one day I am impressed by the almost unlimited 'success' of operant conditioning and behaviour modelling, another day by the dogged tenacity of Man's instincts and talents, whether evil or virtuous, and a third day by his unique, unpredictable curiosity and creativity.

I find it interesting to note that self-profiling is not only an inclination of the individual, but also a strong tendency in *groups* which in turn leads to further profiling of the individual. Although the proverb reads 'birds of a feather flock together', daily life proves that it is equally valid to observe that 'birds that live together develop similar feathers': people on islands develop a culture different from those on continents; Labour supporters have developed norms and values different from the Tories; readers of *l'Humanité* are a different lot from readers of *Paris-Soir*; the organizational norms, values, and styles are quite different in ICI, Shell, IBM, and Philips. There is truth in generalizing and stereotyping. Such 'flocks' with similar features in semi-closed environments develop their own language, style, values, etc., as much for survival, convenience, or comfort, as for assertive or aggressive purposes. Again, there is nothing wrong about the strengthening, specialization, or self-profiling of groups and organizations, as long as it does not lead to prejudice. Some organizations tolerate much less differentiation in 'feathers' than others. Kolb *et al.* found that most effective learning takes place in groups that enjoy variation and perspective (1974: 41).

However, and putting it mildly, there is not enough awareness of what this predisposition implies until the moment of encounter with another flock (for example in multicultural and multinational groups). There are too many disappointments, surprises, and unexpected 'culture shocks'. Birds of one feather are surprised when discovering that other birds can also fly. Even Man learned to fly! Managers discover that there is no 'one-best' style of learning or of doing business, except perhaps that a flexible developmental style is better than a dogmatic, static one. A recent study in the USA is titled: 'If Japan can, why cannot we?'

In conclusion, learning-style and traits tests can be eye-openers, they may prevent or break through myopia. However, if we are to improve our learning capacities such *static* psychological categorizations are not good enough. To manage ourselves in a turbulent future, to make progress with our development in everyday life, we have to understand learning as a *dynamic* cyclic and interactive process. In the world of education and training the obvious professional assumption is that Man is never too old to appreciate new and different things and to become wiser in the end. But can we really improve and manage the learning-to-learn process? Can we rise conceptually and practically above the behaviouristic, humanistic, cognitivistic or what-have-you doctrine? A critical examination of the process model is called for.

2

Experiments with Learning *Models*

In the early 1970s my interest was aroused by an explicit model of learning presented in a workbook on organizational psychology by Kolb, Rubin and McIntyre (1971). It became popularly known as Kolb's learning model. It advocated an *experiential* approach through the interaction of concrete experience and abstract conceptualization. It required active participation of students through the use of a companion instrument: a self-scoring 'learning-style-inventory'.

Of the various models that I was using at that time, Kolb's model and instrument was invariably appreciated as 'very interesting and useful'. It was conceptual and general and also readily related to the user's behaviour in work and daily life. It was acceptable because it appeared neutral, it did not give a value judgement about one's level of learning (or wisdom), nor about which style was the better one, nor did it suggest that one's behaviour should change. Indeed, the test and model always triggered substantial discussions with and between participants of courses, seminars, etc., as well as between us trainers, at that time. (I have already suggested in Section 1.5 that the reader should familiarize himself with the subject by doing the test of Appendix 3 and plotting the score in Figure 1.)

When the initial excitement wore off, some persistent difficulties emerged. Even serious objections were raised. The following sections describe my experience with various adaptations and with different versions of the model through the response of a wide range of people in different organizations in the Netherlands as well as overseas. It soon became clear that I had stumbled right in the middle of the fundamental issues about learning, theoretically as well as practically!

2.1 Kolb's learning model and style-inventory test

Kolb's manual of 1976 is the best reference. Like other educationalists (see Chapter 3) he conceives Man's learning as a four-stage cyclic process as depicted in Figure 2. To be effective a learner must be able to involve himself in new concrete experiences (CE); he must be able to observe and reflect on these experiences from many perspectives (RO); he should be able to create abstract concepts (AC) that integrate his observations into logically sound

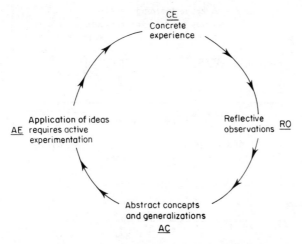

Figure 2   Kolb's experiential learning model

theories; application of ideas requires active experimentation (AE). All four abilities are considered essential, no one is in principle more desirable or more useful than the others.

However, few people develop all four abilities equally well. Experiences at home, school, and work are very personal and therefore learning abilities develop in unique ways. People learn through these stages in their own individual style, pace, and manner; they continuously have the choice of what learning ability they apply in any situation.

Kolb's important contribution has been to make this explicit and visible. He designed a self-scoring questionnaire (see Appendix 3) to let a person identify his individual learning style which can be visualized relative to others in a kite-type picture. Figure 1 in Section 1.5 gives a few actual examples of kite-type learning profiles of managers I have worked with.

Much emphasis was placed by Kolb on seeing the four stages as two polar pairs.

More specifically, there are two primary dimensions to the learning process. The first dimension represents the concrete experiencing of events at one end and the abstract conceptualization at the other. The other dimension has active experimentation at one extreme and reflective observation at the other. Thus, in the process of learning, one moves in varying degrees from actor to observer, from specific involvement to general analytic detachment. (Kolb, 1976:3)

He went as far as reducing a person's learning profile via only two scores: (AC—CE) and (AE—RO) to a *one*-point presentation in a matrix (see Figure 3, copied from Kolb and Wolfe (1977), Figure 3). The four quadrants thus assume specific meanings which Kolb labelled accommodators, divergers, convergers,

18

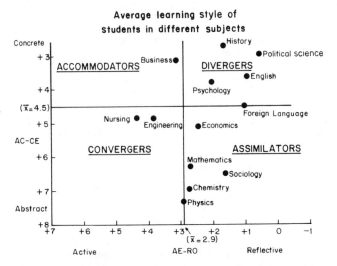

Figure 3   Average learning style of students in different subjects

and assimilators (for detailed descriptions see Kolb, 1976:5–6). Figure 3 also
shows some interesting results from his early research on identifying learning
styles of students. A worthwhile quotation is (Kolb *et al.*, 1974:33): '. . . managerial education could be improved through a more elaborate, structural
integration of the scholarly (reflective, abstract) learning style and the
practical (active, concrete) approach'.

From all these experiments Kolb concluded that 'individual learning style
does not only affect how people learn in the educational situation but also in
the broader aspects of life, such as decision-making, problem-solving and life-
style in general . . . How one learns becomes a major determinant of the course
of his personal development' (Kolb, 1976:7). This became exactly the theme of
my investigations. But contrary to Kolb, I found that more insight was
obtained by expanding the human learning *process* rather than by reducing a
profile to one point in a two-factor-matrix with the inference that people have
'semi-fixed' (genetically determined) personality traits.

2.2   A struggle with semantics

As Head of a Regional Training Centre for management training in Holland
during the early 1970s, I was confronted with the very real difficulty of having
to translate and transfer organizational and management concepts and models
from American and British literature into the Dutch language and culture.
Initially I was reluctant to 'fool around' too much with the semantics of
models. But, as I had worked in six different cultures (Holland, Indonesia,
Venezuela, USA, the Oman, and the UK) I realized that if one wants to know
how something works: change it! Words and their meaning play a crucial role
in any learning situation. This proved to be an essential step in the experimental
research.

Kolb's style-inventory test is based on a rather limited number of 24 words and 12 dummy words, see Appendix 3). Any translation is critical with respect to the validity of the instrument. Therefore in addition to consulting linguists and official translators, I decided to experiment more freely with words that are used in colloquial Dutch, adapting the questionnaire to the circles and levels of the organization I worked in. Through the co-operation of some bilingual persons I could run a number of duplicate tests, in English and in Dutch, by the same persons. I could thus establish a Dutch version of Kolb's learning style-inventory test that would, for all practical purposes, produce the same profile as Kolb's questionnaire in (American) English. During these experiments I found that simple labels for the four learning stages such as listen—think—plan—do, were often clearer than the original and officially translated psychological terms of Kolb's model. Even rather loosely defined popular series like: he?—aha!—try—show it!—were very meaningful.

As an illustration of learning about learning: when using the model to increase supervisors' awareness of the need to train their subordinates, the polarity between and the complementarity of 'know-how' and 'show-how' became a catch-phrase; it led to the valuable insight that a supervisor requires a substantially higher level of understanding and operational skill in order to be able to instruct others. The reason being that it is not easy to explain a particular action clearly as well as executing it exemplarily. He has to tell-how and show-how at the same time.

On the other hand, experiments with higher level staff often led to discussing the philosophical background of the model and the principles of development. Consequently it proved impossible to use only one type of 'label', I had to make a *range* and *series* of words available for each of the four learning stages. Thus I came to see it as the task of any facilitator when using any model, to clarify the core meaning of the concepts and to help his clients/students to select those words from their *own* repertoire that are most significant for them.

This is what I did; I collected verbs and words around the learning cycle that denote modes of learning and which were brought forward as meaningful by participants in group discussions from many corners and levels of the organization. Figure 4 shows the English version of that early Dutch working paper (this collection is used for the actual revision of the model in Section 3.1). Figure 4 clearly illustrates that there are many everyday words that are used in a learning sense. Therefore I need not be too fussy about finding the exact cultural equivalents of Dutch and English. Any reader can add his own. Words in the same language can have different meanings in different groups and even for different individuals within groups. This is not a particularly new idea, but it told me that adopting only one label for each of the stages of the learning cycle is only justified as a symbol.

It was often necessary and important to make it clear that two people engaged in the same activity (may realize that they) are not at the same stage of their personal learning cycle. For example two persons are reading: one is

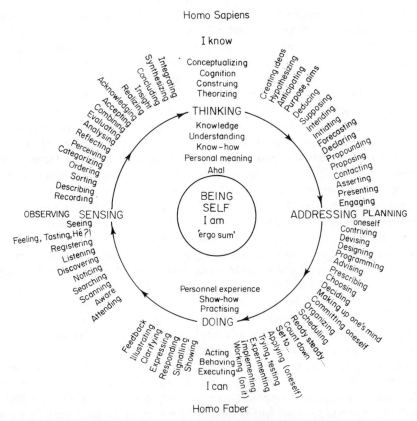

Figure 4   Words denoting modes of learning in the process cycle

learning to read, exercising that skill, the other is just reading as a means of getting information. A testing-out activity for one may be old hat for another. A manager at a conference may consider himself to be in an unusually reflective, theory-forming situation whereas a scientist in the same discussion at that conference may find himself swinging out to an exceptionally concrete, perhaps too practical diversion from his normal learning process. The stage of the learning cycle one is in, is determined by the next higher level of abstraction of what the (un)declared or unconscious learning purpose is (see Chapter 9).

In conclusion, these experiments with semantics convinced me that such a model could be far more effective for managers, supervisors, and students if Kolb's semantics were changed to functional speech, preferably into the actual language of the learner. Generalizing further: educators and facilitators who are serious about accelerating learning should develop empathy and ability to communicate *within* their *students'* and clients' language and *not* the other way around. L cannot be supposed to understand and work with the thought-constructs of scientists. At the time, I saw this principle as being advocated by Rogers (1969). Only much later, during my sabbatical, did I learn about

Kelly's Personal Construct Theory (see Chapter 7) which advocates even more convincingly that communication and learning depend on understanding each others' system of thoughts and values.

2.3 Main objections to Kolb's definition of the stages

It was not only because Kolb's labels were too academic that managers and supervisors found it difficult to grasp the core meaning of the stages and basic polarities. The stage labelled 'concrete experience' was too similar to the stage called 'concepts in new situation' (or 'testing implications' or 'active experimentation'). Their difference is not self-evident and is hard to translate into practice. To discriminate between them in the perceptual world of my students, I had to underplay the connotation of experimentation in the 'testing' and emphasize its role in designing, planning, engineering, organizing or, as Kolb and Wolfe themselves suggest (1977:8): 'making decisions and solving problems'.

I remember a late afternoon's discussion when a participant contended that *all* four stages could be 'active', especially in the mental sense of learning; for example, 'active listening' and 'hard thinking'. Other participants asserted that they could have unforgettable *concrete experiences* not only in one, but in *all* stages, for instance when watching TV, through meditation, when planning a vacation. Indeed, Man can be mentally active in all stages and also be aware of 'tangible' experiences in all four stages.

Discounting the dummies, Kolb's test uses only six words to score on concrete experience (see Appendix 3; these are: receptive, feeling, accepting, intuitive, present-oriented, and experience. None of these six words, except perhaps the last one, has a connotation of concreteness in the achievement-oriented worlds of supervisors and managers. This explains why some managers could not recognize their own profile and were 'disappointed' that they had not scored higher on Kolb's so-called 'concrete' dimension!

If Kolb wants his 'CE' stage to mean concreteness, then, said the managers, it just misses that very element not only in this stage but in the whole test. For us, concrete learning is applying, executing, practising, overt physical doing. Manual, physical, and motor skills do not appear in the vocabulary of Kolb's model! Kolb himself acknowledged this weakness: 'The fact that the CE scale shows the lowest and most variable coefficients across populations may also suggest that the LSI is somewhat biased against obtaining accurate measurements' (Kolb, 1976:15, Table 1); 'the CE scale in particular may need to be supplemented by a more concrete measurement approach in order to achieve greater reliability' (1976:16).

Others have run into similar difficulties. Mrs Kim James (in Beck and Cox, 1980:55–71) found that Kolb's inventory was quite 'inadequate' for her research on the development of senior managers. 'Most British managers would not understand or respond to the categories used by him.' She reworded her questionnaire rather drastically. Beck and Cox (1980:223) have similar objections.

The reason for most anomalies lie in the fact that Kolb's model is based on the theories of Kurt Lewin of the 1950s and 1960s. What is active and concrete in the professional circles of psychoanalyses and sensitivity training need not to be perceived as concrete in the world of industry or business organizations. Morris (1980:114) states that Kolb's model

> shows clear signs of its origin as a learning theory derived from responses to sensitivity training . . . (in which 'activity' is a strongly emotional experience when trainers pull the rug from under people by refusing to meet their conventional social expectations and thereby precipitate a rash of reflective observations) . . . . But if one starts with a different kind of learning in which the activities are those of agents, not patients, and are related to achieving an interesting task rather than recovering from unpleasant feelings, the phases of the model subtly change: . . . one finds a continuous process of planning, programming, monitoring and reviewing novel action . . . . The labels that I would propose are 'project planning', 'active achievement', 'reviewing progress setbacks', and 'interpreting activities' . . . .

Freedman and Strumpf summarize the objections against the use of Kolb's learning style theory for theory building, research and pedagogical advice as follows (1980:445-7):

> Supporting evidence comes from an unreliable instrument designed so that its results spuriously corroborate the theory. Independent research has not supported the theory and suggests its normative use should be suspended . . . . There is a need in management education for theories that integrate situational elements with pedagogy—in particular, a theory that accounts for variance in learning styles among individuals. This need still remains to be satisfied.

And that is exactly what I am setting out to do.

2.4 Other observations. Distinguishing activities and skills

During discussions it became necessary to make the distinction between learning *activities* and the resulting *skills*. Therefore I defined a 'process-stage' as a particular group of activities where Man learns identifiable skills. People recognize that they have learned something when they realize that a skill or an opinion or their memory has changed. The continuously accruing knowledge and the lifelong accumulation of skills are the *products* of the learning process. Strangely enough Kolb has done little to relate the process with the emerging skills. As mentioned in the previous section, manual, physical, and other skills do not form part of Kolb's model. Neither does he discuss the growth and nature of the ensuing body of wisdom ('constructs' in terms of Kelly, see Chapter 7).

Not only had the stages to be redefined but experience demanded that the model also be extended to distinguish both activities and skills in all four stages (see Figure 5), and that the labels or 'names' of the skills and activities of each stage should be readily recognizable and self-evident *in terms of those* who want to do the test and use the model.

2.5   Inserting an 'Undiscovered Self'

One more major lacuna was frequently felt. The learning cycle represents mainly the explicit, visible, and conscious activities and skills. What about all those powerful psychological factors that do influence the human capacity to learn but which are *in*visible and mostly *un*conscious? What about the important role in Man's learning process of the elements that constitute his psyche, such as talents, motivations, instincts, values, will, emotions, etc.?

To account for these inner faculties, I started to write SELF in the centre of the circle (see Figure 5) and let people fill in for themselves what they wanted this to mean. When asked, it turned out that this 'Self' was considered to represent a 'mixed-bag' indeed of the above-mentioned factors and others, like: one's heart and guts; libido and 'dark faculties'; centre of emotion; manager of the process; vitality and ambition; curiosity and serendipity. It dawned on me that this addition to the model would account for the *mutual* influence between learning (activities and skills) and the characteristics of a person's personality.

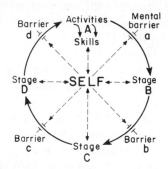

Figure 5   Skills and Self and Barriers in the learning cycle

I was able to make this idea even more useful by visualizing the effect of 'Self' as mental barriers, or filters, or psychological projections in the learning circle (see Figure 5).

These barriers represent both familiar and unexplainable blockages in Man's development process. Once I had introduced this concept on an experimental basis, each barrier gradually acquired further specific meaning and significance. They explain whether or not a learner's mental energy can or will proceed from one particular stage to the next. This is discussed at length in Section 3.2.

Initially I was still unfamiliar and not very comfortable with the centre area of 'Self'. I had to leave it 'undiscovered' (Jung's 1958 term, meaning unexplored and unarticulated), until my sabbatical at Bath University. Then I had the idea of explaining Man's unconscious and subconscious learning with a more fundamental general development model.

2.6 Whirling cycles within a lifelong spiral

Before summarizing the experiments, one more aspect must be clarified. The notion that Man's learning is a *cyclic* process is widely accepted, but it remains a simplification. Authors like Kolb, Hampden-Turner, Hutton, Kelly, Mangham, Morris, Pedler, Rowan, the NPI and many others (see Appendix 5) use a circle schematically to symbolize that Man's mental focus of awareness, the centre of his attention, moves continuously through various active and reflective stages in a never-ending cyclic pattern. The concept of focus is also a simplification, yet very appropriate. It means choosing consciously on what to concentrate one's attention and effort. It is very difficult, if not impossible to focus our efforts mentally or physically on more than one identifiable subject, event, place, or time simultaneously.

> Our common personal experience of being aware only of what we are focussing on either in our reveries or in the outside world, rather than of being aware of all qualities of experiences at once, raises the question whether these really exist and whether our attention can attune itself to their interplay. (Torbert, 1978:112)

The gestalt theory (Section 7.6.7) propounds that Man is dynamically selective, continuously choosing a 'figure' within the context of a background; that he is inclined to deal with it now, to 'finish business' before moving on to raising or selecting new points or issues. It is thus meaningful to accept that Man's focus is inclined to follow a cyclic pattern sequentially. That does not mean, however, that it is restricted, programmed, or has to come back to the same point. On the contrary, it is very dynamic, mercurial, agile. It can scan quickly, move over all thinkable places and flash backwards and forwards through time and history. It will never come back to the same object/subject without having experienced something.

Letting the imagination go beyond recurring cycles, I find myself most attuned to those who conceive development as an *upward widening spiral*. Quoting Hampden Turner (1966:369):

> If, as I have argued, the cycle develops so that one successful cycle helps

to generate the experience and motivation for a further successful cycle, then we may think of the development process as an 'upward spiral', the higher reaches of which represent more mature levels of interpersonal functioning.

And Morris (1980:113): 'This is not a closed circle of repeated experience, so much as an expanding spiral of enlarged experience at levels of heightened awareness'.

Limited to pencil and paper let me try to picture in Figure 6 how I visualize the multitude of learning cycles to be connected with each other and how they are spaced out in time. Possible qualifications are whirling cycles within a life spiral, wheels within wheels, a system of helixes, untidy coils, with loops within loops, etc. Though still a simplification, this presentation incorporates at least the notions of time and progress, of exploring new fields, going on to

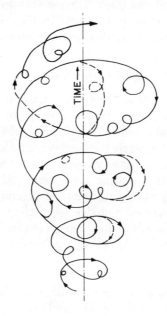

Figure 6   Whirling cycles within a lifelong spiral

higher and lower levels of abstraction; this picture allows us to envisage incidental learning circles within a spiral, and mini spirals within an ever-growing macro one. I visualize that one act can possibly serve multiple purposes, that business and thought constructs can be kept unfinished for the time being; losing track of where awareness is during routine behaviour or during sleep, the spiral can accommodate creative short-cuts, and so on.

It is impossible to depict some *qualitative* learning aspects of the process: that some people like to move quickly through the stages; that others prefer a clear, deliberate, step-by-step progress; or to dwell intensively on certain activities; or to skip stages; that some feel confident while acting; or conversely, feel uncomfortable when reflecting or powerless when planning. All those who have written a programme for a computer will realize how difficult it is to break down even straightforward instructions into well-defined steps. No wonder that learning to drive a car, for instance, consists of many, many intermediate cycles, short-cuts and flashes of observing, thinking, planning, and doing; it will take the learner a long time before he has learned to reduce all the required physical and mental activities into easily manageable and unconscious routines.

The enormous complexity of the real movement of one's focus cannot even be pictured by a million coils. In this connection I should like to mention the BBC's beautiful, evocative film *The Magic Loom*. It makes us realize that any learning model remains a gross simplification of the very complex learning processes in Man's brain and body. Having acknowledged this, and keeping the complexity in mind, let me now summarize the learning in order to redesign the cyclic model in Chapter 3, starting from the basic human learning activities.

2.7 Summary: What the experiments led up to

I admit that during this field research I was often worried about the dilemmas which kept emerging, about the further drifting away from official theories, and about the substantial ambiguity which I was tolerating. The need to clarify important issues and to formulate the concepts and ideas behind the experiments had become so pressing that at a certain moment I actually stopped using the model and the test. At the same time I realized from the response and discussions with managers and students the potential benefit of designing a better and more comprehensive model. My feeling was that it could be very significant and useful for advancing human learning and for the promotion of self-development. In short, I felt that it would be worth my while to take time out to:

(i) redefine the basic stages, in terms of daily activities;
(ii) relate them with the accruing skills and knowledge;
(iii) provide for mental barriers between the stages;
(iv) introduce and account for a central 'Self'; and perhaps
(v) redesign a learning-style-inventory test.

This is done in Parts II and III.

PART II

The Theme

3

Remodelling the Cyclic Learning Process

With the ideas acquired from the above-mentioned experiments I shall redefine the cyclic learning process as I now see it after more study and thinking. I was surprised to find so many writers who have proposed or who have expressed themselves in a multistage/multidimensional learning/development process model. I did not have to scan the literature exhaustively. While digesting their theories and concepts I tabulated them in two groups: authors who propound a four-stage cyclic process (see Appendix 5), and those who stress the multidimensionality of development (see Figure 20 in Section 5.0). The reader may recognize some of them, but he need not be familiar with them at this point. Splitting them up between Appendix 5 and Figure 20 may seem to be somewhat arbitrary, but it is based on what the authors themselves have emphasized, which I shall come back to later. I listed them only to show that (a) many have concerned themselves about this subject in very different ways, and (b) few have bothered to compare or synthesize their thinking with that of others. I shall do this via the major symbols and key words of their theories.

I noted around the learning cycle (see Figure 7), the words (labels) from Appendix 5 and Figure 20, in accordance with the intended meaning of the authors, in the same way as I had done with the many verbs and gerunds collected from the experiments, that is from the persons who analysed and discussed their learning styles (see Figure 4 in Section 2.2). Three important points emerged. Firstly, there is quite an amount of similarity, overlap, and synonymity between them. They are also complementary. Secondly, they are not tightly clustered together, but rather distributed all along the whole cycle; this means that the learning process has essentially a fully continuous cyclic pattern. Thirdly, the authors of Appendix 5 have simplified the process by leaving out most synonyms and selecting particular names for 'stages' as they considered appropriate for their theory, argument, or specialization.

Of course, nobody can escape from simplifying reality when formulating a model. It is the only way in which real life can be represented on paper. (Maps!) I intend to do likewise; my simplification, or bias if you wish, is to make the model generally applicable and useful for self-development. But I will consider *all* terms and expressions and then search for the *core*-meaning of the stages and barriers in the cycle.

30

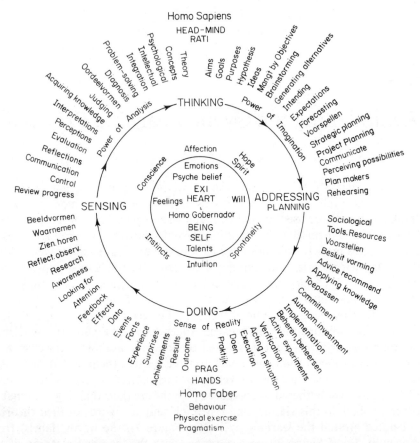

Figure 7   Other authors' labels and concepts around the process cycle

One more general remark: there is quite an amount of play with semantics in the following sections. I hope that some readers enjoy this (even after leaving out colourful shopfloor diction), but word-play is not a purpose in itself. The idea is that through explanation, clarification, and juxtaposition of plain words and ordinary meanings the sought-for concepts will emerge so that the language of the new learning model will largely be self-explanatory to managers, engineers, supervisors, and students.

3.1   The core meaning of the stages

I think that I found the key to the core meaning of the stages by the following procedure: first a reiterative reshuffle into a logical sequence of the words around the circles of Figure 4 and Figure 7; then the distinction of activities *and* skills at each stage and making sure that they are congruent. I base this on the premise that the learner is active, mentally and/or physically, all around the circle. Therefore it should be possible to name specific activities at each stage. Equally, since the purpose is to learn something recognizable, it should be possible to name the *skills* that are the result of the activities. It seems that neither Kolb nor the other authors have applied this check of congruency between activities and skills at each stage.

Thus I propose a general learning-process model (see Figure 8), that consists of:

(i) the learner's mental focus which goes continuously round the learning process circle (LPC for short); whilst
(ii) activating and guiding particular activities (selected from a large series) which are thought to be 'variations' of four activity-categories;
(iii) resulting in four repertoires (or reservoirs) of skill-categories that are acquired during life;
(iv) a central self that is represented by four barriers in the LPC, which regulate the speed, the style, and the intensity of the learning.

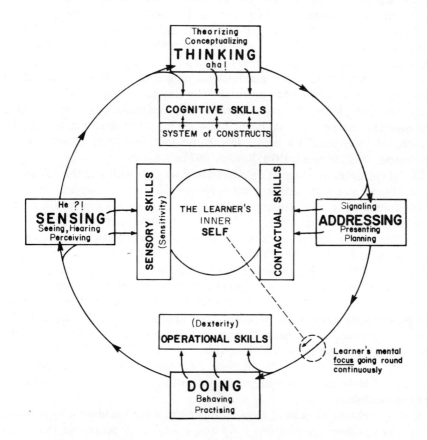

Figure 8   Stages in the learning process cycle. Activities and skills

I shall leave the (*un*conscious) learner's Inner Self as a general, unexplored domain until Chapters 5, 6, and 7 where Kelly, Jung, Bateson and others provide the psychological and philosophical bases for expanding my empirical learning model further into a model for personal development.

3.1.1 The 'doing' activities and the motor skills

The most obvious group of learning words are those that denote *physical* activities and motor skills. Man learns to walk, talk, play, etc. at the behavioural stage of the LPC. We spend much, if not most of our time and effort around the 'Doing' stage in practising and accumulating our extensive repertoire of 'operational' skills. In the beginning is 'Learning by Doing'.

The many synonyms in use (see Figures 4 and 7 and the 'D' column in Appendix 5) can cloud the core meaning of this learning stage. For instance, there are quite a number of verbs on the upstream side of this stage that have a transitional connotation between planning and executing: applying, organizing, implementating, etc. On the downstream side words like showing, expressing, illustrating, feedback are used. Kolb has contributed to the confusion by not considering physical skills and by leaving vague at which stage he envisages these being acquired. Actually none of the authors of Appendix 5 are specific in this respect.

I can visualize a realistic, practical learning model which has a readily recognizable stage where Man practises daily (the co-ordination of) his motor skills, whether physically rough, operationally controlled, or finely attuned and complex, as when playing the piano. When managers are asked to rank the sources of managerial learning, 'Doing the job' invariably comes on top (Burgoyne, 1975; Stewart, 1978; Revans, 1971).

Defining this major stage in an operational way not only has the advantage of relating to accepted parlance, but is also justified by the physical make up of the human body. Penfield and others were able to draw a map of the motor homunculus of the brain (Sagan, 1977:35); it shows that there are distinct areas allocated for sending impulses to activate and co-ordinate the movements of all body parts. These are different from the areas that receive neural-sensing information (see the next section) and different from the areas in the brain that regulate the metabolism of food, the functioning of blood, hormones, etc.

The essence of this stage is nicely expressed by *Homo Faber*. The cultures of the western hemisphere hold this active stage in high esteem: working, achievement, performance, even being busy or just doing something. Dexterity skills are of major importance for blue-collar workers. Titles like 'executive-president' have prestige in themselves. Applying one's talents diligently is called the Calvinistic work ethic. Pathological, compulsive doers are referred to as workaholics.

Radical behaviourists have elevated this part of the learning process to the dominant position (see Sections 4.5.3 and 4.5.4). They propound that overt behaviour is what counts and that learning = behaviour change, which results from subjecting pigeons and rats and humans to operant conditioning.

Subtle distinctions should be recognized. For instance, a child learns to read by the activity of reading, whereas the purpose of a consultant's activity of reading is likely to be the collection of data = 'sensing' (see the next section); for him an actual *intervention* will be 'doing' in the context of his job. In other contexts other labels may be appropriate, like 'applying knowledge' (Jung, 1958), 'acting' (Mangham, 1978) or 'autonomous investment' (Hampden-Turner, 1966). In conclusion, I consider the popular and collective name *'Doing'* fully representative for the core-activities of this stage; this is where Man's physical/motoric and operational skills are practised and developed.

3.1.2 The 'Sensing' activities and the sensory skills

The development of the sensory skills is part of the natural maturation of Man's genetic endowment. His sensory system comprises not only the five commonly known ones: seeing, hearing, touching, tasting, smelling (visual, auditory, tactile, gustatory, and olfactory senses) but also his senses of movement, balance, and viscera (interior organs) (see Figure 8).

Some senses are being exercised already in the womb and in the cradle, even before a newborn infant is aware of the world around it and before it practises its physical abilities. There is enormous scope for learning sensory skills that do not develop naturally, like reading, 'reading' music and Braille, piloting a plane, sensing artificial gravity, etc. Penfield has made an interesting sensory 'map' (Sagan, 1977:34–5) that shows the relation between the anatomy of the brain and the relative importance of the sense organs of our body, for example our head and hands occupy about half of the sensory homunculus of the cerebral cortex. Although there has been much research (for example in space programmes) and popular interest in recent years we still do not know to what extent we can broaden and heighten our sensitivity and what the ultimate limits are of developing new skills in and with the human sensory system.

Man accumulates understanding about (people in) this world 'only through the mediation of his senses' (Jung in Jacobi, 1953:266) 'Everything must be anchored in actual sensation, else there is no belief' (Hume). 'All our ideas refer to data that have been presented through our senses or to operations of mind reflecting upon them' (Locke). These quotes reflect the great importance that the phenomenologists have placed on this group of learning activities and skills; they stress that only 'sensible' factors are admitted to the human system.

Searching for a succinct and suitable name for this stage, I did not get much help from the writers about the learning process (see column 'stage A' of Appendix 5). They cover a very wide range of meanings. Kolb's term 'reflective observation' is definitely not general enough. Both 'perception', which implies interpretation or evaluation, and 'reflection' are too close to the next stage 'thinking'. The simple word 'observing' appears attractive in so far as it relates with the prime sensory activities. However, it suggests visual activities only, and it can be confused with adhering to (for example 'observing' the law) or making comments. Nevertheless I am using 'observing' for simple presentations (see Appendices 6 and 7).

A third choice could be: attending, noticing, becoming aware, being aroused, or being struck (see Hague in Appendix 5). A special form had some popularity in a few supervisory groups: the Dutch word 'Hé?!' which is translatable into something like: 'Well I never!' or: 'I say!'; its essence being that something or some event captures the learner's attention as something new, or as a deviation from the normal or expected pattern.

A frequent and serious suggestion was to use 'feeling' for this stage. I rejected this word, not only because the popular usage of 'feeling' is inconveniently loose, but because it can assume fundamentally different meanings and be mistaken for the emotional dimension. Let me illustrate this with a few expressions:

'I am feeling fine.'
'I am feeling him out.'
'I don't feel like eating.'
'I have no feel for poetry.'
'There are hard feelings about that issue.'
'I feel that we should warn him.'
'It is soft to the feel.'

Only the latter pertains literally to this stage. The others need clarification and are more related to the mental barriers, the Inner-self and Being faculties (see Section 3.2).

Therefore I concluded that the *central* significance of this stage in the LPC is: *sensing* data from the world around and recording them as such without processing them yet within the cognitive system. *Up* to this point judgement is suspended, the signals have physically entered the body, the electrochemical 'data' are still empirically verifiable. *From* this point onwards *meaning* is attached to the recorded data and the learner starts to evaluate, synthesize, and digest them, turning them into information of personal significance to him.

On this basis I shuffled to the best of my understanding all relevant words used by course participants and writers along the cycle (see Figures 4 and 7) and it appeared very logical that words like attending, noticing, listening are located *up*stream of the 'sensing' and words like ordering, associating, evaluating, *down*stream of it. I am aware that the word 'sensing' is not unequivocal either, especially the derivative 'sense'. That word can, for example, be used in the sense of: a sense of humour, losing one's senses, sensing that something is wrong, etc. 'Sense and nonsense are merely manmade labels which serve to give us a reasonable sense of direction!' (Jung in Jacobi, 1953:282).

Yet, provided that it is used in the biological, signal-receiving meaning, I consider *sensing* the most suitable label for this learning stage, for this large group of activities that develop and increase the sensitivity and diversity of the human sensory skills.

3.1.3 The 'Thinking' activities and the cognitive skills

The *centre* of this stage is the bridge between the two halves of the learning process: making sense out of what Man has sensed and of what he expects to happen. This stage links what he has experienced and what he intends to do next, it connects retrospective thinking with prospective thinking (see Figure 12 in Section 4.4).

As can be seen from the many activity words assembled and sequenced in Figures 4 and 7, I see the 'thinking' stage as *finalizing* the processing of the sensed data: generalizing our experiences and integrating them with the acquired system of thoughts, where we do accept and understand them (aha!) or realize that we do not. And this stage is at the same time the *beginning* of producing new ideas: hypothesizing and visualizing future events and behaviour. Here Man exercises his intellectual, cognitive abilities, he expands and differentiates further his skills of reason and logic, abstract theories and symbolic conceptualization.

The fact that we are aware of our thinking process, that we are self-consciously connecting the now with the past and the future is essential and unique for the human species *Homo Sapiens*. Or, with Descartes: 'Cogito ergo sum'. 'Learned' men are in high esteem. The maintenance and further development of the human race is intrinsically interwoven with the educational and scientific institutions. In the foreseeable future demand will remain high for people with educated brains.

Compared with the other stages we have here to distinguish *two* types of results. Not only does Man develop a repertoire of cognitive *process* abilities: skills in storing and retrieving data, in logic and reason, in processing and integrating them. There is another type of *product*: a 'memory', a reservoir of knowledge and thought constructs which builds up during a person's lifetime. This body of intricately interrelated memories and concepts is continuously being up-dated and changed and differentiated. It overlaps with and becomes an almost indistinguishable part of the individual's mental faculties and subconscious dispositions.

The name for this most important product of Man's thinking activities: *'system of constructs'* is from Kelly, whose *Personal Construct Theory* (1955) I found most helpful for understanding how learning is related to the accumulation of Man's personal theories, concepts, and opinions. He, Kelly, also developed techniques to explore, to explain and to make explicit (some parts of) one's personal construct system (see Fransella and Bannister, 1977). I consider it worthwhile to review this whole subject in more detail in Chapter 7.

In summary then, I propose to distinguish in the new model (Figure 8) a stage called *'Thinking'* with three boxes which represent:

(1) The thinking *activities* themselves, ranging from and linking the retrospective and prospective modes of reflection and imagination through processing. The stage where the learner may take time to focus and process his thoughts deliberately.

(2) The repertoire of intellectual and cognitive *skills* built up from performing these activities and from exercising one's thought-processing abilities.

(3) The *system* of *thought constructs*, that is a network of related data and of interconnected subgroups of memories, propositions, values, opinions, theories, etc.

3.1.4 The 'Planning' activities and contactual skills

I have spent the most time and effort on this *fourth* stage in sorting out suggestions and in formulating justifications for useful labels. During the experiments described in Chapters 1 and 2, participants experienced most conceptual difficulties in this part of the cycle, and produced most diverse opinions about it. I received at least twice as many 'synonyms' as I have been able to cram into the available space of Figure 4. To my question: 'What skill would you say is most important for you in this stage?' I received descriptive answers like: (a) foreseeing potential problems; (b) predicting coming events somewhat earlier; (c) presenting my ideas and proposals to my boss; (d) making strategic decisions; (e) being assertive and playing the power game; (f) spelling out what I have in mind; (g) planning 'interventions' in co-operation with others; (h) involving and motivating my subordinates; (i) being pro-active; (j) creating the right climate for concerted action. Had I done the experiments with persons from other types of organizations I would surely have had an even larger 'embarras du choix'. Also the authors in Appendix 5 show a wide spread in concepts under the 'stage C' column: expectations, decisions, advising, committing, rehearsing, project-planning, tools, etc.

If there are so many significant activities and words in daily use for the learning steps and skills between the 'thinking' and the 'doing' stages, what makes it so difficult to grasp and define the central core meaning of this forward-looking part of the cycle? I believe that there are two reasons for this. The first one I found best expressed by Hampden-Turner (1966:374): 'The crux of the cycle is the act of investment, the act of offering our self-related meaning to others for acception or rejection, which is decisive for the achievement of growth. Investment must have the quality of autonomous creativity, of authenticity, of anguish and risk.'

The second reason is that the manifestation of this 'psychological investment' is indeed very diverse in daily life because it covers the whole field of social psychology. It may be that I developed an eye for it, but it seems that during recent years quite a number of authors have been writing on exactly this very subject. To name a few major variations and elaborations on the general theme: 'How Man applies himself' (see also the list of references):

Ackoff: *Redesigning the Future*
Aronson: *The Social Animal*
Berne: *What do you say after you Say Hello?*
Brakel: *Social intelligence*
Buber: *Ich und Du*
Eden (and many others): *Decision-making*
Emery and Trist: *Social Ecology*
George: *Bridging the Gap between Theory and Practice*
Goffman: *Presentation of Self in Everyday Life*
Hampden-Turner: *Radical Man*
Holland: *Self and the Social Context*
Hutton: *Assertions, Barriers and Objects*
Jung: *Man and his Symbols*
Karras: *Give and Take. A Guide to Negotiating*
Mangham: *Interactions and Interventions in Organizations*
Morris (and many others): *Non-verbal Communication*
Sartre: *Nausea, the Dreadful Freedom of Choice*
Vaillant: *Adaptation to Life*

Most of these studies are concerned with the need and abilities of Man to be in or go out into this world, either individually or as a group with the implicit or explicit intention of behaving to his advantage in interaction with things, nature, and/or people.

I would not favour the name 'interaction' or 'communication' for this stage because these would draw the learning cycle too exclusively into the social field as if there were no learning by oneself with things. Man does not learn exclusively through and with people. Also, social skills are not limited to this stage.

In groups of managers, their rather pro-active activities like propounding, proposing, promoting, designing, prescribing, contriving, organizing, etc., were readily recognized and often suggested as symbols for this stage. Most of them, however, were not sufficiently tentative, not general enough. 'Decision-making' was frequently suggested but decisions take place in all parts of the learning cycle. One's mental focus continuously decides to focus or to move on —learning itself is an ongoing series of making decisions.

What is needed is a label that suggests that the cognitive abilities are still of back-up assistance *and* foreshadow the operational skills, that is a proper name for the category of activities *after* declaring one's intention and *before* committing oneself. It is still a (mental) *simulation* from the socio-psychological field of self-development I could accept 'presenting oneself', 'contacting', 'asserting' or 'addressing oneself'. From an organization/ management view the label 'planning' fulfils the criteria best.

My first choice for a general symbol for the core-meaning of this learning stage is the typical English word: *addressing* in the sense of the learner 'addressing himself to'. I consider it to have advantages over those mentioned above. 'Addressing' can be applied to:

(i) people and tasks and things;
(ii) the what and how (= content and process);
(iii) the level and quality of the addressing skills: for example clumsy, honest, eloquent, diligent.

Unfortunately there is no straight synonym in Dutch for 'addressing oneself'. The gerund 'contacting' could be appropriate, it has a widely and fully accepted term in Dutch for the skills: *Contactual skills*. These words may be too limited for the English and too much on the upstream side of the cluster.

Planning is more widely acceptable. Usually, though not always, it has a social connotation. Moreover it implies correctly that people learn through elaboration of ideas, through mobilization of resources and preparation for action, whilst not yet crossing the boundary of commitment to the stage of 'Doing'. I have used 'Planning' extensively and successfully. It serves very well its purpose of recognition, clarity, and significance for this group of activities in the world of engineers, supervisors, and managers. For the general educational application of the model, 'Planning' may be seen as related too much to work and organizations. At least, it is second-best.

3.2 The barriers and gateways to learning

Discussions and counselling repeatedly resulted in the conclusion that a person's learning *style* cannot be explained fully by his profile of *abilities* of doing, sensing, thinking, and addressing. Neither will the amount of time and effort spent ensure that a person becomes well qualified at any particular stage. It is the fundamental power of natural endowment, of talents and dispositions, that determines the learner's attitude and interest. These play the all-important role of shaping up his individual style and skills during life.

From the innumerable motivation questionnaires that I have seen, run, and been connected with, I remember that pay or any other external reward was seldom on top of peoples' lists. If people have some freedom of choice they always prefer to do what *interests* them, whether they are already good at it or not. Preference may cause a person to dwell *at* a particular learning stage, but the reason may equally be that he/she is *not* interested in moving to the *next* stage. Also, people may habitually *skip* one or more learning stages if they do not like them and can get away with it, whether in a private, an educational, or a work environment.

This led me to make provision for an influence *between* the learning stages, for a force that is triggered by our mental attitude or genetic disposition: a sort of threshold or keenness to go from one stage to the next, a reluctance or readiness to embrace the next mode of learning. I introduced four barriers on an experimental basis as projections into the learning process from Man's unspecified Inner Self (see Section 2.5 and Figure 5). Through discussions in courses and from consultancy work, each barrier gradually acquired a very specific meaning, even to the extent that each of them assumed a popular *nom de théâtre*.

This addition may seem to complicate the presentation of the learning process, particularly since the barriers and skills and inner faculties influence each other mutually, subconsciously. However, these barriers became accepted quite naturally, often as the fundamental cause of an unbalanced profile or of a particular strength. The model's significance for diagnosis increased considerably. It became richer and a more practical guide for learning-to-learn and self-development. This is described in the following sections.

3.2.1 The 'Window'

The barrier that acquired most significance in the groups of managers was the one between the Doing and Sensing stages (see Figure 9). This barrier regulates what a person is perceiving, what he takes into his world of Sensing and Thinking. It was soon dubbed the *'Window'* because it symbolizes a person's mental state of openness. Through it he hears and observes the world and receives feedback from events, others, and himself. This barrier represents Man's conscious effort to focus receptively on something; it is related to the sensitivity or selectivity, the keenness or reluctance with which a person makes his attention available.

With the overwhelming variety of signals being broadcast continuously by people and events around us, we need to control the input. We cannot exist without applying an adaptable filter, a dynamic selector. Don't we all wear blinkers or tinted glasses? This barrier can also be conceived of as a 'road-crossing' with 'traffic signs' (see Figure 9), where a person's focus has a choice between:

(1) Making his attention actively available, passing on the information about what happens here and now in the world around him, sensing and consciously recording the stimuli that present themselves, while suspending temporarily the processing (analyses and evaluation) of this data.

(2) *Not* paying attention to what presents itself or deliberately shutting out information. This may be in the form of neglecting (non-legere = not choosing) or ignoring (= intentionally disregarding). A person may remain inactive or put too high a threshold for the entry of information. By closing his window, his attention and interest can be diverted to something else.

(3) Going straight to the next act or plan without perceiving or reflecting, for instance because he prefers to stay active in the outer world, or to go back to planning, etc.

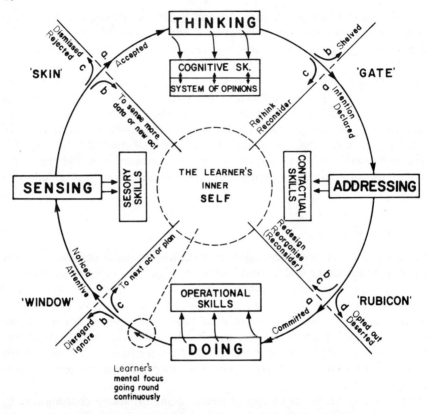

Figure 9   The learning process cycle with the four barriers

The actual wording of the 'traffic-signs' is somewhat arbitrary and can be made specific and significant for an individual in any particular case. Examples of expressions that were used are 'keeping one's ear to the ground', or 'keeping a finger on the pulse', or conversely 'living in a closed system' or 'pulling the blinds down!'.

It is quite easy in a work environment to forget the reflective mode of learning. Interruptions and telephone calls direct one's mental focus away from what happened, leaving no time to sit down and think. Attention is required for the next activity and is kept on the sequence of events. A person can thus be confined to the extrovert mode; learning continues through interaction or by doing a particular action over and over again. If his window stays closed or if he continues to filter out unwanted information, or if being too busy to take time out for reflection becomes a habit, his learning process becomes permanently deflected and his profile will become distorted.

Any habitual constriction of one's aperture (to left or right) may lead to impeded development. If the inflow of impressions is reduced to a trickle, Man can become a stunted closed system. Sometimes a person's physical appearance may show such a defensive attitude that it reminds us of a barred office—or a box-office-window that is only unbolted for selected privileged customers.

On the other hand, *everyone* is faced with the fundamental predicament that his focus cannot possibly take note of the *whole* world. Therefore we all have the very individual responsibility of choice and selection: Sartre's frightening freedom. Of necessity we develop an elaborate selective window to hold the 'traffic' down to a manageable level. Man must be a 'Discriminator' (see Section 8.7). The selective nature can be categorized as follows:

(1) Priority setting. Anyone active in the hassle of modern business (and science I am assured) faces the real danger of overload, of being snowed under by too much information and demand. Any person has to recognize his limitation, whether of brain or body capacity. Since time is limited, and not replenishable, it is all a question of priority: attending to one matter means missing out on something else. When collecting data a cut-off point must be made, consciously, before the point of diminishing returns (the equi-satisficing principle of Simon). Or, in daily parlance: not biting off more than one can chew: (In Dutch: Niet te veel hooi op je vork!)

(2) Negative selection. This means screening out data that could have been helpful in learning. This barrier often operates as a first line of defence for Man's ego, which is mainly protected by his second line of defence (see Section 3.2.2). However, self-imposed blinkers have the tendency to shut out too much.

(3) Dormant selection. Then nothing is noticed because the interest is not educated (yet). Examples: A young child cannot (yet) distinguish the symbols in a book; I am unaware of much that a forester notices during our walk through the woods. This pseudo-barrier relates to the sensing skills as the 'chicken to the egg'. What comes first?

Man's focus can be educated and blinkers can be removed by deliberate training. For instance, in the 1960s and early 1970s there was a boom in courses and seminars, especially in California, to enhance the awareness of participants by sensitizing their vision, hearing, smell, touch, through practising all sorts of non-verbal communication.

It is worth noting that this concept of the window-barrier also applies to the development process of organizations and groups. This is obvious from the more than symbolic 'Iron Curtain' and the physical erection of the Berlin Wall. Pope John XXIII's obituary in a Dutch newspaper (June 1970) used the same symbol: 'He has acquired his place in history for throwing open the windows of the Church to let in light and fresh air!'

In conclusion, a learner's focus, going around the learning cycle, repeatedly encounters a mental barrier between the 'Doing' and the 'Sensing' stage: his 'Window' on the world, on others and himself. This barrier can be deliberately opened or closed or passed selectively, its threshold be lowered or raised. The learner is relatively free to manage this to the best of his preference and purpose; I say *relatively* free because he is restricted (a) by his own genetic disposition and (b) by external constraints and stimuli thrust upon him. In organizational jargon: The Window is the mechanism for boundary management that promotes *and* controls the information and the feedback input for the system.

3.2.2   The 'Skin'

Located between the 'Sensing' and the 'Thinking' stages in the LPC this barrier may not always be as clearly distinguishable as the 'Window' (see Figure 9). It is a filter *within* an individual's inner world, thus rather elusive, imperceptible. Yet it can constitute a very important barrier to learning. It is the barrier that determines whether the empirically sensed data which passed through the window are considered to be relevant. They will then influence and be integrated with one's existing store of knowledge and opinions. It is very much a judgmental *filter*. It may be wide open (normal in young people), or selectively open, or biased by experience, or rendered almost completely impervious by prejudice. Its main purpose is to serve as a second line of defence against facts or against outcomes of analyses that would 'change' the person for better or for worse.

This barrier acquired the name *'Skin'* since it can be conceived as a protective layer around the personal opinions we hold dear and because there are a number of popular sayings that use the word 'skin' in this sense. For example: thin or thick skin; get under a person's skin; change one's skin, save one's skin, etc. These denote that one gets very close to a person's sanctuary, his/her holy treasure of opinions. This barrier, like the 'Window', can be visualized as a cross-roads (see Figure 9), where the person's focus has the choice between:

(1) Accepting the information as meaningful and proceeding with updating, confirming, or changing one's accumulated conceptual thinking.
(2) Skipping the integrating thinking stage completely to go on to the stage 'planning', 'doing', or 'sensing'. More experience and data may be required before the analysis can be accepted or trusted.
(3) Rejecting the information as irrelevant, as unbelievable, or as too threatening for one's identity.

This barrier is perhaps the most critical filter in our learning process, for three reasons:

(1) No-one else can influence it or be blamed for how it operates; it truly is a *self-appointed censor.*
(2) It is intricately related to the effectiveness of our long-term memory;

retention is better if the passage of the barrier causes some pain or joy ('Perturbations', see Pedler and Boydell, 1980:181).

(3) It may change its characteristics dramatically during one's lifetime.

A person's 'Skin'-barrier becomes much more selective during life. Young children are assimilating enormous amounts of information without much analysis. Teenagers become more critical about what their parents, teachers, and heroes say and stand for. Adult people gradually screen the incoming data more 'painstakingly'. They search for new bits, trying to find some gold among the dross. How to prevent the baby being thrown away with so much bathwater?

Some adults conclude too readily that there is not much for them to learn any more. Others become cynical and develop a defensive callosity against the harshness of life. I have met managers boasting that they could learn a few new 'tricks' which would, however, they said, not change their personal opinion about the matter in question. Dogmatically-oriented managers are especially susceptible to self-inflicted learning impairment by making it very hard even for facts to penetrate their tough skin-barrier (myopia of section 1.7).

On the other hand there is a limit to the amount of new and relevant information one can digest. How desirable is a culture shock? Developing countries especially run the real risk of a shake-up of the existing culture by too much penetrative news and merciless exposure to the 'goodies' of the West. The avalanche of environmental change can grow beyond many persons' capability of keeping their thought-constructs reasonably integrated, which in turn may undermine people's sense of identity and stability. Then the 'Window' barrier may have to be activated as well as a first-line physical pre-selector.

It is not easy to judge, either for a person, or for a culture-group, to what extent this should be done. Is it for fear of overloading or to defend the (static) system of beliefs against undesirable 'contamination'? This self-appointed censor of this Skin-barrier could be held accountable for apparent blindfolding of individuals and in groups, as Don Juan blames Castaneda (1973) and the Bible warns in several places, for example St Matthew 13:14-15: 'By hearing ye shall hear and shall not understand, and seeing ye shall see and shall not perceive; for this people's heart is waxed gross, their ears are dull and their eyes they have closed'.

3.2.3 The 'Gate'

The barrier between the thinking and the addressing stage acquired the name of *'Gate'* because it represents the opening through which an individual goes out mentally into the outer world (see Figure 9). At that point he 'makes up his mind', whether he will or will not go on to the public stage from the wings and declare his *intentions*. This barrier represents the mental difficulty of taking the intitiative, of making contact, of exploring opportunities for realization of ideas. There is the inherent risk of becoming vulnerable by becoming visible, by sharing one's purpose, by 'showing one's hand'. It comprises the mental dilemma: the wish to assert oneself and the fear of rejection; the freedom of choice of what type of appearance to make.

At this point in the learning cycle, the 'Gate' again represents a cross-roads (see Figure 9), where the learner's mental focus can choose between:

(1) Going public, that is declaring his purpose or intentions openly. This means being pro-active, planning the intervention, acting-out one's scripts (Mangham, 1978) in the hard real world of other people, of limited resources and unforseen situations.

(2) *Not* pursuing his view publicly, shelving his idea temporarily or 'forgetting-it' or 'just doing nothing'; he diverts his mental effort to other business.

(3) Reconsidering the idea/hypothesis/objective and/or the intended action without addressing oneself to the practical application. Taking this diversion, the learner remains in the introvert/theoretical mode.

As stated in Section 3.2.1, all mental barriers are to a certain extent influenced by the level of skills already acquired. This one is influenced by the contactual and planning skills that have to be called upon. If a person has difficulty in speaking-up in public, he may think twice before taking the initiative in lodging a protest, he would not grasp the opportunity as a welcome exercise. Hampden-Turner (1966:369) describes this part in the learning cycle with a neat example of 'Investing Man', or 'Radical Boy' rather who dares to invest and risk part of himself: 'John decides to kiss Mary more ardently and adventurously than she is likely to expect. He thus invests autonomously and risks her displeasure by exposing himself to rejection.'

For many people this pro-activity is a serious psychological barrier. On the other hand there is a lot of crossing of this boundary unknowingly and willy-nilly, since we send out signals and present ourselves often without being aware of it (Goffman, 1971). There is no way of *not* communicating (Watzlawick *et al.*, 1974:42).

Awareness can lower or raise the barrier, hence our liability to lose spontaneity in adulthood, often as a result of negative experiences (rejection and ridicule). People may become very experienced in putting up a front or in making deceitful appearances. As Man is self-conscious, 'People play games' (Berne, 1972) and they can play at playing. This part of the learning process will be studied further from quite a number of aspects later in the book.

3.2.4 The 'Rubicon'

The fourth barrier, between addressing and doing, is more visible and easier to identify (see Figure 9). This is the point where a follow-through, a commitment is required, or inversely where people can opt out, may desert the plan, can call it off at the last moment. It is the end of the preparation and organization phase, the start of the count-down. It is the mental barrier of assuming responsibility, of being committed to go through the 'point of no return'.

For some people this barrier may constitute no more than an imaginary line, or a light-hearted: 'Nothing ventured, nothing won'. For others actually committing oneself to the execution of a (risky) plan might be a formidable mental barrier. It may feel like sticking one's neck out. Or, using another metaphor: declaring one's intention is only stepping on to the ladder, but then one gets the real perspective on the 'diving-board' where one has to decide whether to jump or not. This symbolizes the real cases in life when one must either take the plunge or climb down the ladder for all the world to see!

At this cross-roads (see Figure 9) our focus can choose between more than 'fight or flight'. 'plunge or climb down' by:

(1) Committing oneself to the execution of the plan/project in order to experience what the actual doing is like and to compare results with expectations; a fight if need be.
(2) Skipping the experience itself, leaving it to others, possibly picking up the process again at the sensing/data-collecting stage. One cannot always do oneself what one has been preaching or proposing.
(3) Reconsidering the whole idea or reorganizing the plan: back to the committee or to the drawing board, doing one's homework again.
(4) The flight: postponing the launching, deserting the project or dropping the whole idea. Realization may not be feasible or be too risky under the present circumstances.

'Rubicon' was suggested to me as the appropriate symbol for this barrier. It is the name of the stream that Julius Caesar crossed in 49 BC. It is more widely known in English than in Dutch through expressions like: 'being at the Rubicon' or 'crossing the Rubicon'. Interestingly, the Concise Oxford Dictionary's explanation of Rubicon defines this barrier precisely: 'the boundary by passing which one becomes committed to an enterprise'.

The Dutch have expressions like: 'De kogel is door de kerk' and 'De teerling is geworpen'. The latter are Caesar's words which he spoke when he crossed the stream: 'Alea iacta est' (the die is cast).

3.3 Diversity and elusiveness of learning goals

The above definitions of the stages and the barriers may have focused the reader's attention so much on the separate parts that there is as yet no appreciation of the totality of the model. The interrelatedness between the learning activities and the skills and the barriers will be examined later. Their interaction is rather complicated since this takes place mainly through the subconscious and unconscious parts of the Inner Self. Learning is not a simple process: consider Thyself! (in Chapters 6 and 9).

People are not often aware that they are learning, or why they are learning what they are learning, or at what level of abstraction. Most sensory, cognitive, and contactual skills are rather elusive and can only be perceived and evaluated via the visible 'doing' stage. Only a fraction of what we learn is accessible for direct verification. Learning goals, whether set by oneself or by others, can be specific and explicit, but most are unconscious or disguised.

Before proceeding to the next highest level of complexity, I will describe in practical terms what happens to this conscious, explicit process when people deliberately or *un*intentionally want to *specialize* in particular skills and what happens when some barriers are impenetrable or become real obstacles.

The cyclic process model described so far already makes it possible to bring order to the large diversity of learning purposes and practices. Most of us have, at certain times in our education and work, come across such learning 'specializations', and suffered or enjoyed them. Let us look more systematically in the next chapter at the most common segmentations of the conscious process cycle.

4

Segmentations of the Learning Process

The previous chapter has not, I hope, left the impression that a learner's focus always rather neatly and diligently follows the fully cyclic process. At times his attention will scan around, follow the whims of the moment. Or he may be fascinated by predominantly outside events or by inner thoughts or feelings. Learning takes place in whirling cycles within a lifelong spiral (Section 2.6).

Hardly anybody has a harmonious, balanced learning profile. Who would strive for this? Domineering strengths and weaknesses, special talents and preferences would not let him. People seek identity by developing specialized skills, they go out of their way to achieve something unique, they concentrate all efforts to break records. 'Nature is not so lavish with her boons . . . . Where one capacity is present in perfection, it is generally at the cost of all others' (Jung, 1958:94). 'Complete persons are exceptions. It is true that an over-whelming majority of educated people are fragmentary personalities and have a lot of substitutes instead of genuine goods' (Jung in Jacobi, 1953:275).

Countless persons are restrained and impaired in their development, millions of children atrophied or disabled through lack of opportunity. Some educational systems are straitjackets. Great talents do die undetected. Segmentation of the process seems to be the rule rather than the exception, both in the positive and in the negative sense: helpful specialization and impairing fragmentation. This made me consider in more detail what it means when one or more barriers are obstacles to learning, when one or more stages stand out, are isolated or neglected. The model helps to distinguish a few characteristic patterns that are more common than others. The following descriptions help to identify these in practice.

4.1 Extroverts and Introverts

Let me start with what I consider a major potential segmentation of the learning process. This occurs when a person's 'Window' and 'Gate' are both rather selective or almost completely closed. The effect can be visualized by connecting these barriers with a slanted line (see Figure 10). This imaginary line divides the learning cycle into two halves. The lower-right is the 'learning-in-public' part because the intention is declared and the actions are visible. The upper-left represents the learning in 'private' as it takes place in the seclusion

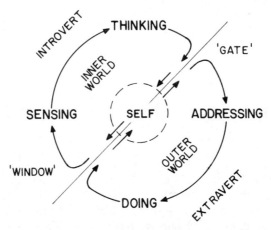

Figure 10   The Inner and the Outer World

of the mind and body of the learner. In other words: there are people who predominantly learn in the 'outer world' and others who learn more or better or preferably in their 'inner world'.

The former group are those who devote their major attention and efforts to the world around them. They will become experienced in dealing with people and tasks and situations in their environment. Their profile of contactual and practical skills is strong. Some may be afraid of new ideas and want to protect their privacy by keeping their 'Window' fairly closed. Others are so busy or pushed by others in modern society that they have little time for reflection. This group run the risk of becoming 'workaholics', who gather plenty of experience, but who may become out of touch with their own inner capacities or purpose in life because of short-cuts they make in digesting their practical experience.

The other group are introspective. Some because they find it difficult to go public with their intentions and prefer not to be too active, visibly or physically. Consequently they will get little practice with their contactual and operational skills. Others prefer to 'specialize' on analyses, evaluations, and/or theory-building; they will concentrate on developing their sensory, analytical, and cognitive skills by monitoring and thinking about events, people, and things, while not testing out their ideas themselves. Potential disadvantages can be indicated with: 'head in the clouds', 'ivory-tower', 'absent-mindedness', 'analyses-paralyses'.

Persons who dedicate themselves to either half of the learning process are often referred to as extroverts and introverts. These psychological terms were proposed by Carl Jung (see further Section 6.1), for which he is best remembered.

The *extroverted* mode orients the individual towards people, objects and events in the world around him; he lives in the present and values his possessions and success and is inclined towards action. The introverted mode orients him towards his own thoughts, feelings and states of mind; he is shy, sensitive, lonely and values his own standards and concepts, he is interested in the underlying forces of laws and nature, prefers reflection and analysis rather than reaching practical decisions . . . . Jung thought of the two modes of orientation as always present in every personality, though one may dominate; he did not consider that either mode was psychologically 'healthier' than the other. (Lindgren and Fisk, 1976:39)

The reasons for developing these segmentations can be manifold. It may be one's upbringing or habitual circumstances, it may be a conscious and deliberate effort, or most likely a self-profiled disposition (remember Section 1.7 on self-profiling?) which is a self-imposed neglect or a short-cut of some parts of one's learning capability. I would not know from my own practice which type runs the greater risk of one-sidedness and bias. In practical terms I would say that managers, supervisors, and engineers are just as often losing out through neglecting the reflective, conceptual, and 'time-to-think' part of their work (and thus on their personal development) as scientists are by underestimating the usefulness of going out into the world of practice (see Beck and Cox, 1980:354). Industry and university could benefit much more from a frequent and intensive interchange between their specialized (segmented) worlds. The result would be, see my Introduction, 'grounded theories and founded practice'.

4.2 Interactions and Transactions

An essential requisite for full benefit from the process is the dual concept of Interaction and Transaction. Man's learning process requires the cyclic interaction between his own inner world and his outer world as he is experiencing these himself. He truly is the 'Window'- and 'Gate'-keeper of his own learning process. The learning process cycle is fundamentally an *Interaction* model: Man can in principle influence the world around him as much as people and things can influence him. Therefore the learning process is also an open *Transaction* model.

The reader must forgive me for finding it important to emphasize and underpin these features of the model with a number of related and fundamentally dialectic concepts of other authors. Buber (1943) postulates with the very simple prime words: 'I—Thou and I—It' that Man can neither find nor develop his own identity without interacting with others and things. He sees life as a continuous struggle between the need for autonomy, to be *in*dependent, to have a domain for one's expanding self and the need for homonomy, that is the ability of relating to others, for enjoying *inter*dependence. Mead (in Bateson, 1978:113) emphasizes as well that Man cannot realize himself through introspection alone, he has to act in the open world and identify himself with a task. 'In setting up *the world* as a field of *transaction*, Self

50

realizes itself' (Zijderveld, 1975:75). Becker (1973:172) goes further in postulating that everybody needs confirmation, independent persons not excluded. Man feels potentially meaningless unless justified by norms outside himself (for example artists from outside the art itself).

Popper distinguishes an inner and outer reality called Worlds 1 and 2 (see Hutton, 1978:11). He argues that there is a causal interaction between them; we form conscious intentions and engage in concrete actions due to the 'purposive nature and mental activity of the conscious-self as the pilot of the brain and body'.

Hutton (1972) presents 'a conceptual scheme for the personal implications of environmental texture' in which he conceives of a person as a system that makes self-initiated assertions in an environment which has varying amounts of control over the person's boundaries. Hutton's schematic concepts are particularly helpful in understanding the subjective feelings of constraint, opportunity, and freedom which the person experiences in the many transactional situations of life.

Emery and Trist classify the nature of the environment (1975: 38–79) in the placid, clustered, disturbed, and emerging-turbulent types, from which they suggest a number of (inter)active adaptations for individuals and organizations: 'the emergence of ideal seeking systems'. Berne developed a theory of 'transactional Analyses' (1972:11–28) which classifies the interactions between two persons on a psychological model of the Inner Self, that is consisting of 'Parent', 'Adult' and 'Child'. Jung states (in Jacobi, 1953:268):

... it is a matter of experience that the man whose interest is directed towards external things is never satisfied with the bare necessities but always aspires to still more and better. In outer human life there is certainly room for many improvements and refinements but these lose their meaning in proportion as the inner man does not keep pace with this. Onesidedness of the psychic diet finally leads to the most serious disturbances of the equilibrium . . . . no-one can escape both realities: if a man turns only outwards then he must live his myth; if he turns inwards only, he must dream his outer so-called real life (Jung in Jacobi, 1953:270)

Reason's 'Human interaction as exchange and encounter' (1977) and Mangham's 'Social interactionism' (1978:14) are equally pertinent to this subject. Their ideas are very insightful for planning interventions in the 'learning communities' of research and organizations.

Trying to see the learning model through the eyes of these authors gave me a number of additional insights, some of which will be used later. The point is that they make it clear from so many perspectives that interactions within oneself and transactions with the outer world are fundamental to learning and development.

4.3 Master and Servant

A second major segmentation of a person's learning process occurs when his/her 'Skin' is (or becomes) rather thick and crossing the 'Rubicon' is a serious problem. The combined effect can be visualized by connecting these barriers with a (slanted) line (see Figure 11), which divides the learning cycle in two halves. The upper-right half represents the short-cut learning process of a person who specializes in thinking and planning, while neglecting the do-it-yourself and the feedback. The lower-left half represents the short-cut loop that is often used to exercise operational skills to higher levels of efficiency and perfection without spending time or effort on thinking or planning.

The first type is found amongst persons whose profession it is to have ideas, formulate objectives, or make forecasts and translate these into proposals, designs and plans. The specialized skills of strategists, 'think-tankers', planners, advisers, consultants, teachers, etc., are essential and very valuable. The natural risk they run is losing the feel for what works and what really matters. If their learning process gets too one-sided their ideas will become unrealistic, their advice be flung to the winds, their white-paper elephants accumulate dust in a drawer. They may become 'backseat drivers', (in Dutch: 'De beste stuurlui staan aan wal').

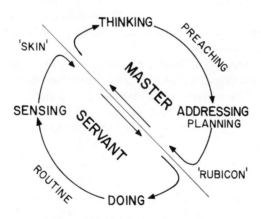

Figure 11   Master and Servant

The second type is found amongst all of us. Every person has to 'reduce' a score of daily activities into efficient routines. This requires many hours of repeated exercises, which are similarly required for highly artistic performances, as masters of crafts, arts and sports will readily testify.

Life would be havoc if our mental focus had to go around the LPC and if we had to make conscious choices for every muscle movement. Our attention must be free for what really matters. Short-cut routines are used for cybernetic-type learning: feedback is not reflected upon, instead we control and adjust automatically the intended, prescribed, or instrumentalized operation (see Instruction in Section 4.5.4). The inherent risk for the learner is that he does not (need to) think for himself, and hence remains uncritical of the purpose and the plan. Lack of participating in thinking and planning leads to alienation; too much routine work reduces the human body to a robot (Charlie Chaplin in his famous film *Modern Times*).

This type of segmentation of the learning process often goes hand in hand with a *value judgement* attached to each of the two halves. Many individuals, groups, and societies hold that those who occupy themselves intellectually are the masters of those who actually carry out the tasks physically. It seems widely accepted that functions such as evaluating, defining policy, planning, and organizing are of a higher level of human activity than performing and controlling the work. Granted, there are exceptions, even reversals, in business, arts, and sports, when those who excel in performance are considered to be the masters. But even then the 'heroes' are often bossed around by their promotion managers!

Not only individuals but also organizations may suffer from this type of fragmentation. A prime example is the ever-present conflict between head office and field-workers, between the planning desks and the factory floors. It is often the combination of the geographical/physical situation and the level of education of the people concerned that separates the 'masters' and the 'servants' into two factions. The 'them-us' syndrome in organizations is typically expressed in reproaches like: 'They don't see the overall picture' versus 'Management doesn't know what is actually going on here' and similar more pugnacious variations.

History books are full of stories of kings, dictators, and political leaders who dug their own graves by surrounding themselves, often unintentionally, with sycophants. The famous role of the jester is to bridge this particular gap and to break through barriers that become too established for the good of master and servant. Quoting *Time* magazine (5 February, 1979, p.10):

> In moments of introspection, the Shah becomes particularly angry at the aides who surrounded him. Out of misguided loyalty, he now senses, they shielded him from reality. 'My advisers built a wall between myself and my people' the Shah bitterly told Sadat at Aswan. 'I did not realize it was happening. When I woke up, I had lost my people. Don't let it happen to you!'

I did not select the title 'Master and Servant' to revive outdated relations or to legitimize the dichotomy between white- and blue-collar workers. It is meant as a warning sign on the personal learning process to keep the 'Skin' *and* 'Rubicon' barriers sufficiently passable to avoid both 'becoming a slave of one's routines' and 'the arrogance of knowing best'. The obvious remedy is to lower the barriers and to appreciate the complementarity of both sides.

4.4   Inductive and deductive learning

A third example of a common segmentation of the process is a specialization in, or a dominance of, either the right or left half of the learning cycle (see Figure 12). In Jung's terms, some people devote most of their effort to *acquiring* information and knowledge, and others predominantly *apply* what they know (see further Section 6.2). From my own praxis I know that there are people who prefer to think (a lot) before they act and others who like to act first and think afterwards (if ever); that there are people who learn best through brainstorming first and then organizing and trying things out for themselves. In courses, the question is where to start the learning process: first an exercise and discussion about practice and then the generalization *cum* theory, or first the principles and then the application and the exercise. It is difficult to predict what will work out best for a group. There are always students and participants who suggest that the other way around would have been better.

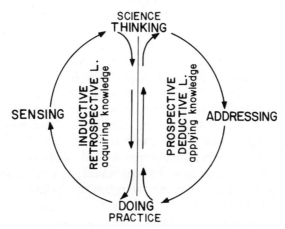

Figure 12   Inductive and deductive learning

But what is better in this respect? Quicker, longer retainment, more insight or skill? Debates on the advantages and disadvantages of starting on either side can go on for ever. My practice is to make sure that the cycle is completed in a *short* time; it is better to repeat the cycle than sequencing two time-consuming halves. This issue is a well-known and recurring one in the educational professions under the names of inductive or deductive learning.

Inductive learning is said to take place from the specific to the general, when the learner starts from the facts of life and proceeds through the stages of analysis and synthesis to arrive at conclusions and/or generalizations. This type of learning occurs *retrospectively*, the person arrives at an insight, upon digesting his personal experience through reflection, in terms and to an extent which could not occur to him and be meaningful until *after* the event. We often make mental simulations of what happened. Sometimes it is a relatively long process (working through many field-data, as in research, as for this book). It may also happen in a flash: the 'Aha!' experience, as when Archimedes leapt joyfully from his bath and ran naked through the streets of Syracuse, crying: 'Eureka!'.

Indeed, there are people who prefer to find out for themselves through practice, observance, and analysis. 'Learning is the awareness of the personal meaning of one's experience' (van Beinum, 1973). This mode of learning is called discovery learning, *post-eventum* or retrospective or inductive learning. The learner has to start with an open mind, accepting others and the world as they are (Rogers, Perls), ready to learn whatever arises from the facts. The importance of this open, unstructured approach to scientific understanding and theory-building has been well argued in Glaser and Strauss' plea (1967) for 'Grounded Theory'.

Deductive learning is said to take place from the general to the specific. In this mode (see Figure 12), the learner starts with a concept, an idea, or hypothesis from which he deduces a plan of action with ways and means of verifying the theory or realizing the objective in practice. All living matter is purposive. But it is typically human that much learning can occur in an anticipating mode, through syllogistic (= deductive) reasoning. Man can consciously direct his focus prospectively from creative thinking via a declaration of intent, through stages of planning, of arranging opportunities and resources into the actual execution and experience. Intensive learning already takes place during the *preparatory* activities, through visualizing, planning, and organizing how an idea may or may not work out. Planning is mental stimulation, planning is learning! Applying theory in this manner is called 'Founded Practice'.

Popper, Kelly, and others have strongly argued that most of our learning is essentially hypothetico-deductive. Popper postulates that hypotheses should be continuously subjected to efforts at *refutation* before they can become scientific theory, if ever. Kelly (1955) has based his personal construct theory very heavily on the prospective part of the process, postulating that 'all our processes are psychologically channelized by the ways in which we anticipate events and construe their replications'. His theory is further discussed in Chapter 7.

The danger of the emphasis on the deductive part is that it can be void of learning if dominated by dogmatic principles. If there are no options considered, no alternatives presented, but only one prescription given, no learning or internal commitment can be expected. This happens sometimes on a large scale. For instance, scholastic theology was concerned with 'precise definition of and deduction from dogma'. This imprisonment of the mind during the 'Dark Middle Ages' evoked a reaction: the periods of Enlightenment and Rationalism of the seventeenth and eighteenth centuries. More emphasis was placed on the inductive part of the learning process, that is on experiments, on empirical scientific methods, and rational analysis. The major debate was on the Nature of Knowledge, on the doctrines of causality and finality, by English philosophers like Bacon, Locke, and Hume, as well as by Descartes, Spinoza, Voltaire, Leibnitz, Kant, Hegel, etc. Can Man rely on innate ideas and deduction from first principles, or is all knowledge empirical?

Fortunately, the arguments and the swings from one emphasis to the other have fostered the development of the sciences. But there is no answer to the issue if it is posed as either inductive or deductive. Because so much is clear from the learning model: deliberate *emphasis* on one segment of the learning process can be propitious at some time and is less harmful to development than denial or exclusion of any segment(s). This I call the *Contingency principle*. And perhaps most essential is the acknowledgment of the *Holistic principle* of the process, that is that the inductive half and the deductive half are each other's natural and essential complements, neither can be left out for any length of time (see the definition of the five principles in Section 4.8).

Let me illustrate these principles with three quite different examples. Firstly, I believe it was C. Handy who formulated: 'Experience without theory is anecdote, and theory without testing is speculation'. At Bath University the title of the 'Centre for the Study of Organizational Change and Development' expresses the intention of covering both the inductive and deductive forms of research, integrating the diagnoses of practice with the application of theories (see Mangham's observing—interpreting—rehearsing—acting in Appendix 5 and Hutton's conceptual—applicability—topicality in Figure 20). Or, in the words I formulated earlier: to be truly professional in any field, one needs to master and combine Grounded Theory and Founded Practice.

Secondly, Kepner and Tregoe (1965), who advocate using systematic approaches to problem-solving and decision-making that are well-known amongst management techniques, define a problem as an observed deviation from a norm for which a cause must be found retrospectively, inductively. And they define decision-making as a prospective activity to transform an idea/objective into reality. Problem-solving is in their terms an exercise in data-gathering, analysis, and logic (what, where, when, who, etc), and decision-making a scanning of possibilities and the judgement of the future outcomes of present choices. They contend that both processes must be systematized and delineated in order to be efficient and effective and to avoid investigating or scanning the whole world.

Indeed there is the bureaucratic danger of turning out elaborate plans and instructions which cover seldom or never occurring instances, and useless details that are already superseded before the event. We have a tendency never to stop looking for opportunities to verify or refute a hunch or hypothesis (Popper's white raven!). People never have enough time to make and study variations in designs and models before proceeding to the realization. Computers are extremely capable of 'presenting' us with almost unlimited variations in worked-out alternatives before any 'first sod need be turned'. Indeed, management techniques which are specially designed for the search for causes *and* for 'satisficing' decisions are very useful.

I found a third and excellent illustration of the principle of the complementarity of the two halves of the learning process in an article by Harrison and Hopkins (1966:17–18) (my italics):

It is not unusual for the returned Peace Corps volunteer to see in his overseas experience a kind of kaleidoscope of impactful, difficult, rewarding, and essentially unconnected experiences. They are unconnected in the sense that he does not see patterns, principles, or generalizations except at the rather concrete level that specific things should have been avoided. They have been through an experience-based overseas assignment without learning anything which they see as clearly transferable to other social situations. *They have not been able to conceptualize their experience.* Hence, they cannot make it available to others. The learning is not lost but is rather latent, waiting for some structuring conceptual framework into which their personal experiences may be fitted in a patterned way. I emphasize the importance of conceptualization because it is possible to become so committed to the primacy of experience, emotion and action, as to devalue the organization of experiences in such ways that they are irretrievable in another situation. Essentially the role for the expert is one of aiding in the *inductive* learning process. He helps the learner to verbalize what his feelings, perceptions and experiences have been and to draw conclusions and generalizations from them. This contrasts with the expert's role in more *traditional* learning settings, in which the learning process has a more *deductive* emphasis . . . .

The last sentence struck me in particular because it applies to my sabbatical period at a university. The 'deductive emphasis in the more traditional learning settings' does not suit mature students. It is wise to exempt them from *ex cathedra* teaching. They need primarily, as do the returned Peace Corps volunteers, to digest, evaluate, integrate and conceptualize inductively all the loose ends of their individual practical experiences. That requires a facilitator in the true sense, someone who provides the guidance to do this not in a standardized but in an individual manner. This last example leads nicely into the next topic: the practices and segmentations in the traditional learning settings of education and training.

4.5 Segmentation in traditional learning

So far we have looked at segmentation in learning in very general terms. The following sections describe specialized modes of formal education and contrived learning. Three opening remarks first. To begin with, it is normal that the educator (the parent, teacher, facilitator, tutor, etc.) is in charge of the learning situation. It is not the learner but the educator who determines the learning goals, organizes the methods, and selects the resources. Objectives and methods are seldom aimed at 'total' education. The emphasis is usually on particular activities and skills via a specialized, partial process.

Secondly, all contrived, formal, explicit learning starts with a stimulus (in this I agree with Skinner) and thus with an input at the 'Window' of the learner. That is the place where the parent, educator, TV, or other medium must get a stimulus into the learner's system, however complete or segmented or impaired or idiosyncratic the ensuing process may be. And finally, it must be said that sometimes quick and efficient learning is brought about by such contrived and single-minded processes. It can also be far less effective, sometimes a waste of effort. In the worst sense it can 'brainwash' and deform the learner (see Freire's *Pedagogy of the Oppressed*, 1972).

When I started to make notes for this chapter I soon realized that the four quadrants of the learning cycle could well coincide largely with the four terms: education, teaching, training, and instruction. This turned out not to hold true in all aspects, but was sufficiently close to warrant such a subdivision. It depends mainly how these terms are understood by the reader. The Oxford Dictionary is not very specific. In fact it legitimizes the words education, teaching, training, and instruction to assume a very wide range of meaning in daily life and in the various professional fields. They are often described in terms of each other.

Accepting some equivocality and overlapping meaning, I still find it important to describe these contrived learning activities as part specializations of the total learning process. Formulating the core meanings of education, teaching, training, and instruction in terms of the cyclic model will highlight the strengths and the professional pitfalls when specializing in educational and training practices.

4.5.1 Education

In its wider meaning 'education' is accountable for a considerable part of a person's development. In its organized, contrived, institutionalized forms it generally means the upbringing of young persons; its lofty aim is to 'educe' their potential. The western-type 'schooling' obviously specializes in providing pupils and students with *knowledge* and understanding about the many aspects of life (on average more about dead things than about live people).

This 'formal' education encompasses the sensory abilities of reading, observing, discriminating, and recording the stimuli as well as the cognitive abilities of categorizing, perceiving, analysing, evaluating, reasoning, synthesizing, etc. (words from Figures 4 and 7). Education concerns itself with the transfer of the accumulated body of knowledge of mankind and the induced generalities and theories. Its activities specialize in all forms of rational understanding within the reflective half of the learning process.

Education is providing input and stimuli about the subjects and guides the learners in processing and digesting the information. The learner is supposed to process its meaning intelligently through his 'Skin' barrier, that is: evaluating the information against the body of knowledge, fundamental laws, accepted rules, and established norms that he has accumulated already, and integrating his insights with it. In short: western education emphasizes the development of analytical and conceptual abilities. In popular terms: 'in school and university I learned to read and to use my brains. Not that I know

58

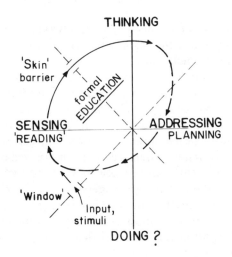

Figure 13   The 'Education' specialization

yet what to do with it or how to apply it all'. In the first instance, the result of education is not visible, it resides with*in* people. In conclusion: the core process of formal education is located in the sensing-thinking quadrant of the learning process (see Figure 13).

We can speak of narrow-minded education if it is limited to a mere transfer of existing knowledge from an existing resource to the memory store of the young learners. Somewhere I heard the story of an auditorium on a campus where one tape recorder was feeding into twelve cassette recorders with no professor or students in sight.

Education becomes *indoctrination* if there is a rigid pre-selection of content, a transfer of a certain interpretation of past experience only, while not letting students find out for themselves or acquire new insights. Staford Beer (1975:24) complains about western education: 'Our tramlines of thought have by now been set in concrete'. Paulo Freire assaults the educational institutions in developing countries: 'The children are thus not prepared for a world to come, they will remain captives of a closed system, the victims of the paradigms of the establishment' (*Pedagogy of the Oppressed*, 1972).

So-called *'Liberal'* education wants to provide options and to promote freedom of thought. The facilitator lets the students discover for themselves (re-search), he avoids imposing too much direction and tries to keep the 'Skin' barrier natural and permeable. This helps the learners to avert prejudice and to integrate what they read or hear or sense into new patterns. The educator can encourage autonomous thinking, exercise the students, critical analytical skills and inductive conceptual abilities and foster the development of the total personality through including some planning and application in the learning process.

The fundamental difficulty is that the unfolding of a learner's ability at a natural pace would not be quick enough. We cannot let the young invent (all) the wheels again. Therefore pre-selection and preparation of content and method are unavoidable. All education is accelerated, it is, 'enforced' learning and development. But in a society that prides itself on being open and wants to prepare itself for the future, effective education requires a rather high level of participation by the learner in setting out the objectives and in selecting the resources, methods, and facilities. However, it is and it will remain difficult to establish the optimum. The art is to determine the right pace and emphasis in joint responsibility for the process. How to select the variety and depth of the content and when does one establish opportunities to branch out and spend more effort on the next segments of the process?

4.5.2 Teaching

Teaching is another specialization of inducing learners to learn. This term is being used for a wide range of activities. The dictionary legitimizes its use as well for general education ('who taught you that?') as for specific instruction ('teach her to swim'). In the world of the specialist, 'teaching' mostly means presenting useful principles and generalizations to pupils, explaining the basic laws and rules that are valid and useful in the concrete world of things and people.

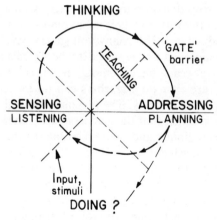

Figure 14   The 'Teaching' specialization

   Teaching starts with *pre*-selected input and stimuli at the 'Window' of the learners (see Figure 14), and it does not leave it to them to sort out and digest the data, it rather presents *'lessons'* on ready-made principles and theories, describing wheels already invented. The assumption of 'teaching' is that the 'skin' barrier is passed without much questioning and that the students can 'efficiently' accumulate large amounts of proven knowledge in a short time. In general, teaching is not meant to induce inductive thinking like education, it often has a clearly deductive, prescriptive slant: to tell what is worth knowing for applying in practice (later). The main aim is to assist people to get through their 'gate', it encourages them to proceed into the direction of practice. Teaching includes exercises to give a feel for appropriate applications, but it normally stays short of developing the practical operational skills. This is left to the specialization of training (see the next section).

The essence of 'Teaching' can be defined as the specialization of the upper-right quadrant of the learning process cycle (see Figure 14). The learner is neither expected nor allowed to do much original personal searching, sensing, or observing; he is not encouraged to do much trying out or getting involved in the real thing. Therefore the major difficulty is to make 'Teaching' interesting and to relate it to the reality of life. Theories may sound irrelevant in the classroom. It is not at all easy to make credible, interesting, and practice-related curriculae. Even when the content material of the lessons is correct, helpful, and practical, the learners may not grasp the meaning and cannot learn (retain the basic material) if they have never seen or experienced the real thing.

Teachers are often constrained by a prescribed programme and by the standardized terminal performance of their pupils (O, A, ONC, HNC and what-have-you levels and degrees). They are liable to lapse into a tedious and boring routine of running a 'sausage factory'. The imparting of prescriptive knowledge may turn into preaching or indoctrination ('this is so, because I tell you'). It is noteworthy that in our 'free' society young persons *must* attend classes *by law*. The (moral) pressures of parents and teachers on pupils are often 'counter-productive'. How many youngsters have experienced learning as fun? Many unemployed are reported to be unteachable and untrainable because their school years have *de*motivated them for life. Also, power relations in society are changing: teachers can no longer demand obedience, nor command long hours of study. The present crisis in the teaching profession is caused in part by the fact that the teachers/tutors themselves have not been taught how to earn credibility and create relevance by the *way* they induce their pupils to learn for themselves.

It seems essential that teachers have their own 'Windows' and 'Gates' open to the world, that they themselves experience in a theory-practice sandwich-fashion what they are going to teach. Only then can they induce students to make frequent little loops through the total learning cycle. *De*fragmentation of the process may have to start with *de*specialization of teachers and with tutors who can teach students how to learn.

4.5.3 Training

The word 'training' has a clear connotation of learning to *do* something. *Chamber's Dictionary* says: 'practical education in any profession, art or handicraft'. The *Concise Oxford Dictionary* says: 'Bring person or animal to desired standard of efficiency by instruction and practice'. For a *trainer* it means arranging opportunities and resources in such a way that specific physical and *operational* skills can be acquired or improved. For the *trainee* it

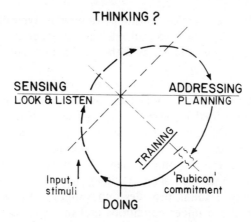

Figure 15   The 'training' specialization

means learning to execute envisaged and/or planned activities under (a variety of) increasingly difficult circumstances, finding the right ways and tools for efficient accomplishment in order to reach the required standards of professional performance.

Sometimes the emphasis is on giving learners confidence to *do* things, reducing their fear of failure: helping them to cross the Rubicon or, to use another metaphor, to step on and take the plunge from the diving-board. Other times the emphasis is more on planning a skilled, effective execution of the task in question or on obtaining better results. Therefore the coreactivities of training are clearly concentrated in the lower right-hand part of the learning cycle (see Figure 15).

Whereas education and teaching aim for a knowledgeable person, the explicit purpose of training is to increase a person's practical competence. It may even result in the acquisition of operational skills *without* congruent changes in attitude or in the make-up of one's cognitive world; for example vocational training.

Training can have an emphasis on contactual operating skills (for example sales-training) or on interpersonal, social skills. In teamwork-training of sports, etc. there is the ever-present tension between three aims: short-term physical results, the longer term development of the 'total' human being, and the contribution to the group. Military and industrial training schemes also have typical difficulties in deciding on the primacy of 'instruction', 'training', 'development', or 'teamspirit'.

The difference with 'instruction' (next section) is that trainees have to retain their personal judgement and that they have to learn to cope with a *variety* of real-world situations in their *personal* way. Therefore it often entails interacting confrontingly or synergistically with other people's intentions and behaviour. That is exactly why it is typically not management instruction but management and supervisory *training*. Business has great immediate interest in this part of the learning cycle, since its main aim is to transform objectives via plans into profitable practice. Business-training is typically done in well-defined subjects and projects so that relevance is ensured and improvements become visible and quantifiable, as with 'Action Learning' as advocated by Revans (1971).

In a narrow way training is sometimes regarded as completely programmable; there are positivistic and rigid training schemes of which the results are not measured in terms of the learner's abilities but in terms of performance standards only (see the recent articles on 'Behaviour Modelling'). There are trainers who claim that measurable output is the only criterion.

From the adult learner's point of view training should not be reductive or prescriptive, but should assist in building his personal competence and confidence. Ideally, training provides opportunities to broaden his skills or exercise them in depth under conditions and in circumstances which occur rather *in*frequently or are too costly in real life (examples are coping with conflict and emergency situations, crash programmes, etc., like training with a flying simulator). Provided the learner's focus is kept on personal judgement, responsibility, and individual skills, there is little chance of the training becoming too mechanistic for development to take place. In order that learning shall continue when the facilitator is not present any longer (having made himself redundant), enough situational and conceptual training must have been given and sufficient learning loops through the *whole* learning cycle have been practised to strengthen the autonomous LTL competence of the manager (see Section 4.7).

4.5.4 *Instruction*

The purpose of 'Instruction' is to improve behavioural operational skills through telling and showing how-to-do-it. The learner is supposed to observe and listen and then to emulate the activity/operation in a similar, if not in exactly the same way: Learning from demonstration and/or modelling. This process is normally intensified by reinforcement, either through personal satisfaction, or in the form of reward or punishment in order to improve the results (Skinner, 1971). Instruction is typically set up so as to shorten the learning process.

From the perspective of the learner both the instructor's activities (tell—show—explain) and his own activities (listen—look—do) are concentrated in the lower-left quadrant of the learning cycle (see Figure 16). The learner is constrained by a strictly structured learning situation and by the pressure of time, so that his mental focus cannot make (wide) process-loops through analysis, thinking, or planning. Such sessions of compact programmed instruction are called 'practice-drills'.

Recognizing fully the negative stigma that 'Instruction' can get by calling it 'classic conditioning' or 'behaviour modelling', let me acknowledge in this section that there are many instances when this specialization is the appropriate learning mode; it can be very functional within the general process of learning and development. Many activities in life have to be executed in one

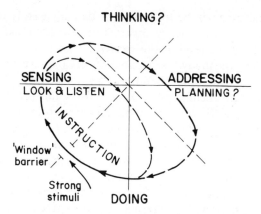

Figure 16   The 'Instruction' specialization

particular way. Many elementary facts and events are explainable by single causes. All of us have to reduce many of our ordinary daily routines to an automatic, repetitive level in order to free our focus for higher level attention. 'To be useful at all, our consciousness must be husbanded' (Bateson, 1978:109).

It is mainly the use of *technology* in a vast and increasing number of activities, that lessens the need for our conscious attention. Many manmade things and symbols are constructed in a particular way and there is often only one straightforward way of operating them. Therefore we need instruction on 'how to read and write', 'how to make a telephone call', 'how to operate a home-computer', etc. We need the 'instructions for use' of the many tools, machines and instruments. It can be dangerous to find out for oneself how they should be operated.

On the one hand there is an increasing awareness that we need *humanized* instruction where the individual learner is and should be involved. For instance the instructions for driving a car should be combined with traffic *education*, that is anticipative and caring behaviour. On the other hand there is an increasing demand for 'programmers' who have the skill of prescribing activities in pure objective, sequential, unequivocal statements with the explicit purpose of *dehumanizing* the activities to a degree that they can be handed over to robotized computer control.

However, it should also be mentioned here that Computer-Assisted-Instruction (CAI or similar techniques) is capable of *individualizing* the learning process to a high degree with respect to method, pace, and level through instructive dialogue. That is why it fascinates youngsters. Computers have an unfailing patience and are indefatigable in presenting options, re-explaining theories, skipping irrelevant parts, assising with exercises, and evaluating personal results, etc., all unmatchable by the most dedicated human instructor. My judgement is that historically we are only just seeing the take-off stage of the software explosion for personalized programmed learning; its application will grow in all fields of education, training, and instruction.

The great challenge will be to satisfy the two apparently opposing requirements: humanness and efficiency. Instructions for use must (of course) be in the language and at the level of the *receiver*. That this is not so obvious and simple is proved by the many 'unreadable' forms and instructions produced by bureaucracies. On the other hand, instructions should be uniform and standardized to keep them simple, to cut costs, and promote wide use (for example typewriter-keyboards, symbols on calculators, information systems on TV, minicomputers, and word-processors).

This dialectic challenge can be largely met, I think, if the person responsible for selecting the specialized mode of instruction is prepared to adopt and apply the five fundamental principles of the total learning process (holistic, quality, etc., see Section 4.8), not only for instructions in the fields of arts and crafts, or for horticultural activities (interplay between green fingers and God) but also for science and for purely technical operational instructions. Pirsig (1974) has given a fascinating and profound account of the issues of quality and value in *Zen and the Art of Motorcycle Maintenance*.

4.6 Negligence of the communicative abilities

The four modes of traditionally organized learning as described in the previous sections are potentially of equally great value. Each specialized mode—education, teaching, training, and instruction—helps the learner to develop a particular group of abilities or combinations of sensing, thinking, planning, and doing. If he wants it, they can give him practice in overcoming any particular mental barrier.

When rereading these earlier sections, it occurred to me that in our western society not all parts of the cycle receive equal emphasis. Adding up the efforts that are usually spent in these four quadrants would not necessarily result

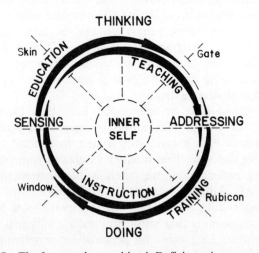

Figure 17   The four modes combined. Deficiency in communication

in an even distribution of devoted time and effort over the whole cycle. It occurred to me that it is quite possible that the specialized modes together could reveal a systematic *under*coverage of one or more sectors. I have tried to show this visually in Figure 17.

Lacking hard data, I have estimated and represented the distribution of the usual efforts in each mode by the thickness of the arrows in the various sectors. Figure 17 can thus be seen as a combination of Figures 13, 14, 15, and 16 but now in a quantitative/qualitative sense of mental attention and explicit practical emphasis. The ensuing picture shows an appreciable overlap and a sort of pairing up, around the thinking and the doing stages. The reason is perhaps, to speak with Jung, that people are primarily inclined either to gather information or to apply it, to concentrate either on intellectual or on physical abilities.

But Figure 17 also implies that the abilities at the two other stages of the learning process, that is the sensory/data gathering and the addressing/planning/contactual skills, do not receive the same amount of effort as the cognitive and operational skills. They seem to get passed over without the same attention. Are the sensing and addressing stages second-rate? Don't they deserve the same explicit, deliberate efforts of our educational institutions?

These two apparently neglected sectors in the learning process cycle can be construed as the two poles of explicit human *communication*. The sensing stage being the input, that is the receiving side for an individual's communication attitude and skills; the window and skin determine how open and sensitive he is for influence by events, people, and information. The addressing stage is the sending, transmitting, or output side of his communicative abilities, the skills of making contacts and proposals, going public and asserting influence on people and events.

Educational institutions require students to be observant (read, listen, search, etc.) at the sensing stage and to be assertive (talk, write, report, and do exams) at the addressing stage. All educational methods rely heavily on the communicative abilities of the student (and no less on the tutor/facilitator), in particular on his searching—reading—listening and his writing—verbalizing skills. The criteria for judging the students' understanding and competence are often exclusively determined and at least critically influenced by their proficiency in a few communicative skills. Students (from overseas) may fail if they do not express themselves in proper English.

However, perusal of the curriculae suggests that very little *explicit* education, training, or instruction is done with respect to skills at these stages. Many learners are just left to themselves to acquire them. Skills of asking questions, searching literature, dealing with and choosing from masses of field data, skills of recognizing or identifying problems, etc. are often frustratingly acquired on an individual basis in a natural, slow, trial-and-error fashion. For instance, few learners are assisted systematically on how to scan the field, how to address themselves to a task, how to present an idea, to advise or counsel others, to make decisions, to plan their work, to deal with the unforeseen, etc.

How important are these process skills for the development and effectiveness of the student's learning capacity?

I am suggesting that the educational professions should pay much more attention to the learning process itself and invest much more effort in a range of supportive skills. The allocation of one hour of the students' first term to data-gathering, to library work, or to note-taking is far too little for the average student. I know that it is not 'the thing to do' at universities to train students in planning and organizing their own learning, but I am convinced that it is the most effective thing to do. It is appalling that there are still lecturers and educators who either ignore or perhaps are ignorant of the basic tutorial principles. It is precisely in these weakly covered sectors of the learning cycle that difficulties are experienced by managers and time is wasted by society as a whole. How are we to cope with the steeply increasing amounts of news, data, books, and reports that are being produced? The problem in the western world is how to deal with and how to digest the available information. When managers are frustrated and complain about the number of memos and files, about the avalanche of papers cluttering their in-trays and offices, about the reports they should read, they implicitly acknowledge that it is not easy to be selective, set priorities, and competently process the ever increasing amount of data that is presented to them. What is frightening is that the information society seems to be in its infancy.

Although great progress is being made in (electronic) data-handling, computers and satellites have not led to a reduction in the amount of data. On the contrary, practice has proved the paradox that dealing with data creates more of it. The danger of uncontrollable overload has already been described some 150 years ago in Goethe's classic story of 'Der Zauberlehrling'. In the sense of Goethe's story, it is indeed the nature of information that it can be multiplied at almost no cost. It is not lost when shared, but doubled or multiplied!

Collectively we are arrogant enough to think that technology will help us to deal with this information explosion quantitatively. The greatest stumbling block, I think, is the qualitative aspect. I am afraid that the deficiency in communicative skills is going to show and is hurting already, mostly at the 'human side of the enterprise' (borrowing McGregor's classic title). Qualitative subjective, emotional, contextual, and other non-rational aspects are essential for working well together.

Most of a person's learning, especially in the early years of life, and much of the human 'interactions-by-encounter' (Reason, 1977) takes place *un*consciously in qualitative, subjective, analogue terms. To understand and transmit appropriate non-verbal communication (gestures, intonations, facial expressions), using the correct metaphors, meta-messages and other emotionally related signals is not easy at all. If two persons say the same thing, its effect on others need not be the same at all! *C'est le ton qui fait la musique!* This is particularly sensitive and deceptive cross-culturally (see Sections 8.5 and 12.1).

I am sure that there will be much resistance to including these qualitative aspects of communication in educational institutions and training practices. It is just 'not done' and not easy to do. Moreover, spontaneous, effective non-verbal communicative skills can only be genuine if they are congruent with a person's Inner Self. Can and should more explicit attention be given to students' and managers' Inner Self and to their intuitive faculties? The educators themselves are all too human (see Section 8.6).

I shall deal with these questions in much more depth in order to understand how Man's subconscious and unconscious inner faculties affect his learning and his personal development. Before doing this in Part III let me first round off the significance of the explicit learning process cycle with a practical and with a conceptual section.

4.7 Management training or management development?

After a few general examples of the various segmentations of the learning process mentioned above, I will now describe some helpful modes of specializations *and* harmful fragmentations that exist in the field of my main interest: the learning by managers.

Firstly, it is worth noting that the learning process cycle has its equivalent in the 'Cycle of Management'. The general words around the learning cycles of Figures 4 and 7 can be replaced by, or be translated into, the typical terms and expressions in use in the world of management. This leads to the Cycle of Management of Figure 18. Most terms are readily recognizable as likely headings of chapters in textbooks on management. The cyclic process of management is indeed a learning process.

Obviously, courses on management often make a choice from these many subjects. In daily praxis certain aspects need more special attention and effort than others. One day the emphasis may be on planning and forecasting, other days on projects, on motivation, or on financial controls, etc. There are specialized management books on most of these topics. Indeed, circumstances may call for segmentation, but for an all-round management education the whole cycle has to be dealt with. Management is the art of perceiving what subjects need special attention when and where, it requires the ability to handle all stages and activities of this management cycle.

I am afraid, however, that management development as organized by institutes is seldom comprehensive; in most cases they are selective and exhibit a particular slant or bias. At universities management education is treated like other academic studies: the students are required to familiarize themselves more with theories than practices (finance, marketing, industrial relations, organization, history of management science, etc.). Sometimes 'cases' are used for problem-solving, for planning and recommended action, but most studies remain typically concentrated around concepts and theories.

Business Schools can easily fall into the trap of fragmented education. Quite an amount of criticism has been levied, even against the *grandes écoles*.

68

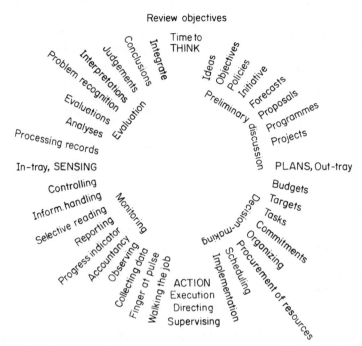

Figure 18   The 'Cycle of Management'. A special version of the learning process

Although many MBAs see themselves as 'the best and the brightest and the most energetic and ambitious as well, a growing number of corporations look on them as arrogant, individualistic amateurs, trained only in figures, in pre-prepared problems and short-term money-making. They lack experience in both the technology of producing goods and the motivation/handling of people' (*Time*, 4 May, 1981, p.37).

Consultants and in-company management trainers concern themselves, by necessity, with the practical activities of managers around the doing stage. The emphasis may shift to the planning side, for example decision-making, organizing projects, etc., or to the observing/analytical side, for example financial controls, but there is seldom enough time for reflection and conceptual, strategic review. They are just as liable to become too one-sided.

Whatever the specialization, whether this is 'Management by Objectives', the 'Case Method', 'Action Learning', etc., nobody can claim to have found the panacea. The universal remedy for any trainee/student is that he is shown and reminded frequently how the specialized technique/topic/practice fits into the *whole* management process.

Secondly, with respect to the individual manager, his specialization and learning profile can be very idiosyncratic. Personal preference, environmental pressure, and organizational requirements can lead to a particular concentration on any part of the learning cycle. This was discussed in Section 1.7 under the heading 'self-profiling'.

In these days of unpredictable futures, of quick social and technological changes, much emphasis is placed on the desirability of entrepreneurship

(Drucker, 1980). In terms of the learning = management cycle, an entrepreneur is most able and puts most effort into the right-hand side of the cycle. He has a vision of what might be. He is creative and pro-active, and optimistic with respect to opportunities. He makes new relationships with people and things in a wide environment. He attracts and motivates his staff to join him in converting plans into reality, to be dedicated and persevere when the going gets tough.

This description, upon which the reader may improve, tries to convey that an entrepreneur has more qualities than the 'trainable' activities of the prospective, deductive part of the process cycle of Section 4.4. It is the spark of life, vitality, risk, courage, etc. which gives quality to the actions of an entrepreneur. These emanate from his Inner Self (the subject of Part III).

Thirdly, with respect to the neglected communicative abilities discussed in the preceding section, I can now be more specific. These insufficiently treated learning sectors largely coincide with the typical management processes under the names of Problem Analyses (PA) and Decision-Making (DM). When we translate PA as perceiving a deviation from the normal or the expected, collecting relevant data, analysing them, drawing conclusions, etc., it is clear that these are synonyms for activities and skills around the sensing stage. Similarly, describing DM as defining objectives, exploring opportunities and resources, formulating alternatives, proposing and organizing the chosen course of action, we recognize these as specialized skills around the addressing/ planning stage.

There is much scope for improving the PA and DM abilities of most managers in most organizations. This is borne out by the extensive attention given to these subjects in management training and literature. Their prominence is partly caused by the increasing complexity (interrelatedness) of the problems, opportunities, and issues in our turbulent environment (Juch, 1978; Drucker, 1980). These can be met only partly by more intuitive approaches. A number of times I have come across a typical profile of what I call the good old-fashioned manager (see Figure 19). Despite an apparent lack of explicit

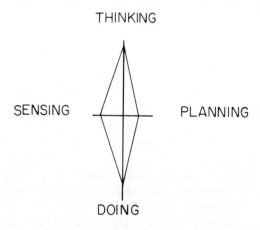

Figure 19   Profile of the 'good', intuitive manager

70

communicative abilities, he is quick in sensing when something goes wrong, while impatient when listening to long stories. He wants a one-page memo. He visualizes remedies and chances intuitively, and is quick and strong in flipping over from thinking to doing, from an idea to application. However, these subconscious skills are only effective in cases where the individual can act *on his own*. Intuitive behaviour is less functional in participative task groups, where data, factors, and judgements have to be shared and discussed; then communicative skills in explicit rational, analytic, that is left-brain fashion, are indispensable. These can certainly be acquired through training in rationally explicit PA and DM, one hopes without losing spontaneity, intuition, etc. (see Section 8.6).

Fourthly, not only individuals but also organizations and societies specialize in *parts* of the learning process. Since Man's subunits (for example his head, hands, and heart) are very successful in their specialized functions, it seems logical to expect that organizations also perform better through functionally specialized groups. Ever since Taylor, organizations have had specialists. There are thinkers and doers, planners and auditors, designers and organizers of resources, those who supervise and those who carry out the physical work. But specializations tend to fragment the total process. If the barriers between the functional departments or between the levels (top, middle, and lower management) become too selective or too tight, 'organization-learning' diminishes and organization development stops.

Finally, the policies on management development vary from organization to organization. The major segmentation is between management-*education* and management-*training*. Some organizations send their managers to academic courses, outside seminars, and sabbaticals in order to reflect and strengthen their *conceptual* approaches. Other companies would rely more exclusively on growing their own timber through *practice*, rotation, and assignments ('action learning'). Management development also varies from country to country. Each seems to promote its own particular pattern and styles. Appreciation of subjects and methods in education and training is quite different. When arranging further education for Omanis in countries as close to each other as France, Germany, the UK, and the USA, one comes to realize how very different the educational systems of these countries are, even within the sphere of business-management.

As said before (Section 1.7) there is nothing wrong with 'self-profiling' of individuals, organizations, or society. The question is whether this is done by design or by ignorance. The latter leads to one-sidedness and myopia at micro-meso-, and macro-levels. Society would benefit greatly from less segmentation between science and industry; experience and feedback should be more readily sensed by academics and new ideas find a more expedient crossing of the 'Rubicon' into business and other organizations. The potential benefit from more cross-cultural appreciation and fertilization is still undervalued.

Whatever segmentation or emphasis seems to be called for in organization (management) education, training, or instruction, it can only lead to healthy, non-deformed management and personal development if the institutions and educators build into their programmes and practices the fundamental learning-to-learn principles. These minimize the disadvantages and optimize the advantages of any particular specialization, as shown below.

4.8 The five fundamental principles

In this chapter I have tried to make the cyclic learning process more meaning-ful by illustrating with the model what happens when one or more barriers are an obstacle to completing the round and when one or more learning stages are isolated or neglected. This common experience induced by each individual's own preferences and talents is amplified because he can remain selective at home, at school, in his job, and in social life, under all types of education, teaching, training, and instruction, organized and directed by others.

What are the criteria by which this diversity of segmentation and fragmenta-tion can still work out all right and when does it trap the learner into a crooked or blind alley? How can we promote learning and development so that they are formative and not *de*formative and so that the process is enjoyable, ongoing, and self-propagating? I believe that this ideal can be fostered by some fundamental principles. These were identified in the earlier sections but they deserve to be brought together now.

4.8.1. *The contingency principle*

This postulates that it all depends! — that it is the combination of the need and talents of the learner, the nature of the subject and task, the prevailing situation, and the available resources that determine where the focus and the emphasis should be at any time and that the appropriateness must be frequently checked with the learner. I hope that the preceding sections have made it clear that all specialized modes of education, teaching, training, and instruction have their *raison d'être*. No teacher/facilitator should be dogmatic or one-sided. The art is to know what to apply and when, to use flexibly and alternatively all techniques and methods when appropriate, that is when effective for the development of the learner.

Educators, trainers, consultants, that is all facilitators, should, I think, be the first to demonstrate this contingency flexibility themselves. Management trainers cannot expect to induce any learning if they are not authentic in advising managers to become more sensitive or reflective, or to be more creative, if they themselves are not able to be pragmatic or reflective, sensitive or creative or productive at the appropriate moments. A facilitator must be prepared to accept that other facilitators/consultants could be more effective than himself in certain circumstances, for certain purposes.

4.8.2 *The holistic principle*

This postulates that the four learning modes are essentially complementary and mutually supportive. No part of man's development can stand or be effective on its own. Each learning stage and each mode is so much more effective if short, quick excursion loops are made frequently around the whole process, to ascertain what and where strengthening and potential gains are possible. Other learning modes illuminate and enhance previous and subsequent learning more often than not. Quoting Hampden-Turner (1966:369): 'the cycle itself is an organismic *whole* from which the different segments cannot be served or isolated without breaking the human mold'. 'Life calls not for perfection but for completeness' (Jung).

The holistic principle is the essential complement to the contingency principle, that is in preventing specialization from becoming counter-effective. All types of educators and learners have a natural inclination to specialize in favourite subjects and to lapse into routines. Some sectors are more favoured or susceptible to neglect than others (see Section 4.6). Learners run a real risk of their skills becoming too one-sided or irrelevant.

At certain situations/moments people learn more from a different mode or resource than from those they have been habitually using. Laudable experiments in this direction are sandwich programmes and *inter*faculty courses for students; the Open University and sabbaticals (recurrent education) for adults; applications seminars, postings, and exchange of specialists, staff, and line personnel.

The holistic principle postulates that the question is not 'either-or' (as in introvert or extrovert, inductive or deductive, theory or practice, mind or matter) but that there is extra gain (synergy) in transcending polarities and in integrating functional specialization.

4.8.3 The interactive principle

The fact that development cannot take place in isolation was extensively discussed in Sections 4.1 and 4.2. The cyclic learning model shows that our mental focus alternates *and* interacts between our inner and outer worlds. It creates the interaction between the learning stages and between the conscious and unconscious abilities all the time.

Exercising both the receiving sensory and outgoing contactual skills is essential for developing the communicative nature of the human being. The interactive principle postulates that transactions with things and people are fundamental for personal growth. Learning by 'encounter' is the real thing. Learning stops when the interaction stops, when people close their system.

4.8.4 The liberating principle

It makes all the difference whether the learner feels liberated or restricted, encouraged or oppressed. If the learner is uninterested or torpid, or has become a drop-out, visibly or invisibly, one may go through all the motions of education, teaching, training, or instruction with little learning taking place.

Outer direction and 'forced growth' will only lead to partial and short-term results. Passive compliance may hide the fact that internalization does not take place: 'You can lead a horse to water but you can't make it drink'.

On the other hand, receiving no guidance, no teaching, or no direction at all is not liberating either, because that would mean absence of interaction and 'abandonment'. Torbert presents (1978:109) 'a theory and practice of liberating structures for an education that moves towards a sense of shared purpose, self-direction and quality work'. Paulo Freire (1972) is spending his lifetime liberating the education of peasants in Latin America; he seeks to do this by raising their political awareness.

In my terms, the liberating principle postulates that facilitators should always ensure that learners progress in the direction of more freedom and more worth. It is essential that they feel empowered and see more options to choose from. All modes, even 'instruction' can and should be liberating, for instance by increasing the learner's competence and confidence without constraining him.

This fundamental difference is expressed in the Dutch words: '*af*richten-*op*leiden', of which the closest equivalents are: 'break-*in*' (as of a horse) and 'bring *up*'. Many a revolutionist (including persons like Freud) originally welcomed as a liberator, actually reduced the options of his followers. The interesting corollary for the educator (teacher, tutor, facilitator, etc.) is that he should promote the learner's independence and his own redundancy. That is not so easy.

4.8.5   The quality principle

The quality of learning has already been mentioned very briefly a few times (Sections 4.5.4 and 4.6). We know intuitively that the human faculties, abilities, and skills have a quality aspect, but it proves difficult to describe, let alone to promote. The explicit, conscious, rational-systems approach to Man's development, which is so 'popular' in the western world, overrates the quantitative and undervalues the qualitative aspects. I share Mangham's concern (1978:77) that this may reduce the quality of academic research.

Quality is extremely difficult to define. Pirsig (1974) has been struggling with it. In daily life it is indicated with expressions like 'green fingers', 'golden hands', 'lucky touch', etc. It is certainly related to the person's existential inner faculties, that is to his mental make-up, his subconscious and unconscious dispositions and personal talents, and it depends on the degree of cohesion and congruency of the person's values, skills, and behaviour.

Quality is perhaps a transcending principle, the Principle of Principles, so to speak. When describing the four others, I repeatedly have the feeling that when I understand and experience the very essence of a principle, I recognize a same (transcending?) point where they all seem to merge. For instance, the positive effect of the contingency principle is that a specialization functions properly when it is needed, it helps, liberates, and strengthens synergistically at the right moment in any situation, which is precisely the holistic principle; the positive effect of the interaction principle is that transactions and cross-fertilization bring about better understanding and different ways of doing things; and that again is similar to liberating from unhelpful barriers, making room for further total development, that is holistic development, and so on.

In other words: the quality principle may well express the fact that the previous principles are inseparable and complementary and that they are essentially only different aspects of the same overall purpose of the human development process, which could be called 'Personal Growth', or 'Individuation' (Jung), 'Actualization' (Maslow), Total Health, Synergy, Quality or whatever transcending value. It is exactly the characteristic of transcendence that 'higher' qualities merge into one and the same (Maslow, 1972).

I want to understand in more detail how these principles are related to and brought about by the mental faculties of the Inner Self. Can they be made to manifest themselves in any or all learning activities and become part and parcel of our skills? Can we enhance their practical impact by a better understanding of Man's subconscious and unconscious? This is the subject of the next four chapters in Part III.

PART III

The Interlude

The previous chapters may have left the impression that Man's learning is mainly a matter of intellectual and physical practice. It is not. It is more than explicit, logical, sequential activities of his instruments (eyes, ears, hands, etc.) directed and controlled by his brain. His personal growth is just as much influenced by what his *'heart and guts'* let him or make him learn. Much of this happens without him being aware. Personal development has more dimensions than conscious learning, it is also a very intricate subconscious psychosomatic process.

In this Interlude I shall digress from the theme of cyclic learning and explore more freely some theories and concepts with the aim of a more fundamental comprehension of Man and his faculties. We need to know more about:

(1) Man's inborn drives and abilities (Chapter 5).
(2) His psychological nature (Chapter 6).
(3) His cognitive nature (Chapter 7).
(4) The nature and function of his brain (Chapter 8).
(5) The roles these play in his learning and development (Chapter 9).

I shall not claim to say much new about the human psyche and brain; the fields of psychology, biology, psychosomatics, neuro-physiology, anthropology, etc. are just too vast and expanding too fast to comprehend completely. My limited aim is to understand enough from these fields to bring human learning and development into accord with the latest insights. Making a selection from the many scientists and writers is unavoidable. I have chosen those aspects that were (a) interesting, (b) compatible with my experience, and (c) suitable (philosophically and functionally) for my purpose of expanding the learning model into a general development model.

At times I will quote and use other writers' concepts and jargon. I may not always explain them. However, the learning and conclusion that I draw from them will be described in terms of the above chapters. I hope the reader may find, as I did, something new from integrating these cross-functional views with my cross-cultural experience.

5

Man's Inborn Faculties

As with so many subjects nowadays the literature on this topic is super-abundant. Where to start? It seemed most worthwhile for me to study the subject from different perspectives. For instance, to name a few, from an evolutionary perspective (Sagan, 1977; von Ditfurth, 1976); from a philosophical (Buber, 1943; Schumacher, 1978); from a historic (Beer, 1975; Friedlander, 1976); from a one-man's-lifetime perspective (Lievegoed, 1979; Lindgren and Fisk, 1976; Hunts and Hilton, 1973); and also from a managerial-career point of view (Muller, 1970; Evans and Bartolome, 1980).

Another difficulty is that there are many protagonists of a 'one-most-important' faculty, but obviously not always of the same faculty. For instance, Man is conceived first and before all as *Homo Sapiens*, or as *Homo Faber*, *Homo Ludens* (Huizinga), *Homo Trudens* (Weyel), *Homo Sex* (Freud), *Homo Hierarchicus* (Dumont), *Homo Gobernador* (Beer), or *Homo Discriminator* (this book, Section 8.7). Others have branded him as the Organization Man, the One-dimensional Man (Marcuse), the Radical Man (Hampden-Turner), Inquiring Man (Bannister and Fransella), Infant Man (Hunts and Hilton), the naked Ape (Morris), the Manipulator (Shostrom), the Scientist (Kelly, Section 7.1) and many more. Others do not agree with any mono-dimensional model and distinguish the predicament of Man as a fundamental X-Y dichotomy, for instance 'Janus' (Koestler, 1978), 'To have or to be' (Fromm, 1978), the 'skating model' (Brakel, 1979), or 'Yin and Yang' (Foy, 1981).

Each author uses his own special kind of language, symbols, and metaphors so that at first reading their approaches appear to have little in common. This is unfortunately confusing for incidental readers. With further acquaintance, their views become much more similar, sometimes surprisingly complementary, as I have come to appreciate.

In Figure 20 I have shortlisted a number of authors who concern themselves with the development of managers and organizations and who propound a 'triune' (3-in-1) concept of Man. I have used the superficial labels of X, Y, and Z dimensions, because although I am looking for similarities the columns have *not* the pretensions of a forced comparison. As a warming-up for a more in-depth discussion later, I would like to summarize three of these contributions in this chapter; they throw valuable light on Man's inborn faculties from very different directions and perspectives.

Author	Propounded by Year	Subject	Labels of development dimensions X	Y	Z
Many	Ancient	Total Man	Head/mind	Hand	Heart/soul
Many	19th century	Education	Cognitive, intellect	Physical, behaviour	Spiritual
Muller	1970	Career potential of managers	Power of analysis	Sense of reality	Power of imagination
Dale & Payne	1976	Development of adults	Awareness	Resources	Ego-strength
Friedlander	1976	Organiz. development	Rationalism	Pragmatism	Existentialism
Berne	1972	Transact. analyses	Adult	Parent	Child
Beer	1975	Aspects of man	Homo Sapiens	Homo Faber	Homo Gobernador
Burgoyne	1975	Learning theories	I know	I can	I will
Boydell	1976	Experiential learning	Cognitions	Connations	Affects
Hutton	1969	Research	Conceptual	Applicability	Topicality
Kagan	1969	Personality	Thoughts	Behaviour	Beliefs
Pedler	1978	Self-development	Thoughts and ideas	Action tendencies	Feelings
Neth. Paedag. Inst. (Lievegoed)	1979	Human development	Thinking	Doing	Feeling
Harrison	1979	Motivation	Intellectual, politico-economical	Physical competence	Affective social

Figure 20 The X-Y-Z dimensions of development

5.1 Power, ability, and sense. A Helicopter view

What are the fundamental qualities that carry a person into a senior position in society? What makes him acquire the necessary skills? Can potential 'high flyers' be detected at an early stage? And how? Do they require special attention?

The need to identify future senior managers as early as possible has long been recognized in the larger organizations. The story goes that Alfred Sloan, General Motors' famous chairman of the board from 1937–56, embarrassed his professional personnel advisers in a wartime boardroom meeting with the question: 'Managers, are they born, or are they made? Where shall we invest most money and effort: in finding them or in training them?'

Since then, quite an amount of thought and experiment have been devoted to this issue. The conclusion remained the same: there is no straight answer to this 'either–or' question. The essential point is that born managers must first be identified and then trained. They should be given the opportunity to develop themselves. Most large organizations allocate roughly the same effort and money to identification/assessment of potential high flyers as to explicit training of their promising staff. That has proved to be a good 'rule-of-thumb' policy.

In the mid-1960s Royal Dutch Shell sponsored an extensive research study by the faculty of industrial psychology of the University of Utrecht, Holland, called: 'the search for the qualities essential to advancement in large industrial groups' (Muller, 1970). The objective was to find the basic common denominators that take managers to Shell's top positions throughout the world. The intention was to probe beyond professional expertise and beyond functions and nationalities. The study wanted to identify the fundamental human qualities that determine managerial potential, especially those which can*not* be *acquired* through training but which can be *developed* through training and through exposure to different opportunities and varied experience.

The research project was very empirical and practical. Muller gleaned from the many 'qualities of personality' which had been used in the past to guide promising people into senior jobs. The study included an identification and validation exercise of the careers of some 500 highly placed managers throughout the world. The data-gathering itself was already useful in that it brought more uniformity and objectivity into the diverse practices of appraisal.

Muller started by identifying, collating, and defining those 'categories of appraisal' that were most frequently used in the assessment of managers, for instance: intelligence, integrity, perseverance, emotional stability, leadership, and so on. Some twenty-eight of these 'personality traits' were defined. These could finally be reduced, through experimental rankings and stepwise multiple regression analyses, to four basic qualities that carried most significance and were independent of each other.

(1) Power of Analysis: the ability and drive to transform, break down, or reformulate an apparently complicated problem into workable terms;

and continue the analysis of the problem until all the relevant aspects have been thoroughly and critically examined.

(2) Power of Imagination: the ability and drive, while remaining pragmatic, to discern the various possibilities and alternatives which are inherent in one's problem field but which are not obvious to less perceptive observers.

(3) Sense of Reality: the ability and drive to select objectively and unemotionally, without becoming unimaginative, a sound and practical solution and display an intuition for the right course of action.

A new and fourth indicator of an individual's potential was formulated as the *Helicopter Quality*, a metaphor coined by Professor Van Lennep of Utrecht University. The concept itself was recognized in (early) literature, for instance it has been mentioned in seventeenth-century French philosophy and appeared under various names like 'total view', 'high-vantage point', 'breadth of mind', 'zooming out', etc. But the word 'helicopter' expresses an extra *complementary* quality, it symbolizes that a person is able to see the relevant detail *and* simultaneously raise his mind above the present and local tumult; he perceives the scene in perspective and with a longer time-span, and he maintains a broad view when taking command of the specific local issues while 'having his feet on solid ground'.

(4) This Helicopter Quality is thus defined (Muller, 1970) as a man's ability and drive to:

(i) look at problems from a higher vantage point with simultaneous attention to relevant details and to shape his work accordingly on the basis of personal vision;

(ii) place facts and problems within a broader context by immediately detecting relevant relationships within systems of a wider scope.

This quality was found to have by far the highest relevance to ultimate career potential. It correlates closely with the *composite* score of the three other qualities. Together they are called with an acronym, the HAIR qualities (*H*elicopter, *A*nalysis, *I*magination, *R*eality).

Shell has based its procedures for the career progression of all its senior international staff on the results of Muller's study. *Every* year *two* reports have to be made up by all immediate supervisors: a Report on Performance and a Report on Development. The first one is a joint appraisal of the work performed during the year and new objectives, tasks, and targets are formulated and agreed for the coming year. The Report on Development (see Figure 21), appraises a person's abilities and career potential and *must* also be *discussed with* the person concerned. This worldwide appraisal and career-progress system has now been in use for over a decade.

It is not my intention to describe this system administratively nor to appraise

			period of
			assessment
			From:
			To:

COMPANY	NAME AND INITIALS OF EMPLOYEE	JOB TITLE	DATE TO
			JG SG
DATE TO COMPANY	TITLE	DATE TO JOB	

FUNCTION/DIVISION/ DIV INDICATOR	DATE OF BIRTH	DATE JOINED GROUP*	PENSION DATE	NATIONALITY	QUALIFICATIONS	GROUP JOB SALARY

I APPRAISAL CATEGORIES
(Full description of the categories are givin on the back of this form)

a. Basic Appraisal Categories

No. Category	below	meeting	exceeding
	present job level requirements		
1 Analysis 2 Imagination 3 Sense of Reality 4 Helicopter			

b. Effective Leadership

Marked ☐   Average ☐   Limited ☐

II NARRATIVE APPRAISAL
Please give clear narrative illustration supporting Section 1: also comments on any qualities considered insufficiently covered by the basic categories. This Section should not be a repeat of the performance appraisal.

III FOREIGN LANGUAGE PROFICIENCY	English			
Speaking				
a. In his own field				
b. General				
Writing				

E = excellent; G = good; S = satisfactory; P = poor

Sections IV and V to be completed in consultation with the highest practicable level of management and with the Pers. Manager/Pers. Adviser

IV POTENTIAL

Express in job groups
assume unlimited available openings

a. Within three years

b. Currently estimated potential.

If CEP is in the lettered categories show whether he/she would develop best in:

1.   a functional capacity ☐

2.   a general capacity ☐

3.   either of 1 and 2 ☐

4.   too early to say ☐

V DEVELOPMENT

Within three years

Show recommended and possible jobs. If employee has reached CEP show desirable lateral moves.

Longer term possibilities

Show recommended and possible development directions

Reporter's Name	Comments by Manager/Division Head	For use by Central Office's Personnel Records
Signed:		
Date:	Name: Signed: Date:	

Figure 21   Report on development

82

its practical utility. Let me only say that it is standing the test of time, it works in such a multinational company. The process is considered beneficial for all parties involved:

(1) Appraisees receive yearly a formal recognition and feedback on their performance, they get an indication of where they stand and what their prospects are.
(2) Appraisers have to formulate carefully and rather objectively the performance *and* the potential of their staff, and they know that they themselves are in turn being appraised by their bosses.
(3) Personnel advisers of Central Offices obtain comparable information about the competence and potential of all senior staff. This makes it possible to plan the 'Human Resources', for example the recruitment, assignment, and promotion of the international staff on a corporate basis, as well as the availability and placings of individuals on the longer term in line with their assessed abilities.

Two interesting and essential features emerged from the study. Firstly, while it is not easy to define exactly what potential is, it seems not too difficult to perceive a person's potential through evaluating his performance and behaviour in terms of the HAIR qualities. The spread in judgement on the same individual by different appraisers is seldom too large to handle. Secondly, while it is very difficult, even for the most experienced appraisers, to assess basic qualities (potential) in *absolute* terms, it proved much easier to rank-order individuals on the HAIR qualities *versus others.*

Most people can make firm, consistent, and reliable judgements in *relative* terms based on practical criteria like: which of the two has more sense of reality; or which of the three can deal with problems within the widest context; or how do Messrs A, B, C, and D rank in order of their power of analysis? This also holds for subordinates appraising their bosses.

This system led Shell to develop a special *ranking procedure* to compare every year the career potential of all senior staff around the world in different cultures and functions and positions. Using benchmarks, these potentials are expressed by ranking panels in terms of equivalent job-*levels*. Each individual's 'currently estimated potential' (CEP) is the highest position-level, whether available or not, which he/she is considered to be able to manage at *some future date* comfortably and successfully without being overstretched. The CEP of each senior staff employee is verified (reappraised) yearly and the person concerned must be informed of any adjustment.

Coming back to my purpose: what is the relation between these basic managerial qualities and the learning/development model of this book? Both studies are concerned with the development of the capabilities of the individual adult and both are supposedly fundamental and comprehensive. Are the four HAIR qualities directly related to the four learning stages, or to the four mental barriers of the model? No, that superficial coincidence has no validity.

By definition and purpose, the HAIR qualities are basic *drives* and mental *powers*, they are neither activities nor acquired skills. Therefore they are located, as inborn faculties, *within* the Inner Self of the learning model. They are driving forces for the explicit learning process. They become discernible operationally as the mental powers that inhibit or activate the process, that decide and regulate where time and effort are spent.

In other words, the HAIR qualities constitute the group of driving talents and mental energy behind the whole learning/development process. They have a similar function to the mental barriers and gateways. On the basis of Figures 4 and 7 it is not difficult to locate the 'power of analysis' in the upper-left quadrant of Figure 22. The 'power of imagination' is, in a similar way, mostly required to activate and guide the process between thinking and planning in the upper-right quadrant. The 'sense of reality' governs a rather large part of the cycle, both before *and* after the actual performance and events. This combination finds confirmation in Muller's description (1971:3) that the sense of reality is both *pro*spective (realistically anticipating circumstances and committing oneself) as well as *retro*spective (objectively monitoring and reflecting on what actually happened).

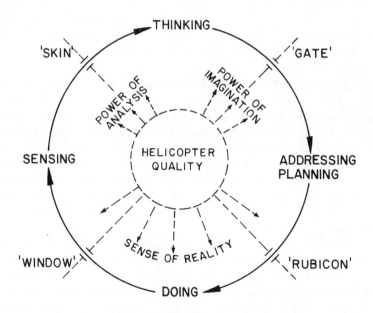

Figure 22   The 'HAIR' qualities in the learning process

This leaves, not surprisingly, the helicopter quality in the special position of being the faculty that combines, integrates, directs, and controls the other three. Therefore, it represents the overall function of the Inner Self. Are there any discrepancies or specific differences between the learning model and the managerial HAIR qualities?

Regarding the five fundamental principles which I formulated for the learning process in Section 4.8, I am convinced from the study and my practice with both, that the helicopter quality subsumes the holistic principle and perhaps the quality principle. But I am not at all sure whether it comprises the contingency, the interacting, and the liberating principles.

Muller distinguishes two interrelated principles. Firstly, the principle of *complementarity*. He found that the HAIR qualities are each other's essential complements:

> A person's power of analysis will remain sterile without simultaneous presence of sufficient imagination and sense of reality; imagination on the other hand without the check provided by the ability to analyse and without good sense of reality, will often lead to fantasy; and finally, a sense of reality without the discipline of logical thinking and without imagination will burden the man with problems he cannot solve. (1971:3)

See also the qualifying additions in the definitions (page 82): 'whilst remaining pragmatic' and 'without becoming unimaginative'.

In other words: these qualities are complementary because the presence of the others is essential to give them their true value. Conversely, each deteriorates in the absence of the other. (I will come back to this principle under the name of conjuncted and disjuncted constructs in Sections 7.6.10/11 and Figure 29.)

Secondly, Muller stresses the importance of balance between the basic qualities because of the *'non-compensatory* principle'. This means that weakness in any of the qualities can*not* be compensated for by excellence in any of the others. It is virtually impossible to rank a person's potential any higher than the 'weakest link' in his HAIR qualities. An individual's helicopter quality cannot be (much) stronger than his power of analysis, imagination, or sense of reality, *whichever is the weakest*. My question is whether this non-compensatory principle, being quite different from the holistic and contingency principles (see Section 4.8) applies only to managerial potential or also to personal development in general.

I have thought a good deal about this. Indeed, real high flyers seldom have a deficiency. Whether especially talented persons can*not* hold special, high-level positions is not so clear. That may be the reason why some corporations (in the USA) have a two-tier career ladder, one for generalists and one for specialists. For some reason I never hear myself telling managers or those with whom I discuss their learning style that a balanced profile is the ideal (let alone a must) for career advancement (in large organizations).

What I find missing in Muller's study and Shell's management appraisal system are the interacting and liberating principles. Any person who is going to reach a senior position in an organization or in society is expected to be an excellent interactor with his environment. He should have inborn qualities for transactions and negotiations and be a good communicator, motivator, and inducer of co-operation and participative decision-making whenever required (see Sections 4.2 and 4.6). Speaking with Muller's own non-compensatory principle: an individual cannot become a much better manager than his interactive and interpersonal abilities will allow him to be.

A first reason for the omission of the interactive principle lies in the actual formulation of the objective of Muller's study. 'The qualities essential to advancement *in* a large industrial group' (as the study is called) are not automatically equal to the qualities essential to the advancement *of* industrial groups. It is not uncommon that managers (and employees for that matter) are promoted without 'promoting' the organization, some may even advance at the expense of the organization. The emphasis is too much on individual traits and personal performance, not enough on interaction and social effects. Which counts more: personal assertiveness or inducing concerted efforts and group performance?

A second reason for this omission can be traced to the study's strictly empirical method: no quality could possibly emerge other than those that *were* essential for making a career in the *past*. Managers may well have been promoted on the basis of their HAIR qualities at a time when the predominant and accepted style of leadership was autocratic and paternalistic. When organizations and society are progressively requiring a more consultative or participative managerial style, then the quality of how a supervisor/manager uses his influence in the organization's environment and how he stimulates and co-ordinates the contributions of subordinates and colleagues and others, become of primary importance. The empiricality of the research method does not, by definition, justify an extrapolation of the 'past' qualities for managers of the future; such a projection is not valid. The question of what qualities a top manager will need in the year 2000 is not, scientifically speaking, answered by Muller's study.

Muller may reason that the (ideal) helicopter quality comprehends everything, hence also the interactive and liberating principles and whatever may be required for future managers. The Shell system had to acknowledge a deficiency in this respect, they incorporated 'Effective Leadership' as an extra appraisal category (see category Ib on the appraisal form in Figure 21, defined as 'a natural, unforced ability to inspire people'). However, I consider this addition not good enough. There are so many opinions about leadership. This appraisal item may even strengthen the selfish assertiveness of an overambitious manager. It does not explicitly request what it should do: explicitly appraise his interactive and liberating qualities. He should be rated not only on his 'genuine interest in people', but particularly on his ability to create *synergy* in the organization, to utilize emerging opportunities, to deal with political/environmental turbulence, to be open for learning under all circumstances.

Brakel (1979:226–34) has also scrutinized the appraisal system of employees and the helicopter quality for managers. He does this from an organizational perspective, and comes to similar conclusions. He suggests that a sociological component, 'Social Intelligence', should be added to the appraisal criteria.

This would add to the helicopter quality, in Brakel's terms (1979:228), a second level of abstraction, that is that the manager has to see himself as part of the field of action.

Looking forward to what will make a future manager, I also postulate (with Emery and Trist, 1975 and Drucker, 1980) that the future will be turbulent and difficult. Therefore I believe that not a trait quality but a *process* quality is the most essential. Kim James (in Beck and Cox 1980:68) came to the same conclusion from her research project in a large multinational company. She recommends that the job assignments and the work experiences of future senior managers should be structured in such a way that they are encouraged to remain *learning* managers.

In conclusion, I would answer the opening question of this chapter: 'What are the fundamental qualities that carry a person into senior positions in society?' as follows. *The best quality the manager of the future can possibly have is the drive and the ability to develop continuously his capacity of acquiring new skills and wisdom in interaction with others and the environment, in order to realize realistic objectives and cope effectively with problems and novel situations.* This holds for whatever talents a person may have and at all position levels. It comprises more than the development of the helicopter quality and it can be operationalized quite explicitly (see Section 9.4).

The short maxim is: '*Learning* managers are the managers of the future'. My task as consultant and management trainer is to: 'firstly identify and coach those managers and employees who have the ability of, and accept responsibility for, organizing their own ongoing development, in particular their HAIR qualities and interactive skills; secondly, create an organizational climate which fosters (the five principles for) concerted performance and collective benefit for all.'

5.2 Domains, dimensions, and levels. An integrative theory?

Quite another approach to Man's inborn faculties is Dale and Payne's report to the European Institute for Advanced Studies in Management. Their opening statement (1976:1) sounds promising:

> The great increase in deliberate attempts to accelerate the development of adult persons and social organizations during the last 30 years prompted us to review these efforts . . . . We believe that the debate is confused because it is very largely a-theoretical, or because the various parties are using incompatible (frequently tacit) theoretical assumptions . . . . We believe that they are inevitably confused and will remain so until the protagonists can clarify at least what they mean by 'development', 'growth', 'intervention', etc., etc. . . . If practice is to be improved, a more theoretical approach is urgently required!

They offer a model of human development (1976:2) in which they distinguish domains, dimensions, and levels. Their word *domain* means area, field, subject; it has the same general meaning as 'world of arts' or the 'financial world'. Man develops himself in many domains along three *dimensions*, with each dimension having three *levels* of development. As dimensions they propose: Awareness (I understand), Resources (I can), and Ego Strength (I will) (see Figure 23). They consider these dimensions independent of each other, at least conceptually. Therefore the co-odinates of the three-dimensional growth model are perpendicular to each other. Each domain thus forms a growth cube. A person develops in a particular combination of these three dimensions in an infinite number of domains.

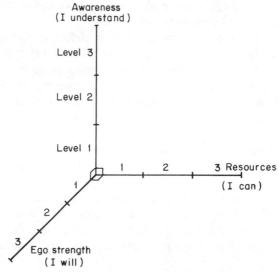

Figure 23   A three-dimensional growth model

The model was developed for use with individuals, but we think that it also applies to organizations. We make no claims that the essence of the model is in any way new: merely that it is a convenient way of representing what has been discovered, and rediscovered about human development in cultures for at least two thousand years. The oldest similar models known to us appear in early Buddhist philosophy. (Dale and Payne, 1976:2)

Their intention of presenting an integrative theory is laudable. Unfortunately they make no effort to compare their 'dimensions' with what other authors have put forward. I refer to the small selection in Figure 20: this shows that it is worthwhile to do so. Some similarities are striking, say with Burgoyne's and Harrison's terms.

Dale and Payne's dimension called 'I understand' (Figure 23), covers roughly the same mental activity as the combined sensing and thinking stage, that is the inner world of the learning model of this book, and the 'I can' dimension is similar to, though not congruent with, the combined planning and doing stages, that is the outer world. Then it is of particular interest to know what they say about their 'will' dimension as this could be the equivalent of what I named the Inner Self of my model.

They do not define the 'will' dimension but convey what it entails in the elaboration of the meaning of its levels 1, 2, and 3; they use key words like power, apathy, inertia, fear of change, rejection, conflict, commitment to norms or expectations, fear of looking foolish, authenticity, self-respect, and self-enactment. These concepts confirm the relation to the Inner Self. However, I am lost again through a statement like (1976:7): '. . . when we have to pin it down—the 'Will' dimension—in a few words, we can say that it is about changing relationship with the outer world'.

Dale and Payne make much more effort to define explicitly the levels of each dimension. In this part of their study (1976:2–10) they refer to and compare with scholars like Alderfer, Assagioli, Jacques, Kohlberg, and Vickers. I was disappointed not to find any reference to, say, Maslow, Kolb, Harrison, and Loevinger who are well known to have studied the levels of development of managers. This led me to make a collection of my own (see Figure 38 in Section 9.1).

There are good reasons to distinguish the discreteness of levels. Any particular dimension is made up by smooth growth ranges (more of the same), which are interrupted at some points by thresholds and barriers. At these points a rearrangement or repatterning needs to take place before growth can continue. There are thus distinct *dis*continuities along any one dimension. Indeed, real development is *not* continuous. It incorporates the fact of life that the death of some elements allows the creation and interaction of new principles.

Dale and Payne's description of 'between-level' development makes interesting reading (1976:28). They regret that many educational and training programmes remain within a given level and rarely lead to, or encourage, a step-jump development. They postulate that to bring this about an individual has to be pushed beyond comfort and that he may lose control temporarily, yet within the zone of tolerance. This reminds me of the assertion of Pedler *et al.* (1978) and many others that there is no development without risk, no substantial progress without surprise, excitement, pain, or other emotional perturbations. Life has its passages (Sheehy, 1976) and crises (Lievegoed, 1979).

Dale and Payne present a diagram in which a learner's level of competence is directly proportional to the degree of environmental pressure. The concept of 'zone of maximum development potential' is helpful, but I cannot accept that a person's response is a linear phenomenon (see the arousal pattern of Figure 36 in Section 8.8). Their one-sided emphasis on environmental pressure is also too simplistic. 'Too much attention to external factors blocks the way to immediate inner experience' (Jung, 1958:48).

I realized two points from Dale and Payne's report. Firstly, amongst the many words that indicate levels of development, there are few that apply to one dimension only, for example dexterity expresses an advanced level of 'I can', and wisdom a high level of 'I understand'. Otherwise, development being multidimensional, most words express level multidimensionally. For instance: 'expert' indicates a level of the combination I understand—I can, and 'assertive' combines I will—I can. This explains why the terms used by the various writers (in Figure 38, Section 9.1) are so different. Maslow's well-known hierarchy is a point in case: the key words of the successive higher and more complex levels of motivation and maturity, that is survival, security, belonging, etc., are combinations of different dimensions and even of different domains. These imply that human beings follow a preferred pattern of growing in particular domains to certain levels before moving over to other domains for further growth.

Secondly, Dale and Payne make the strong point that identifiable barriers must often be crossed in order to progress to higher levels (of maturity) in any dimension or domain. Such breakthroughs and emotional factors are represented in the cyclic learning model by the four mental barriers between the learning stages. 'Whirling cycles within a lifelong spiral' of Section 2.6 picture the pathway of a developing individual through the various dimensions and domains to higher levels.

I shall come back to this concept of *level* of development more specifically: with respect to Man's construct system in Section 7.4; to the functioning of the brain and memory in Section 8.3; and most systematically in combination with sub- and unconscious learning in Chapter 9.

5.3 Ancestry-roots of personal development. A parable

I remember that a number of my colleagues were rather excited about Friedlander's Parable on the Ancestors of Organization Development (in *JABS*, **12**, no. 1, 1976). Discussions were at a peak about what Organization Development (OD) actually was, what it could do, and what it wanted to grow up to; whether it was a passing fashionable theory or a practice that was taking hold. Friedlander's vivid account of the roots and nature of human development was very illuminating for me because I was in the midst of reorienting my personal commitment to the purpose, values, and methods of OD.

Chronologically speaking, it was not Friedlander's article but my own experiments that made me expand the cyclic learning model with an 'existential Being' dimension in the centre (see Section 2.5). And now, by hindsight, it is still fascinating, although not surprising, that Friedlander's 'Ancestors' of OD, Pragmatism, Rationalism, and Existentialism, are fundamentally the same dimensions as I am using in the personal development model presented in this book.

When I reread the article last year, it struck me not only as lucid and convincing, but also as profound and applicable to development in its widest sense. It was a delight and a new experience for me, grasping the significance of the Parable not only for *OD* but also for *PD*. Therefore I decided to take the liberty of selecting and paraphrasing those parts of his article that describe more convincingly than I could have written myself the relationship between the conscious explicit learning process (like Doing = Pragmatism and Thinking = Rationalism) and the elusive 'Inner Self' = Existentialism. His specific contribution was that *OD* 'reaches adolescence and maturity if it integrates not only theory and practice but *also* our underlying values, our existential being'. That holds also for my *PD* model.

What follows now, with acknowledgement to Friedlander, is a shortened version of his article (1976): 'OD reaches adolescence'. I gradually adapt it more liberally towards the end. For instance, I introduce various 'descendants', amongst them the adolescent boy 'Pede' which is an acronym for Personal Development. More about him later. Here is the parable:

The grandparents of present-day generations of theories, ideas and methods with names related to the 'Human Development' family, can be traced back to their philosophical ancestors: Pragmatism, Rationalism and Existentialism.

The *pragmatist* grandparent (whom we will call Prag) made sure his children saw the paramount importance of usefulness, effectiveness and the inherent worth of anything that *works*. Prag was a kind but stern parent. He would often sit his children down and impart such wisdom as: start with what you know — that which is accepted for the time being; there are several meanings to what people say, and it is important that we *test* those meanings to arrive at a common understanding; meaning for each of us emerges from practice, if it works, not from definition. The learning or knowledge-getting model proposed by Prag was essentially: practice → experiment → insight → testing → reality → better practice.

The *rationalist* grandparent (whom we'll call Rati) stressed upon her children the importance of logic, consistency and determinism. Rati was a cool and somewhat distant and disengaged grandparent. Often she lectured her children with such proclamations as: There is a cause for everything; there is only one meaning to every message; every one who is competent reaches the same answer; all events are reproducible and determined; propositions should mean what they say and say what they mean. The learning model for Rati was somewhat different. Information, reason, data and logical consistency were the essential ingredients in the search for truth. Then she would draw conclusions or make predictions. Prag, on the other hand, was most motivated by the immediate situation and the pressure for improvement and effectiveness.

Thus Rati and Prag, two of the major ancestors of the Human Development family, each confronted life quite differently. Rati's search was for the 'ultimate truth', the plan, the nature of things. Her mission was to describe the universe as it is, no matter how distasteful her findings. Prag's mission, was to fashion the universe according to a desired set of characteristics. Neither Prag nor Rati were terribly involved in the here-and-now meaning of their existence; both relied more on their vision of the future. Prag would continually ask 'how', while Rati would ask 'why'.

The courtship of these two was respectable and seductive. On their dates, Prag would sense all sorts of solid possibilities in himself and in her and Rati would enjoy her feeling of being attractive to and wanted and needed by Prag. They generally guided their relationship away from disagreements, of which they had many. When things got too warm, close or intense (which could lead either to fight or to genuine contact), Rati would pronounce, 'Let's not get emotional', and Prag would be provisionally satisfied with the state of affairs.

They engaged in a reasonable, if not exciting, marriage and bore a number of offspring. They bickered a good deal about the name of their first child—each one wanted it to symbolize his or her dream—and finally Rati suggested a compromise. They called their first child 'Scientific Management', or Sime for short. Sime showed a reasonable blend of his parents' genes, always aiming at scientific, *rational* support for managers in *practice*. As it turned out, Sime, like many offspring, did not (and perhaps could not) live up to the expectations and values of his parents, he started to limit himself to observable, quantifiable standards.

After Sime came a second child that they called: 'Operations Research' (nicknamed Ops) and a third child: 'Management by Objectives' (Embio for short) and many more in quick succession. All these brainy children resembled or borrowed in some degree from both parents. They all tried to apply their rationalistic heritage pragmatically to real-life situations, and to build these experiences back into better rationales and revised models.

So went the marriage of Prag and Rati; and their offspring did partially achieve what the two parents were not able to accomplish as partners. Today all live in the same neighbourhood, accept each other's short-comings, but devote much of their energy and attention to quite separate worlds of their own.

Time passed and interests faded. Then, one fateful day when he was frustrated with his lack of progress and development, Prag met a stranger: Existentialism. *Exi*, as he was later to call her, came over him like a wave. She was an aesthetic, sensuous experience he had never before encountered. For Exi, everything began with her *own* experience, her *own* subjective sense of events as she personally percieved and experienced them. It was fruitless and meaningless to define concepts, said Exi. When she found another person whose experience was similar to hers, then she became aware that a sort of resonance took place between whoever spoke and whoever listened. It was feelingful communication, which she called 'good vibes'. When she was asked by strangers to describe an experience, she would frequently reply simply that she could not do so. 'I guess you have to experience it to understand it', she would say. Only her here-and-now existence had primary meaning for Exi; the past was over and the future was not here yet.

Exi, unlike Rati, became easily bored with analytic discussions, particularly about people. When someone encouraged her to analyze her own behaviour, her personality characteristics, her life style, she would pause, smile and respond: 'My existence precedes my essence. Experience precedes concepts about the experience'. Propositions, for Exi, could have many meanings, and different people would derive different conclusions, perhaps even self-contradictory ones. Her concepts arose out of her unique human processes of perceiving, of pattern forming, of symbolizing, of conceptualizing. But none of these is necessarily a conscious process. For Exi, experience is broader than the experiment. The latter implies boundaries, controls, rules of evidence, initial purpose, whereas experience has no *a-priori* relevance and is open to uncertainty.

Exi's learning process was: experience → awareness → choice → commitment → becoming. Her interest in such fields and movements as humanistic and transpersonal psychology made her participate in encounter groups as they occurred in a variety of personal growth centres: body therapies, sensory awareness, massage, dance, yoga, spiritualism. Oriental meditations and even some drugs.

Exi had known several lovers, but Prag represented a new and different way of extending her personal experience into the interpersonal domain. He changed her mode from being with herself in the presence of another into being *with* another. Prior to this she had not seen relationships as opportunities for learning as much as for experiencing. Exi represented so much that was completely new to Prag: her very personalized experience, her focus on the here-and-now, her free, lively, subjective reality touched him to his pragmatic depths.

Clearly, these were attractive differences, but they did cause difficulties. For example, Prag's frequent emphasis on achievement and success, which he defined in terms of performance; progress, not personal experience, was his most important product. Prag was quite insistent that he knew the meaning of success in this world. He defined it in terms of external criteria: recognition, power, status, and money and what it brings. This could irritate Exi, who would reply (borrowing from her school days undoubtedly) that 'underachievers have more fun'. At other times, Prag would impatiently complain to Exi: Don't just stand there —do something'. Exi would reply calmly: 'Prag, don't just do something—stand there'.

Prag and Exi begot several offspring. It was never quite clear whether some of them were perhaps the result of Exi's experimental other encounters, but this does not seem to have influenced their enduring relationship. Most of them were a visible mixture of existentialism and practical humanism like 'Traps' (Transpersonal skills) or 'Trans' (Transactional Analyses) or 'Coco' (Co-counselling) or 'Asser' (Assertiveness training) or 'Esp' or 'Est' (I have already forgotten what these stand for). They turned out to be a rather close-knit sibling group, who traded learning between each other. Some of them liked to live in communes and there were times that some of the bolder offspring of Prag and Rati joined them for a period of caring and sharing and for fierce debates about what matters in this world. As could be expected, more offspring were born as a result of these relationships. And as time passed it became clear that a number of the youngsters were exhibiting characteristics of all three grandparents.

One of today's promising adolescents is *'Pede'* (short for Personal Development), who seems to have inherited the best part of all his ancestors. Pede is a strapping youth, eager, energetic, confused, looking for an identity, looking to prove himself, wondering what he will be and do when he grows up, wondering if he ever will. He is proud, but insecure, strong but clumsy, boastful but shy, interested in meeting many people but often preferring solitude, wanting to get on with others but not knowing how, sowing his wild oats but hoping he was not wasting his talents, amazed and excited by his obvious potency but a bit frightened by it also.

Like many adolescents, he is the product of both his socio-cultural environment and his heritage. Many of the current dilemmas, conflicts, issues and imbalances within him are the representations of the dilemmas and struggles between his ancestors: rationalism, pragmatism and existentialism. To understand his ambitions, let's trace these ancestral themes as they are enacted today.

Rationalism pushes the young, contemporary Pede toward becoming more scientific, more theoretical and conceptual, more logical, more mathematical; toward abstract models, toward building theories; toward understanding the determinants of our organizational, social and personal worlds. Pragmatism pushes him in the direction of becoming more useful. How can he increase effectiveness, performance, productivity, and how to organize his life so as to reduce the gap between the way it is now and the way it would be better? Existentialism within Pede pushes him to enjoy life today and tomorrow, to become more humanistic, more aware, more emerging, more growth oriented. *As a rationalist he likes to learn by thinking; as a pragmatist by doing; and as an existentialist by becoming aware of what he is able to become.*

Pede realizes that he obviously cannot represent his ancestors Rati, Prag or Exi as ideal or pure types any more, he rather draws on all sets of values as clarified and epitomized in their biographies. He knows that he is a blend of practical and cognitive and existential potentialities which

Components	Rationalism X*[a]	Pragmatism Y*[a]	Existentialism Z*[a]
Purpose	Discover truth	Improve practice	Experience, choice, commitment, exist
Basic activity	Think, knowledge building	Do, acting	being
Terms are defined	Precisely	Tentatively	Need not be
Meaning from	Definition of concepts	Practice and results	Experience and perception
Learning from	Concepts and logic	Experiments and feedback	Awareness of existence
Reality is	Objectivity and truth	Workability and practice	Subjective perception
Good communication	Semantic precision	Consensual listening	Shared feeling and resonance
Locus of knowledge	Conceptual model	Organizational practice	Individual experience

[a]*Added to compare with Figure 20 (X-Y-Z dimensions of development).*

Figure 24 Set of values of organization development (copied from Friedlander's article, Table 1, in *JABS* 12, no. 1, 1976) (conceived by Juch as equally relevant to *Personal* Development)

have to mature naturally and to be developed deliberately at certain times.

Situations and resources, or just his mood, can be such that the development process takes after one side of the family to such a degree that his behaviour seems unbalanced. Pede cannot but agree whole-heartedly: he feels *ir*responsible when his cognitive abilities are denied full rein; he is likely to get guilt-feelings if he has not been doing useful things for some time or when he becomes alienated from himself and from the many important others around him when he is not in-touch, not caring and sharing here-and-now. He continuously feels the urge that these ancestral dispositions should be realized, they stretch and burden him, especially when he is denounced for failure of living up to a proper blend of these traits.

However, it does not seem to do Pede any harm to live under these pressures. He thrives upon the ancestral faculties he fully realizes he has inherited. He is becoming more mature, more competent and confident all the time.

Here ends the parable.

It is quite remarkable that Dale and Payne consider their develop-ment model for individuals to apply also to organizations and that Friedlander's distinction of the ancestry roots of 'Organization Development' is equally significant for 'Personal Development'. This is not only obvious from the above parable but also from Friedlander's explicit set of values which he published in a table, copied in Figure 24, showing close resem-blance with the dimensions of personal development which I collected in Figure 20.

It is also noteworthy that the holistic and contingency principles which I formulated in Section 4.8 are supported by Friedlander's view that in the ultimate evaluation it is no use arguing about the primacy of either rationalism or pragmatism or existentialism or any form thereof. Because for real development to take place all three components are essential in the long term in a synergistic and contingency manner, that is to say that a blend of them is needed at any one time and circumstance to further the whole.

My conclusion is expressed in the description of the energetic strapping young named 'Pede'; that is the explicit learning process based on rationalism (thinking) and pragmatism (doing) should be completed into a model of total personal development by incorporating the existentialistic Inner Self.

Friedlander's description of the existentialistic Inner Self (see 'Exi' in the parable and the Z component in Figure 24) is more reminiscent of the optimistic Anglo-American phenomenological, humanistic, and gestalt values than of the European existentialistic views; the parable brings out Man's positive and spontaneous faculties much more than the primitive, instinctive and repressed parts of his psyche. Therefore I shall have to consider, in analogy of Plato's symbol of the white and dark horses which pull the cart in different directions, both the light *and* the dark side of Man's Inner Self. Together they constitute the 'control centre' of the model. The question is, subjectively and existentially, which of the inner parts of Self is operable most of the time. This is the subject matter of the next chapter.

6

Know Thine Own Self

I had to introduce the mental barriers in the learning cycle on empirical grounds. They account for the passages and deflections of Man's mental attention, for the hurdles and breakthroughs in his learning. They are conceived as the manifestations of the complex conglomerate of powerful psychological factors which make up the individual's inner self. It is, however, too simplistic merely to draw an inner circle in the cyclic learning model and label it 'Miscellaneous — Inner Self'.

In Chapter 5, we got to know this black box in the centre of the human development process somewhat better under the name of helicopter quality, will-dimension, and as the sprightly 'Exi'. Do these cover all the psychological factors that play a role in Man's lifelong learning? To what extent can a learner discover his own 'Undiscovered Self' (Jung, 1958)?

The *Concise Oxford Dictionary* defines Man's psyche as his soul and spirit or mind. Looking further for the definition of these terms leads into a vicious circle. Moreover, the meaning of these terms has changed between primordial and modern times. To mention a few: the immaterial, immortal part of Man, his animating principles, spiritual endowment, moral conscience, emotional feelings, instincts, willpower, basic drives, talents, values, aspiration, libido, Angst, etc. All these different names are too important to be left unidentified and uncategorized.

Making an extensive study of the psychological and philosophical theories of Man's psyche is off-putting; they already fill tens of packed pages in the *Encyclopaedia Britannica*. But understanding the fundamental outlines and functions of Man's most personal inner world should be a minimum ambition. At least one has to come to terms with extreme views. For example: Freud is afraid that Man is dominated by his libido (hidden instinctual drives) and caught up between his biological urges, sexual impulses, and aculturated superego; Skinner (1971) contends that we develop predominantly through conditioning, that is to say by responding to repeated rewarding and punitive stimuli from our environment — he maintains that a rational experimental study of this mechanism is the best way to determine how Man's nature operates.

Most helpful for my purpose were the views of Carl Gustav Jung, for three reasons:

(i) he clarifies many concepts of Man's personal traits, especially the differences and interactions between the conscious and unconscious parts of the psyche;

(ii) he advocates a dialogue with one's own unconscious in order to uncover more of one's Inner Self;

(iii) his suggestions for the development of the healthy individuated person are most compatible with my own experience.

6.1 Jung's individuated person

At the turn of the century Sigmund Freud discovered Man's 'libido', the unconscious reposition of instinctive biological needs and drives. He founded the famous Wednesday Circle and the psycho-analytical school in Vienna based on the tripartite division of the human psyche in id, ego, and superego. His analyses of neurotic minds and his findings from sexually repressed persons came as a shock to the medical world and to the 'civilized' culture which comfortably held more rational and moralistic views of the human being.

Carl Gustav Jung was a Swiss psychologist and psychiatrist, whose research findings confirmed many of his colleague Freud's, leading to an early and close association. Their collaboration ended after some five years, partly because of difference in temperament but mainly because Jung became convinced that Freud was severely and dogmatically overstating the primacy of sex and aggression as unconscious drives in all affairs of human behaviour.

Junt wanted an open research of all functions of the human mind and body; he explored all possible techniques, including open-minded confrontations with his own unconscious, searching out the importance of instincts and desires, dreams and phantasies, aspirations and fears. He developed a school of theories of his own, called Analytical Psychology. This includes concepts about life in general and about the process of growth and development of Man's personality in particular.

Later in life he spent most of his time on the psychology of the *healthy* personality which emerges from the *free* development of the *un*conscious and from its integration with the conscious world of the individual. While acknowedging the many obstacles in life, Jung was convinced that the process of 'coming to selfhood' was so natural and strong that it was an instinct. He called it the process of *individuation*.

The danger of a poorly developed Inner Self, says Jung, is that it leaves the personality piteously disjointed:

We readily assume that growth only comes from the outside world and base on this the assumption that we can become a personality if we succeed in cramming in as much as possible from the outside. But the more we follow this recipe, and the more we believe that all additional growth comes from without, the poorer we become inwardly. Therefore we should realize that a great idea can only take hold of us because something within us comes to meet it half way and corresponds to it. Psychic readiness is what signifies riches, not the piling up of hunting trophies . . . . A man grows with the size of his task. But he must have *within him* the ability to grow, otherwise the most difficult task will be no use to him; at the most he will break himself upon it. (Jung, in Jacobi, 1953:276)

The greater number of his books are written for professional analysts and difficult to read. Late in life he wrote a few shorter and more accessible works like: *The Undiscovered Self* (1958). Through the comments and elaborations of many, for instance Jacobi, 1953; Lindgren and Fisk, 1976; Schultz, 1977), his concepts and theories are now better understood and more widely accepted in the USA and in Europe than at the time of his death in 1961.

Jung is best remembered by the concepts of extraversion (outward-looking) and introversion (inward-looking) as two major types of people according to their attitude and orientation in life (see sections 4.1 and 4.4). Later he differentiated four functions of the mind: thinking, feeling, sensation, and intuition (very different from Freud's tripartite concept) which became known in the professional literature as the Jungian typology of personality.

In the heyday of psycho-analytical tests during and after the Second World War, several personality tests were based on his theory. A well-known example is the Myers–Briggs-type indicator (copyright 1976), a self-scoring questionnaire with 166 forced choice questions which classifies any person into any of sixteen psychological subtypes. These tests may help in the psychological assessment of people, but my criticism that people's personalities cannot be divided into such hard and fast classifications should not be directed at Jung, since he meant his typology as a simplification. He wished to illustrate how one-sided dominant types would interact with people and environment, not to provide an instrument for people to be psychologically pigeon-holed.

Jung may have given cause for categorizing people psychologically, after all he conceived and extensively described the concept of 'archetypes', but he would certainly have taken exception to the view that people's personality traits are fixed. He asserted that a person's personality is both unique and continues to develop, it undergoes crucial transformation throughout life. '. . . at least we are not condemned to be prisoners of our early experiences' (Jung in Schultz, 1977:93). This confirms my experience (see Section 1.7) that it is far more helpful for any person to realize that he has a unique (maybe idiosyncratic) but influenceable learning and development process which goes on as long as he lives, than to perceive himself as a particular psychological type which is fixed and/or should be changed.

Jung never ceased to emphasize the uniqueness of every person:

The individual is the true and authentic carrier of reality, the *concrete* man as opposed to the unreal ideal or normal man to whom the scientific statements refer. The real person consists of nothing but exceptions to the rule . . . . There is and can be no self-knowledge based on theoretical assumptions, for the object of self-knowledge is an individual: a relative exception and an irregular phenomenon; hence it is not the universal and the regular that characterizes the individual but rather the unique.

(1958:12)

Man is *not* to be understood as a recurrent unit but as something unique and singular, which in the last analysis can neither be known nor compared with anything else. (1958:9)

6.2   Jung's undiscovered self

The main reason why I had to leave the centre of the learning cycle as an indistinct Inner Self is that most of its content is *un*conscious; it is neither directly available nor accessible for observation, it is unknown territory for our awareness, a black box. Yet without subscribing to the Freudian view that the unconscious is 'the cellar to which fearful and painful memories are consigned by a process of repression', we know for sure that this Inner Self is not a blank space, a *tabula rasa* either. In fact:

Our psyche, which is primarily responsible for all the historical changes wrought by the hand of man to the face of this planet, remains an incomprehensible wonder, an object of abiding perplexity, one of Nature's secrets . . . . Psychology is the youngest of the empirical sciences, it has great difficulty in getting anywhere near its proper object. It had to be freed first from the spell of mythological ideas and then from the prejudice that the psyche is a wholly unapproachable and recondite matter. (Jung 1958:44)

For more than 50 years we have known, or could have known, that there is an *un*conscious as a counterbalance to consciousness. Medical psychology has furnished all the empirical and experimental proofs of this. The unconscious psychic reality demonstrably influences consciousness and its content. All this is known but no practical conclusions have been drawn from it; we still go on thinking and acting as before as if we were simplex and not duplex. Accordingly we imagine ourselves to be innocuous, reasonable and humane. We do not think of distrusting our motives or asking ourselves how the inner man feels about the things we do in the outside world. But actually it is frivolous, superficial and unreasonable of us, as well as psychologically unhygienic, to overlook the reaction and standpoint of the unconscious. (1958:84)

This is exactly what needs to be established in the next few pages: the practical connection between the conscious Self—which can be understood and managed by the cyclic learning process — and the unconscious psychic 'reality' which I have so far labelled 'Inner Self'. Jung describes this connection (in Jacobi, 1953:272, 280) as follows:

> The human personality consists of two things: first, of the consciousness and secondly of an indefinitely large hinterland of unconscious psyche. The former is more or less clearly defined and delimited [as I think I did in Chapters 3 and 4] but so far as the sum total of human personality is concerned one has to admit the impossibility of a complete description or definition . . . . Within this whole, consciousness is continued, as it were, like a smaller circle within a larger one.

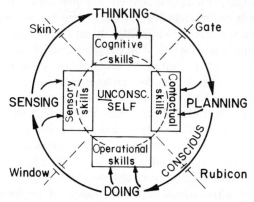

Figure 25   The conscious and unconscious Self

For convenience my pictorial model shows this the other way around ('inside-out') in Figure 25: the Unconscious Self as the central area within the larger conscious circle. The reason for showing the boundary as a dotted circle is to indicate that it is permeable, that it can be crossed radially. It is not an iron curtain. This boundary runs *through* the reservoirs of knowledge and skills, since they are partly conscious and partly unconscious.

> The unconscious is a useful storehouse of material which is no longer conscious but which can easily rise to the conscious. This material consists of memories and thoughts and skills which have dropped out or have been pushed out of the conscious awareness because they were unimportant or routine or threatening. (Schultz, 1977:88, about Jung's
> theory)

The model in Figure 25 pictures the reality that we are not aware of all the physical, sensory, cognitive, and contactual skills which we either inherited or acquired. A person is not and need not be aware of a portion of his memories, beliefs, or values. He may not (yet) realize that he holds them or he may have 'forgotten' them.

These subconscious thoughts and abilities are not just stored away to be used only if they can be made conscious (radially). No, they are often put to (good) use *un*consciously in combination with each other, without the person being aware how this all happens. Thus, there is also an inner cyclic process that links the subconscious thoughts and skills together. I have shown this in Figure 26 with secondary cyclic arrows. This secondary process is not directed or controlled by our mental effort, its activities are (mostly) imperceptible. It produces Man's intuitive insights, his dreams, and phantasies, and creative ideas. The functioning of the subconscious process, often intangible and unsteerable, is essential for human survival, for living and working together.

Since conscious and subconscious processes are connected radially and laterally at the stages, it means that there are alternative routes between the stages. In the words of Ornstein (1972:180): 'There are two major ways, then, in which men have approached knowledge about themselves and the nature of life. One, the scientific and logical, employs the steady input and accumulation of information; the other the intuitive, attempts the development of another organ of perception'. Ornstein makes an analogy with radio and TV signals which are always in the air but for which a proper receiver is required to tap this resource and to transform these signals into audible and visible information. Or, in Jung's words: 'Knowledge about the world and our environment is accessible to attention through mediation of our senses *or* through intuition: insights may also come spontaneously' (Jacobi, 1953:266).

Defining these processes in terms of the model, see Figure 26. There are two discretely different alternative routes to update or to form thoughts and opinions: route *a* directly via the sensing to the thinking stage with the explicit use of our senses and cognitive skills, and another, short-cut route *b* which does not follow the explicit, conscious path, but is intuitive, and takes place *through* the Inner Self.

Similarly there are *two* discretely different routes to acquire/improve operational skills: one route via the conscious, explicit-planning, decision-making, and organizing activities (route *c* in Figure 26) and an alternative, spontaneous, or impulsive direct route *d* via the person's inner, unconscious process.

In other words 'in-tuition' is an introvert unconscious process. Insights and meaning are derived from events, relationships, and things without being aware of how and why; one is not aware of the sensing, and explicit analyses and evaluations are by-passed. Similarly, *impulsive or spontaneous* behaviour is an extravert unconscious process, things are done without our being aware of reason or purpose. The conscious mental activities of addressing, planning, contriving, organizing, etc., are by-passed.

Referring to the difficulties I had with distinguishing between sensing and feeling (see Section 3.1.2), it is now much easier to understand that Jung's notion of 'feeling' does not mean the explicit feeling with our tactile senses but the *un*conscious *stirring of the mind* or the *emotionally* related feelings of the contact-ual skills, as in 'the general feeling was against us', or 'don't hurt their feelings'.

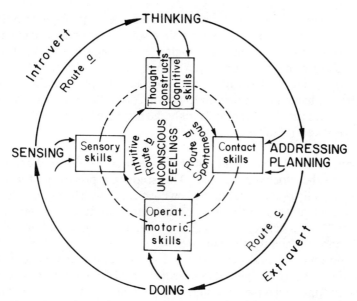

Figure 26   Alternative *un*conscious routes, intuition and spontaneity

Watzlawick says (1978:21) that Jung defines 'feeling' as a distinctly different way of experiencing reality, not through a step-by-step, logical, methodical analytic approach but as a global holistic perception of reality (= route *b* in Figure 26). Since one can also have a feeling for how to do it (route *d*), the word 'feeling' covers both the intuitive and spontaneous *un*conscious routes.

Quoting Jung (1958:94): 'The discrepancy between intellect and feeling, which get in each other's way at the best of times, is a particularly painful chapter in the history of the human psyche'. He does not advocate a subordination of reason to the control of the 'heart' or vice versa, but demonstrates the possible duality (even conflict) between the *outcomes of the two equally valid routes:* the unconscious and the conscious one.

Expressed in this manner Jung's well-known four or eight psychological types are not seen as different additional stages or *areas* in a learning cycle (as Kolb or Margerison have applied them) but as notations for (individually preferred) alternative *routes* in Man's multilayered process. And Jung's prescription of having dialogues with oneself means: to connect deliberately and keep in touch with both parallel routes; to check the congruency between the conscious and subconscious processes, not trying to suppress either but letting them strengthen and enrich each other.

I found a practical description of how to activate and explore these subconscious routes in Ann Robinson's article 'How can intuition help trainers?' (1980:54):

We seek a quite place, . . . go through our favorite relaxation exercise . . . .

Then we wait, . . . we try to remain relaxed, we simply remain open to our alternative source . . . . After a time we reiterate our assignment to the subconscious; we re-enter our logical, reasoning, coping world. If we have not received hints or help we may achieve answers or insights later . . . what we have done is to deliberately activate the intuitive process; we have set it in motion to gain access to the immense, treasure-filled storehouse of the brain's right hemisphere, that portion which knows not how it knows . . . .

In Chapters 8 and 9 we shall explore further how learning and development take place in the *sub*conscious level. This secondary process is, for instance, almost exclusively operational in the newborn child, which can raise its awareness only gradually up to the level of self-consciousness. Conversely, many adults may have to deflect their mental awareness and relearn how to explore their subconscious and use their Inner Self.

The importance of intuition, creativity, and spontaneous functions in adult life is gradually being recognized (and rediscovered) in many realms of western societies. Putting subconscious abilities to good use is not limited any more to music and arts, but applies to science (Phillips, 1973: abandoning method), to sports (Gallwey, 1974: the inner game of tennis), to flying (Bach, 1973: Jonathan Livingstone Seagull), to training (Ann Robinson, see above) and also to technology (Pirsig, 1974).

In conclusion, a secondary, alternate/alternative process in Man's Inner Self modifies and strengthens many *sub*conscious skills, and links them with thoughts and feelings and memories. This process goes on without our being aware of it and without being directed by our mental focus. Yet we can make it (easier to) happen more frequently, to improve and/or accelerate the healthy development of the total person. The reader may have noticed that I have referred mainly to the *sub*conscious, that is to the *top* layers of the *un*conscious. What do we know about the real unconscious, about the inaccessible powerful motives and instincts that we can*not* account for? Is the core of the model a 'black-box' after all?

6.3 Beast and man

From early literature we know that throughout the ages people have regarded the deepest levels of Man's unconscious as of a bestial nature, a sort of refuse bin for all inexplicable instincts and unethical 'dark' motives. Plato uses the metaphor of Man as a chariot-rider who guides but sometimes is being guided unpredictably by two horses, a white one and a dark one, always trying to pull in different directions. A quotation from him (Book 9, *The Republic*) sounds like a description of Freud's libido:

When the gentler part of the soul slumbers, and the control of Reason is withdrawn, then the wild Beast in us, full-fed with meat and drink, becomes rampant and shakes off sleep to go in quest of what will gratify its own instincts. As you know, it will cast off all prudence at such moments. It will go to any length of shamelessness and folly.

Darwin, who devoted his lifetime to understanding the descent (or ascent?) of Man, sums up his opinion somewhat differently: 'With his godlike intellect which has penetrated into the movements and constitution of the solar system —with all these exalted powers—Man still bears in his bodily frame the indelible stamps of his lowly origin' (in Sagan, 1977, prologue). Who has not been profoundly shaken by Stevenson's story of Dr Jekyll and Mr Hyde's schizoid double life?

According to Jung (1958:78) both *under-* and *over*valuation of the 'dark' side of our psyche is groundless and can be dismissed as mere prejudice 'In animals the instinct is the spiritus rector of all behaviour, . . . whereas in civilized Man, the instincts are so split up and modified that only a few of the basic ones can be recognized with any certainty in their original form . . . . It is highly probable that all man's psychic functions have an instinctual foundation'.

Desmond Morris (1967) has tried to convince us in another way that Man, the 'Naked Ape', has inherited a great number and variety of instinctual behaviours from his evolutionary forefathers. Human beings display an enormous number of genetically determined patterns, some amusing and some less pleasing ones, not only in anatomy or physiology but also in psychology and sociology.

Mary Midgley, in her excellent book from which I borrowed Plato's quotation (1978:37) and the title of this section, argues as a zoologist that there is no such Beast in Man as Plato and Freud and others would have it. Animals are 'neither incarnations of wickedness, nor sets of basic needs, nor crude mechanical toys, nor idiot children. As a species, they would not last long . . . . If then there is no lawless beast outside man, it seems very strange to conclude that there is one inside him' (1978:39). I found her detailed study of the similarities and differences in the instincts of animals and Man very useful for our purpose. She distinguishes (1978:52–57):

(1) Closed instincts. These are the automated behaviour patterns, reactions which are fixed genetically in every detail. They are also called 'wired-in' reflexes or involuntary responses, for example the honey dance of bees or the production of adrenalin in mammals and humans when threatened. These *instantaneous* reflex reactions are 'triggered' without any possible influence of future needs.

(2) Open instincts. When triggered, these instincts lead to programmed behaviour with a possibility of modification by circumstances and experiences. They are typically *conditioned* reflexes which are partly genetically determined or as a starter only; they are changed by experience and aculturation. Examples are the homing instincts of animals, the

breast-seeking and sucking of babies, and some sexual reactions of adults.

(3) Learned instincts. These are transitional combinations of innate and learned abilities like the hunting skills of the higher animals and the walking and talking of the human species. There is often an optimum period for their training and development in the early life of the species. Conversely, they can be stultified and atrophied when repressed at the wrong moments.

Midgley argues that it is neither true that Man is little more than an animal (not to speak of a Beast), nor that he has switched over to intelligence and reason altogether. He certainly has a hard-to-define mixture of the whole range of closed, open, and learned instincts, but he does not need as many closed instincts as the creatures at lower levels of evolution. She propounds that the automatic skills drop off higher up the evolutionary scale; the more adaptable the species is, the more choices it has. *Development takes place in the direction of greater choice, of freedom to follow other options.*

Midgley found that 'what replaces closed instincts is not just cleverness, but strong innate general desires and interests. (1978:332). The higher animals have acquired the desire and capacity to play for pleasure, including counter-playing aggressive tendencies. 'Social life rests on this capacity of peace-making' (1978:336). I fully agree with her that the antitheses between Beast *and* Man and Beast *in* Man are quite false and that most of the arguments about 'Nature or Nurture' are not very helpful. She rejects any forced choice between 'loyal innatists and faithful environmentalists'. I like her simple analogy (1978:20) that such polarization seems much like arguing whether the quality of a meal is determined *either* by what you buy *or* by how you cook it. Of course, it is both. And it all depends on which factor dominates in the given circumstances.

Accepting that Man's unconscious consists of a hard-to-define mixture of closed, open, and learned instincts, and that the species evolves anthropologically to less closed and more learned skills, it still leaves me with the problem of idiosyncrasy. That is: to what extent are personal preferences and individual traits genetically determined? Are outstanding intelligence, ambitions, special talents, homosexuality, criminality, extraversion and introversion, male and female traits, inborn or conditioned? Since many of these issues are still under fervent debate in the scientific world, I realize soberly how far we are still away from fully grasping all ramifications of human development.

An optimistic view is that Man's instinctive nature itself is a great ally in self-development. Jung observes, in rather guarded language (1958:79): 'We shall probably not be wrong in assuming that the learning capacity, a quality almost exclusive to Man, is based on the instinct for imitation as found in animals. It is the nature of this particular instinct to disturb other instinctive activities and to modify and differentiate them'.

Others, like Adler and Maslow, have asserted that some (semi-) innate instincts constitute Man's urge to learn and develop: the drive to survive, to belong, to fight boredom, to challenge, to investigate, etc. Whether in the form of 'individuation' (Jung), 'self-transcending' (Frankl), 'fully-functioning' (Rogers), self-actualizing (Maslow), or more mundane 'self-developing' (Hague, 1979), the drive to become what Man is able to become is so natural and strong because these processes are part and parcel of Man's (open?) instincts. Quoting Bertrand Russell (in Phillips, 1973:165): 'Curiosity is the instinctive foundation of intellectual life'.

It is clearly my curiosity to establish whether personal development is a learned instinct.

6.4 Self on the couch?

Turning now to the individual, one of the oldest dictums for Man to grow up, to become competent and wise is: 'Know Thine Own Self'. However, 'most people confuse self-knowledge with knowledge of their conscious ego personalities, and take it for granted that they know themselves. People often measure their self-knowledge by what the average person in their social environment knows of himself, but not by the real psychic facts which are for the most part hidden from them' (Jung, 1958:7).

Numerous psychic disturbances are occasioned by Man's progressive alienation from his instinctual foundation, by his uprootedness and identification with his conscious knowledge of himself, by his concern with consciousness at the expense of the unconsciousness. Modern Man knows himself only in so far as he can become conscious of himself, orienting himself chiefly by observing and investigating the world around him. This task is so exacting and its fulfilment so advantageous, that he forgets himself in the process, losing sight of his instinctual nature and putting his own conception of himself in 'place' of his real being. In this way he slips imperceptibly into a purely conceptual world where the products of his conscious activity progressively replace reality.

(Jung, 1958: 80–1)

Jung experimented extensively with dialoguing with himself, trying to understand the composition of his 'Self' *by himself*, searching and confronting the unconscious, as he advocated, boldly, openly, without reservation or inhibition, always asking why, and how? His prescription for humanity is precisely what it is for the individual—a confrontation with the unconscious psyche. 'Individuation' is a process of reaching progressively higher levels of (a) self-knowledge; (b) acceptance of Self; (c) integration of the conscious and unconscious; (d) Self-expression (described in Schultz, 1977:99).

This programme requires discipline, patience, persistence, and many years of hard work; it balances all parts of the personality: 'assimilating the conscious and unconscious process such that the *centre* of the *personality shifts* from the ego to a point midway between the conscious and the unconscious. Thus, material from the unconscious becomes a more active part of the personality' (in Schultz, 1977:92). A much wider personality emerges step by step from this constant self-dialogue with the unconscious, whose frontiers are continuously being pushed back but not defined; therefore the 'scope of the personality which can be realized is practically illimitable. (in Jacobi, 1953:273).

In the 1960s, this process became known as *personal growth*. A wide range of training programmes caught on, especially in California: sensitivity training, transactional analyses, transcendental meditation, body therapy, encounter groups, biofeedback, Yoga, extra-sensory perception, and some other twenty odd methods to help persons 'grow'. These humanistic movements created high expectations of change (for a 'Greener' America and world) and not only amongst the hippies and the young at universities.

This euphoria has now ebbed away. But as a result (reports *Time*; 2 April 1979)

> through all the popularized do-it-yourself techniques, psychiatry—the medical speciality holding exclusive franchise for Man's psyche—is actually itself 'on the couch' as a sincere, trustworthy, useful science. It has always suffered from public misconceptions, but now TV and other media are merciless in exposing crises in mental hospitals, embarrassments of major errors in public trials, with distinguished psychiatrists completely contradicting and even ridiculing each other (Kesey, 1973: *One Flew Over the Cuckoo's Nest*). After psycho-analytic chic ran high in the 40s and 50s there is now, with 27,000 psychiatrists alone in the USA, an obvious post-Freudian deflation. It is predicted that the classic psycho-analytic treatment: prodding the lonely patient on the inevitable couch, to let his unconscious difficulties break through into conscious coherent thought, will soon be extinct. On one hand such one-hour-per-week treatments become even too exclusive for the established clientele, and on the other hand acupuncture, neurophysiology, biochemistry and psychopharmacology are gradually but surely changing the future scientific outlook in this field fundamentally.

Indeed, people grew impatient with the classical psychiatry. Its esoteric terms and doubtful results were rather confusing and suspect for the short-sleeved engineer and the straight-tie-and-striped-suit-wearing Organization Man. New semi-scientific literature on these subjects started to enjoy pocket-book popularity, for example Berne, 1972; Harris, 1973; Eysenck and Wilson, 1975. One thing is sure, management is not the same any more. Management training and OD programmes give a good deal of attention to interpersonal skills and feedback, that is how one sees oneself and how others experience one's actions, words, and influence.

One of the many exercises that elaborate on Jung's advice and the dictum:

'Know Thine Own Self' is the well-known concept of 'Johari Window'. The window is a simple matrix of four areas which are known and unknown to myself and others respectively (see Figure 27). The idea is to explain the possibilities of enlarging the area (I) which contains the opinions and skills about which people can communicate openly and honestly with each other. It can be enlarged through a deliberate process of disclosure by myself (arrow *a*), that is by showing or telling others about my personal characteristics, interests, beliefs, etc. (private area II); it can also be enlarged through feedback (arrow *b*), in which others inform me about my behaviour and about the influence I have on the environment which I have not noticed or cannot perceive myself (area III, the socalled blind spots). The combined effects of *a* and *b* are also important: parts of my unconscious self are uncovered to myself (arrow *c* in area IV).

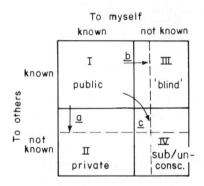

Figure 27   The 'Johari Window'

This short schematic description (see further Pfeiffer and Jones, 1974:65–9 and 1978:170–8), serves to illustrate that any person can use the feedback from someone else who knows him from work or otherwise, to enlarge and accept his Public self, and reduce his Blind self and Unconscious self. It is my experience that this simple matrix demonstrates very well to technical and managerial persons that for understanding one's own functioning in an organization one must (a) let others know something of oneself (arrow *a*), and (b) let or ask some trustworthy other persons to give honest feedback (arrow *b*) to open up areas III and IV.

The disadvantage of this exercise is that it suggests that the Other can see and tell me how I am. This is not true, he/she has only *impressions* from my behaviour. And secondly, it does not relate to the learning process of interpersonal skills. Therefore I prefer my own model, which in Figure 28 shows that one needs factual data from audio or video playback and the *impressions* of others in addition to one's own observations. Figure 28 also shows what can happen when a person puts tinted glasses on or when others give him/her distorted impressions. This process model can be combined with any self-searching questionnaire and impression-giving questionnaire on

110

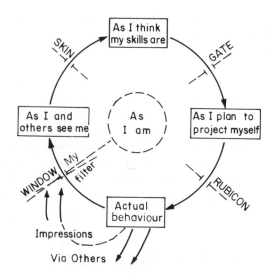

Figure 28   Learning interpersonal skills from feedback

any specific subject. For those interested, I have attached (see Appendices 8 and 9), the ones that I have put together for improving lateral relations between colleagues, for example for horinzontal co-operation between departments.

On an earlier occasion I discussed the practice of feedback in an organization (Juch, 1979:50-2). I presented there the so-called 'eliciting guide' for a deliberate dialogue about one's behaviour with a trustworthy Other, initiated and controlled by oneself. This is, in my experience, an excellent method for exploring the effects of one's interactions. It may be rather unusual to put oneself on the couch but the advantage is that one remains in charge of the process.

Before returning to the interacting processes of the personal development model, let us first follow quite a different approach to the understanding of one's Inner Self, namely the cognitive route of George A. Kelly. He and others assert that opinions, values, memories, feelings, beliefs, preferences, norms, etc. are just *thought-constructs* in a person's mind. Self can be put on the 'Grid' instead of on the 'Couch'. Man and his development can be understood via the brain instead of via the psyche.

7

Personal Constructs

So far we have made some progress in exploring the existential (irrational, emotional, intuitive, and instinctive) aspects of Man's psyche and in formulating the workings of Man's Inner Self in the development model. However, I am still curious about what difference there is, if any, between the psyche and soul and mind. I do mind since it seems to matter!

Therefore in this chapter I approach Man's Inner Self from an opposite end, namely via his conceptual, cognitive nature. Terms like motives, drives, talents, fears, beliefs, values, etc., can not only be seen as forming the irrational psyche, but also be conceived of as part of a person's mind in the sense of: 'people develop a mind of their own'; or 'I could not read her mind'; 'my mind is set on'; 'they could not make up their minds'; 'bearing in mind' . . . . etc.

With excuses for a further simplification: I shall use the word 'brain' mainly for the physical substance ('hardware' in computer terminology) and explore its make-up in Chapter 8. This chapter is concerned with the 'software' that is with the workings and the products of our mind.

I named this chapter after the theory of a typical representative of this approach: George A. Kelly. His basic statements (1955) aroused my curiosity:

(1) A person's processes are psychologically channelized by the way in which he anticipates events.
(2) Persons differ from each other in the make-up of their 'personal constructs'.
(3) The concept of learning evaporates.

These enticed me to investigate his views further and I came to agree with Bannister and Fransella (1977:17) that his Personal Construct Theory is rather comprehensive; it has such a wide range of convenience that it explains much that was not envisaged at the time he formulated his statements, which is the proper criterion for a practical theory. On the other hand there is also a good deal of criticism of his philosophy and methodology, with some of which I concur. In balance, however, my appreciation is great, at times I don't know whether some arguments are his or mine. Anyway, they substantiate the understanding of the cyclic process model of Man's development.

111

7.1 Kelly's theory

I read his books with pleasure and increasing appreciation. I found his theory original and elegant in its formal logic, his philosophy is optimistic, his methodology and definitions are fresh, new and precise, his language is rich in imagination. My sympathy also relates to his career, or rather to his personal development. Born in Kansas in 1905, he studied mathematics and physics and graduated in engineering. He also received an MA in educational sociology and a PhD in psychology. Initially he earned his living as an aeronautical engineer. When starting to work in an impoverished area, he found the official theories of psychology, behaviourism, and psychoanalysis not very useful. Being intensely concerned with how people make sense of the world they live in, he gradually developed experimentally a tailor-made humanistic, individualistic psychology. This comprehensive theory, described systematically in a monumental two-volume book (1955), brought him the recognition of the academic world. In short his theory is as given below.

Man wants to make sense out of his experiences and give purpose to what he is doing in this world. Every person tries to bring and keep order in the events in which he is involved. From earliest childhood we learn to differentiate in an increasingly refined and abstract way: first between food and things, between mother and father, later between grey and gray, and between abstractions. In the course of life Man develops and accumulates an enormous amount of discriminations, categories, labels, concepts, ideas which he or she orders, connects, reorders, and (sub)ordinates continuously. He/she continuously develops *mental maps* to fit the events in the world. One's personal impressions of reality model the world as one perceives it.

Kelly proposed (1955:9) to give the name 'constructs' to these patterns of thoughts and mental stimulations. They enable man to chart a course of behaviour, explicitly formulated or implicitly acted out, verbally expressed or utterly inarticulate, consistent or inconsistent with other courses of behaviour, intellectually reasoned or vegetatively sensed. The fit may not always be good, but even a poor fit is more helpful than nothing at all. In general, Man seeks to improve his constructs by increasing his repertoire, by altering them to provide better fits and by subsuming them with superordinate constructs or systems. He will continue to test and adapt his constructs by finding out how useful they are in predicting future events, thus building a 'map' of reality as he perceives the objects, their qualities, their connections. No map is inherently right or wrong, the question is how useful it is to the maker and whether it can be made to stand the test of time and situations.

Kelly himself qualifies his theories as 'a psychology of the human quest—a theory of Man's personal inquiry'. They grew out of a necessity to explain the 'obvious': Why do people respond differently to the same event? Each individual differs from anyone else in how he perceives and interprets a situation, in what he considers important about it, in what he considers its implications, in the degree to which certain things, events, or people are considered clear or obscure, threatening or enjoyable. Even when people behave similarly, they will attach their own unique meaning to their experiences, 'construe' (= digest) them differently and then behave differently as a consequence. Each individual develops a mind of his own, an idiosyncratic model of the world around him.

Behaviour is as much a proposition as a reaction. People always have a reason and an explanation for their actions. They are always consistent in their *own* terms; everyone lives in his own world. Hence Kelly's strong emphasis on *Personal* Construct Theory. Man always tries to explain what happens in terms of what he understands already and prepares himself in accordance with how he anticipates coming events. Man is a self-directed explorer and interpreter of the world around him. Kelly's adages are: 'Man-the-Scientist'; 'Behaving is experimenting'; 'Man's aim is to predict and control'.

Kelly argued that a response is not evoked by the stimulus itself but by the meaning attributed to that stimulus by the person who responds. The reasons for adapting one's constructs are confirmations and disconfirmations of one's predictions; these are often accorded greater psychological significance than rewards, punishments, or other reinforcements. Man responds to what *he* interprets the stimulus to be. This is very much a refutation of Skinner's arguments!

Kelly defines *construing* as transcending the obvious: representing an event by means of a construct is to go beyond the meaning of the data, it gives insight how that event could possibly happen again in the same way or differently. 'We can do more than point realistically to what has happened in the past; we can actually set the stage for what may happen in the future' (1970:4).

Kelly built his personal construct theory on one fundamental postulate and eleven corollaries; he defined all formal aspects of his theory and classified the type of constructs, for example super- and subordinate, comprehensive, core constructs (see further on). He also coined new terms which qualify the *nature* of the constructs like permeable, pre-emptive, tight and loose constructs (see the glossary of terms in Appendix 10).

What is more, he defined a number of (pure?) psychological concepts, like threat, anxiety, dependency, guilt, hostility, in terms of his theory. Although I regret that he did not also define some 'positive' psychological concepts, like enjoyment, excitement, ambition, assertiveness, I consider this part of his theory as very important. It reaches beyond Man's strictly cognitive nature; these definitions bridge the mind and the psyche, relate the rational and the irrational characteristics and connect the intrapsychic parts, that is the conscious and unconscious layers of the Inner Self.

For the praxis of psychologists and other counselling professions, he and others designed a number of enquiry techniques and instruments (see Bonarius, 1979; Hinkle, 1970; and Fransella and Bannister's Manual, 1977). Best known are the various forms of the 'Repertory Grid Method' which systematically elicit the opinions of individuals, how they think and feel about some topics in their *own* terms. It compels people to verbalize what they have in mind, in such forms that this can be understood by and discussed with other persons as well.

Finally, Kelly elaborated a philosophy named 'Constructive Alternativism' (1970:5) which I could well embrace as a development philosophy. This states in short that we know nothing for sure. There are no givens. All our present interpretations of the universe are subject to revision. If the history of human thought teaches us something, it is that there are still a lot of alternative constructions to come. His constructive alternativism is 'an invitation to immediate adventure. By not insisting on disproof as a precondition for initiative it should release a great deal of scholarly manpower for more productive and less disputatious occupations'. This, and other quotes like: 'We are concerned with finding better ways to help a person reconstrue his life so that he need not be the victim of the past (1955:23) remind us very much of the liberating principle (of Section 4.8).

Recently the Personal Construct Theory and its practices have enjoyed renewed and widening interest, especially at universities in the UK. The papers presented at the seminars organized in Oxford, 1977, in Brunel, London 1978, and in Breukelen, Holland 1979 are evidence of an increasing diversification and usefulness in the worlds of academics, of education, and of industry.

7.2   Kelly's fundamental postulate

Two little points as a prelude. In line with the philosophy of constructive alternativism, Kelly invites people to 'join in the good life of exploring and inventing different ways of seeing the world'. Following his advice, I will happily listen to him as well as to his critics and myself. And I acknowledge his warning: 'bear in mind that the moment we bring a postulate in dispute, we must recognize that we are then arguing from other postulates, either explicitly or implicitly believed' (Kelly 1955:47).

Here then is his *fundamental postulate: A person's processes are psychologically channelized by the way he anticipates events.* This means in Kelly's opinion that prospective activities and anticipatory skills play the dominant role (1955:18, 19): 'This theory provides a basis for an active approach to life, not merely a comfortable armchair from which to contemplate its vicissitudes with detached complaisance. Man can only play active roles in the shaping of events'. Bannister, a major advocate of the Personal Construct Theory in the UK, underlines this stand: 'Man is not reacting to the past as much as reaching for the future. Man is not a ping-pong ball with a memory' (Bannister and Fransella, 1977:19).

Kelly goes very far when he states with italics (1970:13): 'Constructs are imposed *upon* events, not abstracted *from* them'. This extreme formulation has the aim of 'cutting ourselves free from the stimulus-response version of the nineteenth-century scientific determinism. I am aware that this is a drastic step indeed . . . .' (1970:10). This is too drastic in my opinion. His neglect of the reflective-inductive part is just as fundamentally unacceptable as Skinner's denial of the element of freedom in the thinking and planning stages in the stimulus-response sequence.

I may remind the reader of Van Beinum's view (1973) that 'learning is the awareness of the personal meaning of one's experience' and Exi's remark: 'Experience precedes concepts about experience'. Boot and Boxer (1980) assert that experience alone is not learning, they place great value on reflection and encourage managers to engage in a dialogue with themselves to realize and update their own constructs on certain chosen matters. I conclude from theory and experience that 'Time to reflect' (left-hand side of the cycle) and 'Time to plan' (right-hand side of the cycle in Figure 12) are of equal importance.

To make my point with respect to Kelly's theory, I propose the following 'constructive alternative fundamental postulate' (!):

A person's activities and psychological processes are channelized by:
(i) the personal meaning he infers from all his experiences;
(ii) the expectations he construes of future events;
(iii) the way he wants to assert himself and to be accepted in the outer world.

In summary, this differs from Kelly in that the model in this book represents a *holistic* process and emphasizes the complementarity of all parts and aspects of the development processes.

7.3 Kelly's view on learning

Unfortunately Kelly's contribution to the educational profession has been small. He does not often refer to learning and development. A few quotes may explain why: 'Learning is not a special class of psychological process, it is not something that happens to a person on occasion, it is what makes him a person in the first place' (1955:75, 76). The clue is that Kelly equates learning with the process of changing constructs as defined in his Experience Corollary (1955:73): 'A person's construct system varies as he successively construes the replication of events . . . . It is not what happens around him that makes a man experienced, it is the successive construing and reconstruing of what happens as it happens, that enriches the experience of his life'.

The consequence of defining learning as a natural, normal, daily ongoing process is that 'the net effect of *incorporating learning* into the assumptive structure of this theory, is to *remove the whole topic* from the realm of subsequent *discourse*. Some readers may be dismayed that learning has been given such a pre-eminent position in the theory of personal constructs that it has been kicked upstairs . . . . *Thus the concept of learning evaporates* . . . .! (1970:29, 76).

This is clear language. The italics are mine. I am not dismayed, disappointed perhaps. Because 'kicking the subject upstairs' meant that it went unnoticed by the educational profession for some twenty years, until a wave of research at universities in the UK brought to light the intrinsic close relation between Personal Construct Theory and learning. See for instance Thomas (1977); Harri-Augstein (1976 and 1978); Beck (in Beck and Cox, 1980).

While playing down learning as a special process, Kelly confirms its cyclical nature. For instance (1970:18): 'The unit of experience is a cycle embracing five phases: anticipation, investment, encounter, confirmation or disconfirmation and constructive revision; this is followed of course, by new anticipations as the first phase of subsequent experiential cycles gets under way'. Combining the first phase (anticipation) and the last phase (constructive revision) in the 'thinking stage', then the others fall nicely in place around the learning model of this book (see Appendix 5).

In short: learning = changing constructs; that is elaborating, loosening, defining, validating, tightening them, etc. See for instance the description of the CPC cycle and the Creativity Cycle in the glossary of Kelly's terms in Appendix 10. To understand this better, we need to be acquainted first with how Man's constructs are interrelated in a complex network called his 'Personal Construct-*System*'.

7.4 Man's construct system

Man's view of the world is composed of many observations, facts, experiences, beliefs, opinions, etc., which are interrelated and intertwined in complicated patterns of logic, feelings, time, sequence, hierarchy, etc. The Personal Construct Theory has found attractive and helpful methods to describe and understand the relationships.

In the words of Bannister and Fransella:

> A personal construct system is a person's guide to living, the repository of what he has learned, a statement of his intents, the values whereby he lives and the banner under which he fights. It is being put to perpetual test . . . . As his anticipations are successfully revised in the light of the unfolding sequence of events, his construction system undergoes a progressive evolution. The constant revision of the personal construct system is a function of incoming validating experience. (1977:27)

Kelly's Organization Corollary reads: 'Each person characteristically evolves, for his convenience in anticipating events, a construction system embracing ordinal relationships between constructs'. That is: a person's system of constructs grows in the normal course of his development through addition, through defining, differentiating, (re)connecting, (re)arranging them in a network of internally organized patterns, groups, and subsystems within a functionally integrated whole.

He distinguishes an inner group, called '*Core*-constructs' which comprises all those constructs which give Man his self-identity and confidence under conditions of change and anxiety. On the other hand Man has '*Fluent*-constructs' which are in the process of being reshaped, defined and/or connected. '*Super*-ordinate-constructs' like 'animal', 'job', 'sport', are labels for a whole group of '*Sub*ordinate-constructs' often related hierarchically in terms of logic, abstraction, and/or sequence.

The complexity of a person's system of constructs has to be expressed not only in terms of the number, differentiation and elaboration, relations and patterns, hierarchy and sequence of the constructs, but also in qualifying terms like their stability, consistency, flexibility, functionality, convenience, commonality, etc. (see the glossary in Appendix 10).

Hinkle's research of sub- and superordinancy of constructs led to a major revision of the theory and the techniques of inquiry (Fransella and Bannister, 1977:42–51). In short: constructs imply and subsume other constructs and are connected in various ways into implication networks. Hence Hinkle's 'Implication Grids'. He distinguishes five different types of connections: parallel, orthogonal, reciprocal, ambiguous, and multiple connections between the 'poles' of constructs.

Relationships can be traced and complex strings of implied constructs can be elicited and investigated through posing systematic series of 'why' questions. This is known as 'laddering-*up*' (in the hierarchy of aims and purposes to the most superordinate construct) or as 'laddering-*down*' (following the string of cause and logic to find the source of evidence or reason). The more resistant to change the construct is, the more likely it is to be superordinate in the hierarchy because superordinate constructs carry a greater number of implications than *sub*ordinate ones. The significance of his views for personal communication in organizations has been explored in many ways, for example by Murphy, 1977; Bonarius, 1979; Boot and Boxer 1980. This is all very similar to Koestler's 'Arborization' (1978: 97:298).

Tony Buzan (1977) applies these ideas by coaching children and adults to sketch their networks, thus giving them insights into thoughts and abilities they did not realize they had. He shows the richness and the vast capacity of the human brain through displays of branched groups and interconnecting networks of thought and concepts. He has demonstrated this in BBC programmes and has been very successful in educational practice.

At this point it is tempting to give some practical examples of the use of Construct Systems and the Repertory Grid Techniques. That would be very useful for those readers who have not yet grasped their practical utility; but a large variety of examples have been clearly described in the books and articles mentioned above. Therefore I shall continue the discussion on the conceptual level.

Whenever complex sets of connected constructs are made explicit, they are still a simplification. It is often revealing to make two-dimensional sketches (grids) of the invisible, complex, operational world of thought, memories, opinions, arguments, feelings, phantasies, etc., about people, things, events.

Yet those interrelated grids and Buzan's networks are still only *static* representations of Man's construct system.

How to deal with the dynamic aspects? How to account for the many *time-related* constructs in the form of roles, rituals, work-routines, plays, and games? People tell and write stories, play music (thousands of notes), and conceive complicated programmes. Our minds contain an enormous history of experiences of how to act and react in all sorts of situations. These patterns of time- and cause-related constructs are hard to describe in their detailed connections.

Berne (1972) has studied and classified many 'life-scripts'. Hutton (1978) talks about 'constellations through which journeys can be made, which cross and re-cross the same points as the exploration proceeds'. Mangham (1978) writes about the dramaturgical aspects of social interaction and speaks of Man as a playwright *and* the actor. Morris (1978) has compiled 'Manwatching' as a 'field guide to human behaviour'. I have parodied, with a serious touch, in Section 8.10, the further evolution of the population of constructs in the human brain.

Here, I would like to highlight three aspects: firstly, these routines, scripts, games, etc., are meant to help, but they can hinder. On the one hand they help us to go through life with ease: in acting out familiar scripts we do not have to make choices every second, through roles we behave predictably and do not clash with each other. On the other hand we can get caught up in habits and become the slaves of our own structures and routines. Efficient practices (of washing the dishes) can flip over from being desirable and convenient into terribly constraining routines. Major efforts may then be required to break out of empty roles and frozen habits. In many situations we have to *un*learn, to *re*learn, or learn-to-learn. 'Rewriting one's own script is a second-order change' (Mangham 1978:107).

Secondly, the concepts and practices of construct systems fit the preceding chapters on the Inner Self: *parts of* Man's construct system are *submerged* in the *sub*conscious and in the *un*conscious. A dialogue with ourselves and others is needed to discover and understand the constructs and scripts of our blindspots. Some constructs are not 'Manmade', they have their roots in his genes. Speaking with Midgley we should distinguish closed, open, and learned constructs (Section 6.3) depending on how much and how strongly they are connected with the unconscious.

Thirdly, the fact that Man strives to keep his construct system an integrated whole means that he sometimes finds it unacceptable to make gradual changes. Anomalies are then discarded until a crisis brings the pieces of the puzzle together and alters (that part of) his construct system substantially. We say then that a conversion, a gestalt-switch takes place. Concepts like 'paradigm' and 'gestalt' are other words for a consistent, semi-permanent group of constructs. Cultural shock, eye-opener, 'eureka', creativity, breakthrough, etc., indicate rather radical changes of such cognitive subsystems. Finally, personal constructs are as much the *tools* as the products of learning.

In conclusion I reformulate: for convenience of understanding and guiding oneself in interacting with (others in) the world and in congruence with one's purpose in life, each individual develops:

(i)   a characteristic learning process which results in and from,
(ii) an extensive body of accrued cognitive learning, conceived as a complex system of personal, ordinally related constructs, which is
(iii) partly accessible by one's mental focus and available for conscious consultation, updating and revision,
(iv) partly submerged in one's subconscious Inner Self and subjected to one's intuitive, spontaneous learning,
(v)   and partly rooted in one's unconscious (closed) instincts.

7.5   Contrasts in constructs

For some years the whole field of differentiations, discriminations, contrasts, polarities, antonyms, antinomies, etc. has intrigued me as a major problem in interpersonal communication. That is why I studied the views of Kelly and others with more than normal interest. After a short review I shall develop my views in Sections 7.6, 7.7, and 7.8 by defining and classifying the various types of contrasting constructs and by describing how they are used in daily communication.

A major concept in Kelly's theory and especially in his repertory grid technique is the bipolarity of constructs. 'A person's construct system is composed of a finite number of dichotomous constructs'. In arguing the validity of this explicit statement he warns (1970:12): 'I know that this is the point where many of my readers first encounter difficulty in agreeing with me'.

Such bipolarity is quite acceptable when an explicit label is used, say black as opposed to white, or north to south, or introvert to extravert. But Kelly's argument is that *all* constructs are sensed as bipolar because we never affirm *anything* without simultaneously denying something. When we call someone 'honest', it is implied that he is not *dis*honest or greedy. This bipolarity makes a construct different from a notion or a concept. He postulates that a person always uses a construct in a *particular* situation or context, to contrast say 'animal' with 'human' or 'beast' or with any particular element in a particular context. 'In its minimum context a construct is a way in which at least two things are alike and thereby different from a third' (Kelly, 1955:61). This principle of constructs being essentially bipolar is retained in all his writings and it forms the basis of the various repertory grid techniques.

Indeed, 'thinking in terms of opposites is natural to the human species' (Osgood *et al.*, 1965:327). Bannister and Fransella say (1977:24) that 'in line with the philosophy of constructive alternativism Kelly is not asserting that constructs *are* bipolar and that they are *not* unipolar: he is merely assenting that we might find it more useful to think about them as if they were bipolar'.

Hinkle came to the conclusion that 'constructs have many differential implications in the given hierarchical context, the number of possible contrasts ranging from nil to infinite'.

Several writers who are not familiar with the personal construct theory have none the less concerned themselves with contrasts, polarities, discriminations, (dis)complementarity, etc. Let me briefly name a few: One of Maslow's central themes is human needs and values (1972). He describes them often in contrasting dichotomous terms, in what he calls healthy and pathological forms. And he defines 'peak-experiences' as when seemingly polarized and dichotomous values and qualities (like selfishness and altruism) lose their contrasting sense and are transcending into unity.

In Perls's gestalt-theory (see Herman and Korenich, 1977) 'figure and ground' is a central concept. 'Figure' is the object or subject on which a person focuses his attention; 'ground' is the background or environment, that is *all else* that is within the individual's scope of awareness. This 'figure' is well differentiated from the background and is dominant in claiming the person's attention. When a person has dealt satisfactorily with the central figure then the total 'gestalt' dissolves and a new figure emerges out of the ground. This relates to Kelly's postulate that nothing is ever affirmed, without denying (= putting in the background) something else.

One of the interesting features which emerged from Muller's study of qualities essential for the career advance of managers (discussed in Section 5.1) was that people form opinions by rushing into comparisons; people have difficulty in assessing other people objectively in absolute terms, but they are quick in ranking and are consistent in assessing contrasts and dissimilarities. Muller also makes the point that throughout history, several writers have acknowledged the 'polyvalency' or 'complementarity' of qualities in character: essential personal qualities cannot stand on their own, they need the connection with other qualities to assume their full value.

Diesing (1971:212) writes: 'Holistic concepts are frequently related dialectically, viz., when the elaboration of one draws attention to the other as an opposed concept that has been implicitly denied or excluded by the first; or when one discovers that the opposite concept is required (presupposed) for the validity or applicability of the first'. This is known to dialecticians as 'the principle of interpenetration of opposites'.

Brakel's major theme is the 'skating-model' (1979: 79–87) which symbolizes the complementarity of 'pairs of concepts' for changing, that is improving an organization. Progress cannot be made in the direction of A only, nor only in the direction of B, but in a direction C that results from the interplay between both 'leg movements', that is from making progress *operationally* in *both* dialectic opposites in a ratio that is required by the context. For instance: organizational changes should be made on macro- *and* on micro-levels, in the objective *and* subjective reality; organization as a structure *and* as a collection of individuals; functionalism *and* interactionalism; the general *and* social intelligence of the manager, etc.

Gurth Higgin gives his own sociological account (1973: 9, 91, 92) of Jung's concept of 'centroversion' which is the tendency in individuals, evident collectively in organizations and in society, to react against overelaboration of some aspect of their development and to pull back to a healthy, more central line of further growth by attending to another aspect.

All the above examples are brought together by Hampden-Turner (1981:20) under the famous twin-symbol: *Yin-Yang*:

> In their profound influence on Chinese and later philosophy they stand for two intertwined, evercycling polarities. Yin, the dark side, represents female, earth, valley, night, absorbing, rest, autumn-winter and many associations therefrom. Yang, the light side, symbolizes male, heaven, mountain, rock, day, forcing, movement, spring-summer and similar associations. Life is a rhythmic movement among opposites. Take any phenomenon or human value to its logical extremity and it will yield to its opposite . . . . Yin-Yang anticipates the whole modern concern in psychology, with gestalt, binary constructs, figure-ground relationships in which behaviours occur . . . . It is our earliest known symbol of integrity.

Nancy Foy (1981) sees many 'scintillating' examples in organizations. This umbrella symbol of Yin-Yang of interpenetrating human values is congruent with the 'holistic, contingent, interactive, liberating, and quality principles for Man's learning and development described in Section 4.8.

7.6   Categories of contrasts

Instead of pooling contrasts and polarities together under the one fundamental twin-symbol 'Yin-Yang', I shall distinguish and define the typical differences between them in order to show the richness in meanings of contrasting constructs used in daily parlance. When I started to recognize and define the various types I came to a most complex one which turned out (surprise, surprise) to be a very general and useful one, on the basis of which I had designed a practical instrument for improving teamwork at a time when I had not heard of constructs.

I just followed the grid technique by asking myself, for instance: 'What do you see as a meaningful difference between the contrast in Brakel's skating model and the contrast in Kelly's and Hinkle's theories?' Or, with an obvious example: the difference between the contrast 'warm-cold' and the contrast 'wife-husband' is that the first is a matter of degree (literally and figuratively) and the second not. The second denotes a distinct biological contrast or a role difference.

In this way some eleven categories emerged to which I allocated an identifying name, a description of the particular relation between the parts, a schematic model, one or more examples from everyday usage, and typical

Type	Description: Relation	Model	Author	Applied functionally: Examples	Characteristics
DEGREE	Scaled		Kelly	Hot-cold, slow-fast, Light-dark.	Can be measured, has in-between positions, relative to each other.
POLAR	Polarized	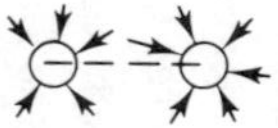	Thom	Magnetic North–South Parties, opinion groups	Cohesive clustering in groups or poles Group-think, loyalty, party-line.
ALTERNATIVE	Either-or		De Bono	Daily snap-choices Decision-trees, matrices	Either–or, mutually exclusive, 3rd choice problem-solving and decision-making. 'PO'
PARTNER	Pair, couple counterpart		Many	Husband–wife, pairs Nut–bolt, coupling	Distinctly different, separately also meaningful, meant to work together
DUALITY	Two-face,		Koestler	Coin. 'Janus' Yin–Yang	Two sides, dual function of one entity. Total construct higher abstraction
IMPLIED	Association part-synonyms	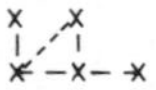	Hinkle	Poor — hungry — ill Ambitious-aggressive	Connected by association, by implication of logic or hierarchy in complex networks
GESTALT	Figure-ground		Perls in Herman	The tree from the woods	Subject/object stands out in context against background. Gestalt switch
PARADOX	Contradictory		Watzlawick	'Ignore this' 'Be spontaneous'	Self-contradictory paradoxes and semantic, pragmatic types ('I lie')
CONJUNCTED	Interpenetrating dialectic values	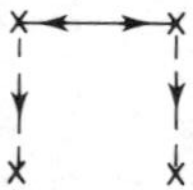	Diesing Juch	Freedom — equality	Antithetic in dialectic tension, not mutually exclusive, impossible to maximize both, integration at higher level
DISJUNCTED	Counter, mutually exclusive		Juch	Shameless Coercive exploitation uniformity	If disjuncted, assume negative meaning, 'cry wolf', indicate undesirable effects
DIALECTIC	Skating moves, centroversion	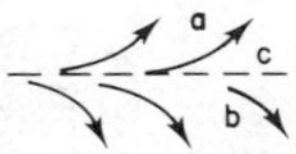	Brakel Jung Higgin	Skating, tacking, Special drives	Alternating, off-centred progress in dialectic contextual tension, yields synergistic results

Figure 29 Categories of contrasting constructs

characteristics. They are tabulated in Figure 29 together with the authors whom I consider closely related with the particular categories. I certainly do not claim that this table is exhaustive, it is meant as a handy reference for recognition by the reader of most types of contrasts used in public communication.

7.6.1   Contrast of degree

This most common type includes all contrasts that can readily be measured or scaled in one way or the other. Examples are: short-long, hard-soft, wet-dry, fast-slow, etc. This category has historically been of most interest to the natural sciences, which developed an enormous capability and variety of methods to discriminate and measure quantity and quality. The human sciences also are trying to develop more ways and means to measure, rate, or scale human qualities and relations. Osgood *et al.* (1965) have written an excellent book about semantic differentiation and the 'measurement of meaning'. Various quantitative enquiry methods, including the many scaled questionnaires and the computerized processing of opinion polls and elicited constructs are being developed further, often with much controversy. Ever since Einstein, we have been aware of relativity in measuring and quantity. And we are slow in adopting worldwide standards. A thousand knots per day, how fast or slow is that?

7.6.2   Polar contrast

This second category (see Figure 29), is *not* referring to Kelly's notion of bipolarity but to the literal meaning of the tendency to polarize. Contrary to the first category above, it is not the scale but the discernible *clustering* effect which carries most meaning. Magnetic poles, both physical and figuratively, are the obvious example.

In the human sciences this symbol indicates the tendency of organisms to form clusters or subsystems in an otherwise more scattered field. For instance, public opinion polarizes into some outspoken groups (say Labour, Liberal, and Tory). Expressions like 'the party line', and 'Southerners', 'autocratic managers' are examples from daily life of contrasts being used in the polar mode.

René Thom's biological-based catastrophe theory (1975) deals with the growth and change of organisms. It provides exciting and promising insights when applied to changing clusters in organizations, to political (in)stability and interpersonal relations. Personal disasters can be predicted and avoided (Postle, 1980).

7.6.3   Contrasts of the alternative: Dilemmas

The third category (see Figure 29), represents the either-or' contrasts, all situations with unavoidable and mutually exclusive choices: 'One cannot have it both ways', 'one cannot have one's cake and eat it', etc. There are no scaled positions in between them, no notion of clustering but a confrontation with cross-roads where one must physically follow one path only.

Although most choices are made by snap decisions, this is the category where 'decision-making' theories are required for the more complicated cases to assess the attractiveness and potential problems of the alternative routes, responses, or solutions. Many techniques apply, both the parallel/matrix types (attributes versus alternatives, for example which car to buy) and the (time-related sequential types like flow charts and 'decision trees' (what course of action and what influences to be expected?).

This category includes Kelly's notion that one side or alternative is unavoidably denied, discarded when accepting, affirming the other. Choice and decision-making are very much part of Kelly's anticipating process, in order, as he says, 'to shape the events'.

This type of contrast is rather simple, clear-cut and easy to handle. Therefore it is often misused; it may take on (in people's minds) more cases and situations than inherently justified. People like to simplify and force a choice: 'are you for or against it?' 'Do you want A or B?', 'Does she or doesn't she . . . .? Also, due to the historic dominance of the quantitative sciences, statements are labelled true or false, exams may consist of forced-choice questions, and computer operation is based on the binary 'on-off' situation of electro-magnetic gates.

This is also the category of real and false dilemmas. A real dilemma is an unwanted forced choice or a choice between alternatives none of which are considered attractive (enough). A false dilemma is a contrived contrast or a falsely formulated choice like: 'Your money or your life!', 'When would you stop beating your wife?'

De Bono (1977:179) has rightly and successfully unmasked self-imposed constraints and advocates lateral thinking. He introduced the new concept of 'PO' (which is listed in dictionaries), which is a *de*patterning device, a provocative rejection of false binary choices. He advocates creative third alternatives to spurious yes-or-no situations.

7.6.4 *Partner-type contrast*

This type is quite different from the previous ones as it requires no comparison or choice. The contrasts are distinct parts, meant to go or to function together, although they can exist separately and have (some) meaning of their own. Mentioning one implies the existence of the other. Therefore I have chosen the word 'partner' to label this type. Words like pair (of scissors, counterparts) and also companions and pendants, express the relationship between the parts. Examples from the physical world are nut and bolt, key and lock, hook and eye, the parts of couplings, etc. (see Figure 29).

The criterion of this category is that a particular (physical) counterpart must exist, while both can exist on their own. This distinction cannot always be drawn unequivocally. Husband and wife is a clear case. Horse and cart is a reasonable example. Interviewer-interviewee may be a borderline case. Body-soul can be considered to belong to the next category.

7.6.5   Contrast of duality: 'Janus'

The major characteristic of this fifth group is that there are no parts. The contrasting aspects are two manifestations. They appear to be separate entities or to behave quasi-independently, but they are essentially complementary and part and parcel of a unity, of one larger whole. The popular expression used for this duality is: 'There are two sides to every coin'.

Janus, after the two-faced Roman god, is the title of Koestler's latest book (1978) with which he symbolizes this particular characteristic of many entities in life. Janus conveys the notion that not only a person, but also a thing, an event, a concept may show two distinct faces, can give two very different, contrasting impressions. For instance, Man himself is both a unique individual but also part of a social group, which itself is part of a larger group, and so on (Koestler's concept: holon). A manager, any boss, is a linking pin in an organization, he is boss *and* subordinate, he represents a section or a department, *and* is a member of a larger unit of organization. There are many multilevelled hierarchies in life, in which order and stability can only prevail when the self-assertive and the integrative manifestations are in equilibrium.

There is no light without darkness, no valley without mountains, no body without soul, no Yin without Yang. All proposals have advantages and disadvantages, buildings have insides and outsides, any conflict two or more versions, looking upwards or downwards in an organization gives different perspectives. Therefore, this duality contrast teaches us to make an effort to view an entity from more than one side to comprehend the whole. Look for the other face, consider the other side of the coin as well.

7.6.6   The contrast of implication

This category is very much related to Hinkle's definition of 'implication' in a person's construct system. A word like 'success' does not stand on its own. If a person calls someone ambitious, it implies more than that, for example he may consider the other to be aggressive as well, or ruthless, intolerant, deft or too sure of himself, he may regard this positively or negatively, and so on. To what extent is the construct associated with other constructs and with which ones? In fact, there are few constructs, if any, which do not evoke associations.

Hinkle studied these networks of logical, hierarchical implications and distinguished some five different types of relationship (see Fransella and Bannister, 1977:49). For instance the terms super- and subordinate are used when constructs are related hierarchically. 'Hungry' and 'ill health' may both be implied by (thus subordinate to) 'being poor'. 'Ambitious' and 'aggressive' may not be connected hierarchically but may be seen as reciprocal, as close synonyms. What about 'rich' and 'happy'? In the table of Figure 29 I have taken the general form of implied contrasts by defining this type as a network of part-synonyms and associated constructs.

7.6.7   The figure-ground contrast

This category is taken from Perls's gestalt theory (see Herman, 1977). I see this also as a special contrast because the 'figure' contrasts with many (all?) other things in the background and is experienced as a total gestalt. The figure can be one leaf of a tree in the woods, one person in a crowd, the sore thumb of a body (a series of) problems and subjects that require attention in a day of business, this planet earth in the cosmos.

This mode of contrast is very natural and exists all the time whether our mental focus is actively discriminating or not (see Section 8.7). That there is a contrast can be made apparent via a 'gestalt-switch', that is when figure and ground are changed or reversed. For instance: I can switch my attention from revising this sentence on this page to the temperature in this room; we may study the power of managers in organizations and neglect the effect of subordinates (or of the type of organization) on the manager(s).

The criterion of this category is that there is always an actual contrast to the 'figure' in mind, that is the existential background, or the context, or the range of convenience. In bipolar grid terms, an opposite pole cannot be named because it is submerged amongst others. It can be elicited by a person himself by reversing the figure and (part of) the ground to find out how the construct is related to the other constructs. For instance: asking oneself whether and why one likes one task/job/person more than other tasks/jobs/persons.

7.6.8   The paradoxical contrast

This category contains the imaginary and (not so many) true paradoxes that are used in daily life; these are experienced as constructs with a self-contradictory 'contrast', like 'be spontaneous', 'ignore this sign'. I am not sure whether the category includes semantic or pragmatic paradoxes like: 'I lie' which Watzlawick *et al.* (1974:167–203) define as absurdities demonstrated with valid premises. For instance: freedom and equality might be construed pragmatically (even be experienced) as a paradoxical pair. Many other constructs can be spuriously construed as paradoxes, especially by schizoid persons, who confuse the levels of the logical types (see Section 9.3).

7.6.9   The contrast of conjuncted constructs

This category and the next seem to account for much of the misunderstanding in interpersonal communication and for much of the controversy in society. The reason is that this type of contrast is characterized by the fact that the opposites get their meaning through being contrasted with each *other*. And the other is not always explicitly voiced or even clear in people's minds. For instance: 'freedom' assumes a somewhat different meaning when contrasted with 'equality' than when associated with 'justice' or 'determinism' and so do the opposites. The contrast changes when paired, or associated, or conjuncted differently. Hence the name.

The second characteristic of this type is that the opposites are in dialectic tension; they can neither be maximized individually nor both at the same time. Although they are antithetic in this sense, they are *not* construed as paradoxical or as mutually exclusive. They are *related in tension*, they are tempered and qualified by each other. For instance: complete, maximized 'freedom' would result inevitably in certain *in*equalities in society and absolute 'equality' would require *restricted* freedom. A sort of optimum position between the two extremes is called for.

Muller has referred to these characteristics as 'polyvalency' and Diesing as 'interpenetration of the opposites'. The latter states (1971:213) that dialective logicians can 'easily show how unity makes sense only as an overcoming of diversity, for example autonomy can persist only in and through consensus, and so on. These relationships have been known since Plato'.

De Valk (1977:28-9) discusses present-day problems as associated with what he calls the 'antonyms': freedom–equality, democracy–efficiency, individuality–group loyalty, substantial–functional rationality, participative education–bureaucratization of organizations, etc. He reviews how these dialectic dilemmas have been treated by various philosophers and postulates that one of the reasons why frustration is on the increase in western society is that a number of these 'antonyms' have an increasing influence on an ever-growing number of people.

I can think of many more conjuncted contrasts which pose problems in present-day life: specialist–generalist, idealist–realist, differentiation–integration (Lawrence and Lorsch, 1969), 'to have or to be' (Fromm, 1978), theory–practice, egocentric–altruistic, left brain–right brain, etc. The point that I shall make is that I named these pseudo-dilemmas: 'conjuncted constructs' because they pose a problem as soon as they become disassociated from each other and/or as soon as people construe/perceive them as being disjuncted.

7.6.10   The contrast of disjuncted constructs

If one side of a conjuncted construct is maximized at the espense of the other, if the mutual support ceases to exist, if the opposites do not interpenetrate any more, then their meaning *degenerates* into a *different* pair, a pair of *dis*juncted contrasting constructs. For instance: equality will degenerate into coercive uniformity if there is no freedom left, and freedom will be construed as shameless exploitation if care for equality ceases to qualify the freedom. In a similar way assertion will be construed as overbearing or impudent if there is no modesty, idealism debased as visionary if disjuncted from realism, uncontrolled differentiation will lapse into disintegration, overinspiring will be called manipulation, etc. These sorts of changes occur in the minds of people through very individualistic perception/appreciation of the contexts.

The relation between conjuncted and disjuncted constructs can be pictured as shown in Figure 30. This picture clarifies that when the umbilical cord of a conjuncted construct is actually cut or experienced as disconnected, its meanings and contrast change drastically and 'flip-over' into disjuncted constructs.

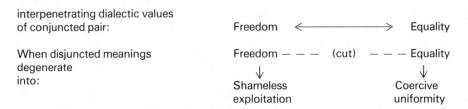

Figure 30   Relation between conjuncted and disjuncted constructs

The reason why these types of contrasted constructs play such a major role in daily talking, reading, writing, listening, and in confronting argumentation is that opinions and beliefs are often unclear and difficult to communicate. How does one know what association and contrast people have in mind? Where do they want the actual or proposed equilibrium to be? For instance: What does he mean with 'more freedom', how much is there now and/or how much does he want in order to retain (how much) equality?

Secondly, people can 'contaminate' a conjuncted and a disjuncted pair by making *crossed* contrasts, by posing mixed dilemmas. For example, equality versus exploitation, and freedom versus uniformity. People have an urge to exaggerate, they use the *tactic* of hyperbole to express dislike, fear, etc. They will point out the dangers of too much of one, or too little of the other, in the debasing terms of the undesirable disjuncted construct. For instance: people may cry 'exploitation' to safeguard equality, or cry 'coercion' to safeguard freedom.

Thirdly, this explains why so often the same acts or facts are perceived differently, that one and the same idea/project is both hailed *and* detested. For instance, any law, rule, or procedure can be perceived by one person as promoting equality and by somebody else as an abuse of freedom. The phenomenon is clearly explained by Watzlawick *et al.* (1974:47) as a matter of 'punctuation'. A practical example of clarifying conjuncted and disjuncted constructs in the practice of management training is given in Section 7.7 below.

7.6.11   The dialectic progress

In the context of learning and development one extra and important point must be added to the foregoing descriptions of categories and contrasts.

Accepting that the conjuncted opposites cannot be maximized either independently or simultaneously, lest they degenerate into 'corrupted' meanings, that does not mean that a happy compromise/consensus must always be fabricated somewhere in the middle.

No, the real chance of improving the optimization lies in making *alternating progress* at *both* sides towards a synthesis at a higher level. For instance, in terms of the freedom–equality construct, greater freedom becomes possible only if there is more equality to build on, not by maximizing freedom itself, and equality can be of a higher quality if based on more freedom. Or, with another example: conceptual thinking is more fruitful and of a higher quality when a person has more experience, and performance can be of a higher quality when a person understands the concepts and purpose of what he is doing, etc. The possibility and need of standing on each other's shoulders applies to most, if not to all conjuncted constructs.

This dialectic holistic-synergistic principle is fundamental for a healthy development process. It is the common denominator of Diesing's interpenetration of opposites, De Bono's PO, Koestler's Janus, Buber's Ich und Du, Muller's complementary qualities, Hinkle's implicative dilemmas, Hampden-Turner's Yin–Yang, Watzlawick's pragmatic paradoxes, De Valk's antonyms, Higgin/Jung's centroversion, Perls's gestalt, etc., and in particular the conjuncted constructs.

In down-to-earth terms sailing to windward requires this very principle: straight into the wind is impossible, tacks have to be made and changed at the appropriate moments. Also Brakel's metaphor of skating movements (1979) is a practical action–model for organizations to make synergistic progress on alternating fronts.

Summarizing the whole section: a person learns and develops through differentiating and expanding his thinking skills and system of thoughts which is a growing network of complexly interrelated constructs. The nature of their relation is defined and categorized in this chapter and summarized in Figure 29. The categories of conjuncted and disjuncted constructs play an important role in society, in interpersonal communication ('punctuation') and in personal development (further discussed in Section 9.4.3).

7.7 Application: a model of teamwork

To demonstrate that contrasting constructs are very much an operating reality, I can present a model for teamwork that is composed of conjuncted and disjuncted constructs. This model, with which I have been working for more than ten years, grew out of the opinions given by supervisors and managers about organization and teamwork, before I had ever heard of bipolar constructs or implication grids.

During 1969 and 1970 I was experimenting in Holland with a diagnostic exercise for teamwork, based on Friedlander's three dimensions in organization development: pragmatism, rationalism, and existentialism (see Section 5.3).

130

I formulated the essence of teamwork as: sharing objectives to be transformed into results through

(1) What the team does: content of work (pragmatism).
(2) The 'team-structure': the procedures, rules, arrangements, organization (rationalism).
(3) The 'team-spirit': synergistic interaction of team members (existentialism).

This helps the facilitator and/or team members to realize at what level the team needs improving/assistance. In general, a gradually more serious intervention is required to tackle levels 1, 2, and 3. It is more difficult to discuss rules and procedures (level 2) than the task at hand (level 1) or to say something about the co-operation or teamspirit (level 3) than about the structure (level 2). Contributions at the work-level are easier to improve than personal interactions. If a team is to operate more effectively, at what level lies the bottleneck? An intervention need not be at a 'deeper' level than where the problem lies. (Principle of minimum intervention.)

When team members discuss their performance and diagnose and qualify their contributions in terms of these three dimensions, the first generalization that emerges is that all three dimensions are construed as *bi*polarities (see Figure 31).

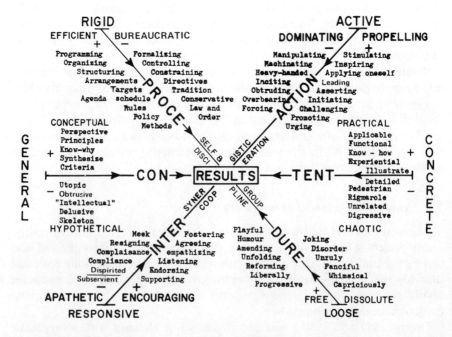

Figure 31 Main aspects of any group or organization (original team building model in Dutch)

(1) Content contributions are judged as concrete or as general.
(2) Procedures are perceived as ranging from rigid to loose.
(3) Interactions are experienced as pro-active or as responsive.

Secondly, when categorizing the perceptions and qualifying each other's contributions, it turns out that team members normally construe these as either positive or negative, as helping or hindering. For example (see Figure 31), a concrete contribution to the work can be construed as helpful when perceived as practical, whereas a very detailed contribution that is just as concrete may be construed by the team members as digressive or time-wasting and thus *not* helpful. At one moment an active contribution can be felt as stimulating, whereas a similar active contribution later can be construed as manipulation, overbearing or disruptive.

Thirdly, these positively and negatively qualified contributions are not limited to any particular dimension or pole, but hold for all six ends of the three dimensions, thus forming twelve categories in all (see Figure 31).

Fourthly, the most interesting feature was that *one* and the *same* contribution can be construed by one member as positive and by another as negative. What one manager qualifies as a useful new arrangement can be branded by another team member as a typical example of encroaching bureaucratization; the quiet attitude of a group member qualified as apathetic and complacent by one colleague can be appreciated as sympathetic and supportive by another.

The above features emerged gradually over one year or more through finding out and keeping notes (in Dutch) on which qualifications were most common and acceptable with respect to teamwork. I was gradually adding 'flesh to the bones' of this model. During team-evaluation sessions, members were quite forthcoming in giving reasons for their qualifications and keen to adapt and complete the model experientially.

By May 1971 I felt confident enough to issue a formal colourprint of the model 'het Kruis' (the Cross) as it was named in Dutch; of which Figure 31 is a simpler black and white English version. At the time I was, as I said, still unaware of any theoretical backing or justification. I saw it as a conceptual diagnostic instrument *from* the practice *for* the practice of teamwork. It proved to be a successful organization-development model and there are now several Dutch and English versions in use by colleagues. Hardly any modification of this original model is needed after writing this chapter on personal constructs.

By hindsight the 'cross-model' is a perfect example of composite sets of conjuncted and disjuncted constructs, that make or break co-operation between people. In short: a contribution to teamwork is construed in a positive manner at any pole of a dimension, when the value of the opposite pole is not denied but supported. Contributions which are considered to be one-sided and perceived as pushing one pole too much (for instance too assertive or too detailed) are psychologically construed as hindering teamwork and then qualified in typically disjuncted, negative terms (for example as dominant or as irrelevant). These qualifications are mostly *sub*conscious but can be made explicit through discussion to serve as valuable feedback on the behaviour of the members.

As a model, the 'Cross' appears complicated at first sight, perhaps cluttered with too many words. But the basic frame of the Cross is simple. Therefore a step-wise introduction is recommendable, starting with the three dimensions: work, procedures, interaction. This applies to all organizations, large and small. I am always surprised by the ease of recognition and acceptance by staff, supervisors, and managers. Team members have an almost unfailing sense for what fosters teamwork and what does not. They acknowledge that progress is made through positive contributions on any of the three dimensions at either pole. Most persons have enough experience to realize that evaluative opinions come in pairs of positive and negative qualifications. They have no difficulty in perceiving the 'Cross' as a useful simplification of their own cognitive map of what teamwork is all about.

This original experiential model has thus found its conceptual justification in Kelly's bipolar construct theory and in my classification of contrasting constructs. It is now clear to me why it is so difficult to bring teams on a higher level of co-operation: a team operates in the dialectic tension of the personal networks of values and opinions of its members. It takes time and effort and lucid communication (and trust in the mean time) to work in and with each other's construct systems. This model serves to get more common ground and explicit understanding.

As teamwork is a special form of any organization, I also see now that many opinions in society and qualifications in the media are of the conjuncted and disjuncted types. Politics and daily papers are using those for propaganda. It is all too easy, especially for exaggerators, cynics, and slanderers to use such negative disjuncted terms whenever they want to put someone down. Any contribution, quality, or motive can be given a positive or a less favourable interpretation. Snappy examples of such flipovers from conjuncted to disjuncted qualifications can be found as 'pin-up wisdom', on office walls. Who would not recognize them in 'The complaints of an underdog':

If I breach a rule my boss calls me 'unruly'
but when an exception suits him, he is 'original'.
When I need time I am 'lazy' or 'slow'
but he can be late because he is 'busy' and 'thorough'.
When I take a stand I am 'hard-headed'
but he holds on because he is 'firm'.
When I go ahead I overstep my 'boundaries'
or entertain ideas above my station,
but when my boss moves on, this shows 'initiative'.
When something works for me it is good luck
but his success is the fruit of hard work.

7.8 Self on the grid

Initially, Kelly's 'Scientific Man' appeared to me very different from Jung's 'Individuated Person'. When Kelly postulates that a person's processes are psychologically channelized by how he anticipates events and construes their replications, it appears that he advocates a rational, cognitive theory in which the person's psychological faculties like emotions, dispositions, and instincts play only an indirect role. He seems to disregard Jung's concern about the reflective understanding of one's inner feelings. People develop a mind of their own through building a personal, cognitive useful map of reality. Jung warns against Man's progressive alienation from his instinctive foundation if he is 'carried away' by things, people, and events in his environment and does not stay integrated with his inherited characteristics and his unconscious Inner Self; this seems a direct criticism of Kelly's 'scientific' theory and methods.

However, from what I read and have written in Chapters 6 and 7 I have come to the conclusion that their two points of view turn out far more synthetic in their practical applications to human development than first impressions suggest. The essence of psycho-analysis ('Self on the Couch', see Section 6.4) is the promotion of a healthy state of mind by letting 'problems of the soul' break through into conscious thought through encouraging intelligent verbalization and acceptance of one's unconscious and semi-conscious experiences. And Kelly's successors have typically expanded the clinical work also in the direction of the healthy development of the individual as a total human being. The 'Self on the Grid' methods of self-organized, self-directed reflective learning (Thomas, Harri-Augstein) have the same purpose of raising to explicit awareness the more intricate, intimate, emotionally and value-related constructs. Several computer-assisted grid programmes are available to explore and order one's own construct system to a depth of personal norms, beliefs, dispositions, and unconscious relations Jung would be jealous of. Boot and Boxer's Reflective learning programmes' (1980) require dialogues with oneself in a most rigorous Jungian fashion.

Are these praxes of analytic psychology and analytic cognition becoming much more similar? Are differences of an erstwhile fundamental nature proving to be closely related? Are these two routes perhaps leading to the same results?

Let me take another example from the teamwork discussed above. When a team does not function as well as the leader or members would like, a psychological approach ('on the couch') through interviews would require a psycho-analytically schooled person to find the reasons why one or more members are hindered in giving their full co-operation. It is very likely that he will find some psychological reasons (level 3) which need to be 'translated' in terms of arrangements/procedures/work/competence (levels 2 and 1). When a cognitive approach is adopted ('on the grid', for instance with the Cross of Figure 31) it is likely that the team itself or a consultant can verbalize in direct operational terms how the task could be done better and/or formulate whether structures/procedures or interaction problems are in the way. These two routes to find the cause and work on improvements are quite different. However, if people are co-operative and reasonably honest the same points are likely to emerge. The 'Grid' approach has the advantage that it is more gradual and natural, the relevance of the follow-up is obvious and shared.

Indeed, it is my experience that the extra insights obtained about one's Inner Self by following the route of 'Self on the Couch' and 'Self on the Grid' are of the same nature and a mutual confirmation. The latter approach does not need a professional psychologist, and is thus useful for *self*-development and more acceptable to managers.

The obvious question arises: are Kelly and Jung perhaps talking about the same thing? Can we draw an analogy with physics where Newton's wave theory and Planck's quantum theory are equally valid for describing the phenomenon of light and radiation? What is the difference between psyche, mind, and brain? Where does Man's Inner Self reside? In his 'heart and guts'? Or within the physical confines of his head? Dennett's 'Where Am I' article (1979: 310–23) about a person with an artificial brain is more serious than a science-fiction story.

Limbs can be replaced by artificial ones. Internal organs, even our ears and eyes and heart, can be transplanted without much change to us as a person. But it seems inconceivable that a (partial) transplant of the brain will ever become possible without a radical change in personality. Is learning and human development then mainly a matter of utilizing whatever Man's brain is capable of storing and processing?

8

The Human Brain

I realized that I could not possibly consider myself to be a credible trainer/consultant without having a knowledgeable answer to the intriguing question of the last chapter. Hence I had to familiarize myself with what is at present known about the brain.

Brain research is snowballing and keeps us on the brink of comprehending the operation of this complex organ much better. The publications range from unreadable treatises to popular articles. For instance: the 'Brain' issue of *Scientific American*, 1979, *Brainstorms* by Dennett, 1979, *Dragons of Eden* by Sagan, 1977, *Right Brain* by Blakeslee, 1980, serious articles in *Time Magazine* and *The Economist*, etc. Neurologist Restak (1979) convinced me that 'the human brain is our ultimate intellectual challenge, the last frontier in Man's understanding of himself'. The intriguing theme of anthropologist Bateson's last book (1979) is that the biological evolution of brain and mind is very much a *mental* process.

There are completely new disciplines, for example psycho-biology and neuro-physiology, which combine brain studies with the 'behaviour sciences'. A wide range of applications already confirm the practicality of deliberately modifying the functioning of brain and body (for example biofeedback, drugs). Artificial intelligence, 'embodied' in computers, seems to be around the corner. Man's idea of himself as the supreme creature will be challenged and tested. *The Economist* (22–28 August, 1981, p.77) cautions:

> The human brain is the most complex puzzle facing scientists and is unlikely to be understood within the next generation . . . . Brain scientists are sensibly concentrating on individual pieces of the jigsaw. It is really much too early to attempt a grand synthesis between the biological and behavioural sciences. They are a long way from any physiological explanation of Man's soul!

It would be presumptuous to pretend that I could keep up with all new information and make this synthesis. The next chapters may become out of date before they are printed. Yet it is a challenge and a necessity to summarize the functioning of Man's brain as best as we know it today with respect to my query: 'How can Man improve his capability of learning and personal development?'

8.1 The evolution

The evolution of the brain can be put into perspective with Sagan's 'cosmic calendar', in which the billions of years of evolution are compressed into one year (Sagan, 1977:13–17). This cosmic year starts with a 'Big Bang'—the creation of the universe. The planet earth took shape in the second half of this cosmic year and remained 'empty' until about mid-September when primitive life started. Special combinations of molecules, amino-acids, and chromosomes were formed and came alive. How this happened is still an intriguing and much debated question.

Just as difficult to understand is how the first living units started to replicate themselves into offspring, that is to say duplicating each time the unbelievably complex amount of hereditary (genetic) information of some 10^{10} bits. This breeding process was not and is not perfect. Sometimes inexplicable 'mishaps' spontaneously occur. These are copied again. Some new mutations and developments are more stable than others and variety thus accumulates. There is no proof but there is reason to believe that the essence of Darwin's theory on evolution has applied from the start: 'the differential survival of the fittest', that is a natural selection of the stable forms with high fertility and longevity while unsuitable and unstable offspring do not survive.

In the beginning was simplicity, but not for long. The differentiation of the flora and fauna continued. If the genes (units of heredity) had embarked not on heterosexual reproduction but on cloning (single-parent identical reproduction) the development and accumulation of variety would have taken much longer, if it occurred at all. The first limbless creatures (invertebrates) did not appear until 16th December. The *Selfish Genes* (Dawkins, 1978) were aggressive and gradually became more complex. Species developed and many became extinct, for instance the dinosaurs in the Mesozoic Era. And finally, amongst the higher animals, *Homo Erectus* began to stand out on 31 December.

As if this evolutionary process was not providing enough excitement and variety on planet earth, a radically new evolution was already under way. What had started as a trifling, inconspicuous small swelling at the end of the spinal cord in primitive fish (to provide a sense of directionality: head and tail), developed prodigiously in reptiles and mammals via distinct lobes into a mighty new complex organ: the *brain*.

The higher animals developed, inexplicably, more brain than they needed or would use for survival. Its capacity for utilizing information had surpassed their own genes. Eventually Man had become 'top-heavy' with more brain in relation to its weight than any other creature. Somehow, around midday 31 December on that cosmic calendar, *Homo Sapiens* had acquired a highly differentiated and active brain system, on top of the still recognizable primitive parts, which gave him the unique faculties of speech and self-awareness. Human civilization started only in the late hours (stone tools at 11.00 p.m.); the conscious accumulation and application of knowledge called science and technology did not take off until the last few seconds of the cosmic year. Viewed from the perspective of Man on earth the acceleration of his evolution is already staggering and overwhelming. What is then the sense of expediting the learning and development processes even further? Would this make humans more humane?

8.2   Make-up and functions of the brain

Figure 32 shows globally the physical make-up of the human brain system. It is a typical 'brain-over-brain' configuration which has great significance for its operation. The most central part is the oldest part and operationally hidden from one's own awareness. It regulates the blood circulation and most other vital body functions, perhaps still in the same way as in prehistoric times, hence its name the Reptilian Complex (RC for short). At convenient and sometimes *in*convenient moments this primal centre produces species-typical impulses. It makes a monkey behave as a monkey and humans as man or woman in genetically pre-programmed, instinctual ways in such matters as survival, territory, hierarchy, dominance, submission, rituals, etc. (see 'Rituals and Deceit' in *Science Digest* of November/December 1980). It may, in so-called unstabled persons, lead to pathological anxieties and behaviour. However, its normal effect on Man's daily life is certainly subdued, tamed, or toned down by the influence and activities of the other overlying layers of the brain system.

The second layer is called the Limbic System (LS for short) which houses the emotional-affectional centres which are mainly experienced as primary sensations. Through it we perceive pain and pleasure, love and care, fear and anger, hunger and thirst, distress, excitement, alertness of the senses, etc. These emotions are induced not only neuro-electrically but also biochemically by tiny glands embedded in these layers like the pituitary, the amygdala, the thalamus and other secreting organs.

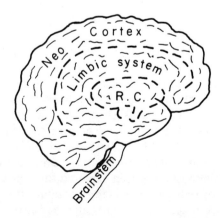

Figure 32   Make-up of the triune brain

The RC and LS systems are jointly referred to as the 'Old Brain', OB for short, because together they contain most of Man's primary, instinctual (some say animal) needs and his basic drives to avoid physiological distress. They control a person's emotional behaviour, his temperament, his curiosity, his propensity for seeking challenge and excitement. If required, in crisis situations, they produce instant gut-reactions and fire off orders (for example adrenalin) through the body. This explains why under difficult circumstances Man's behaviour is OB controlled and biased towards short-term physical well-being ('here and now'), without much rational direction from the conscious.

This combined OB is capped and crowned, literally and figuratively, with two voluminous, predominant lobes in Man's skull, called the Neo-Cortex or *Neo-Brain* (NB for short). These, in evolutionary terms the most recent ones, contain the astonishingly complex processing and command centres of Man's multifunctional (sensory, motoric, and cognitive) nerve system. In themselves unassuming, not much more than 'two fistfuls of pink-grey wrinkled tissue with the consistency of porridge, are able to store more information than the libraries of this world can hold' (Rose, 1976:21). Over 15 thousand million neurons can interact with each other more intensively than a generous telephone system for every person in this world would permit.

One particular characteristic of this NB, which is different from all other organs of the body, is that the cells do not regenerate; some 20,000 neurons are formed each *minute* from conception to birth, some 10,000 die each *day* from birth to death, fortunately adding up to less than 5 per cent of the total. Although a new-born brain is physically closer to its adult condition than any other organ, the number of connections and pathways (synaptic contacts) greatly increases during the first two years of life.

Much progress has been made in mapping out in substantial detail, for instance by Penfield (Sagan, 1977:33–6), the locations where the neural information from all parts of the body is received and transmitted. Such is the direct link between the nerves, receptors, and terminals in our body and brain that the brain feels with the nerves of the skin and 'the eyes are the brain's instrument of seeing'.

The right and left halves of the Neo-Cortex (RB and LB for short) are intricately connected by nature's most compact communication cord, the *Corpus Callosum* (see Figure 33). It consists of some 200 million nerve fibres which facilitate instantaneous, continuous, conscious, and unconscious switchovers from LB to RB and vice versa. This cord has a 'consultative exchange' capacity of more than a thousand million bits of information per second.

The combined capacity of the NB is so large that it has never been used or tested to the full. It is the most *under*utilized natural library and information system. Not all its possibilities have been explored, its limits are not even in sight. This high degree of redundancy has the advantage that the function of damaged parts can be taken over by the remainder; its plasticity and versatility are very high, especially at a young age.

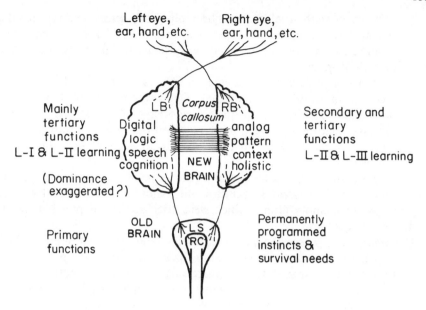

Figure 33   Schematic diagram of the left and right brain

The total weight and volume of the NB shows significant differences between male and female and between some races, but it is noteworthy that volume has no (significant) correlation with basic intellectual ability. All human brains are physiologically astonishingly similar in structure, anatomy, texture, and physical substance, both philogenetically (between the races) and autogenetically (development from embryo to adult). However, all brains are astonishingly different with respect to their programming and processing capacity and even more with respect to the contents of 'the archive'. In computer terms: we all have identical hardware but no two people have the same software. Not even identical twins are alike with respect to the state and content of their brains. The human mind demonstrates its uniformity *and* uniqueness at the same time.

8.3   More about Man's phenomenal store

I was tempted to call this section 'Memory Matters' after Brown (1977) because the function that memory plays in matters of learning and in daily life is very important. But I shall not and cannot deal with all aspects of the human memory in this section. I will only give a sort of overview and summarize one aspect, the process of recording. Other aspects will be dealt with successively later.

The simplest definition of memory is: 'Man's faculty of keeping things in mind and recollecting them'. In a wider meaning memory encompasses many more aspects:

(1) *Memory as content:* all that has been physically sensed and registered as 'facts' during life, including personal memories of feelings, emotions, thoughts, ideas, phantasies, and one's 'episodic' memory that relates everything in time.

Man's archive is phenomenal: hundreds of thousands of words, scenes, sounds, events, persons, etc. One's second half of life would not be enough to write out all one's memories of the first half. Research indicates that there is much more recorded than we are aware of or are able to use later. It is 'all there, if only one could find the way to retrieve it'.

Some would also include Man's genetic 'memory' under this heading, that is the unconscious faculties, the (semi-) instinctive and cultural collective memory (Jung) which were discussed in Chapter 5 as Man's inborn faculties.

(2) *Memory as process:* the handling, storing, and retrieving of all available information. Actually, the brain's *speed* of sequential processing is rather low compared to the processing speed of computers, but its 'software' capacity for high volume (for example visual) perception and instantaneous recognition and parallel retrieval is ingenious, immeasurable, and inimitable. The difference in perception and processing of the left brain and right brain is worth a few separate sections (8.4, 8.5, and 8.6).

(3) *Long-term and short-term memory:* many experiments have been carried out to pinpoint the influencing factors. Popular books have been written to identify and improve the reader's memory. It depends not only on the mechanism of recording (see below) but also on association and contexts (Section 8.5), individual selectivity (*Homo Discriminator*: 8.7) and on how the brain is turned on and off (Section 8.8).

(4) *Memory as awareness:* another approach to the above aspects, for example, combining content and process, is to consider memory as levels of awareness, that is of delegating knowledge and learning to the subconscious, or combining with and retrieving it from pre- and post-consciousness. I have come to view the ability of crossing these boundaries of such importance for creativity, for the levels of learning and development, that a separate chapter (9) will investigate this further.

For a better understanding of all these aspects it is indispensable to summarize here how the actual physical recording of 'engrams' (= units of information, see Rose, 1976:252–60) takes place. It is most remarkable that the ongoing experiments keep producing substantial evidence that more than one process operates at the same time. Some five theories are accepted:

(1) The electrical pathway theory. The multiple connections between the synapses of the neurons can be selectively opened up and closed electrically into particular patterns. So-called alpha waves and typical rhythms have been distinguished under conditions of sleep, dreams, and activities

while awake. Electro-encephalograms are used for medical and psychological diagnosis. Electro-shock treatments are a contested practice. The electro potentials are, however, not permanent enough to account for fixed programmes and lifelong memories.

(2) Biological and chemical theories explain how nerve cells thicken and shrink and change the synapses (semi-)permanently. Experiments have identified particular chemicals that can make fixations. The artificial influence with drugs is well known. The change from short-term to long-term memory especially depends on these processes but how they are regulated is still far from clear.

(3) The memory molecules. Amino-acids with information along the chain have been identified. Although this research has been put in disrepute by articles like 'Brain abstracts from professor to students?', transfer of learned behaviour from rats to hamsters, for instance, has been achieved with extracted substances.

(4) The distributive theory. It has also been established that learned behaviour is registered at various places in the brain. Destruction of an identified learned engram (brain imprint) does not wipe out learning. Information is apparently recorded at a number of different locations at the same time. This has given great support to the gestalt theories. The brain can recognize a pattern instantly, perhaps in a similar fashion as a hologram, of which the image-forming property is diffusedly dispersed throughout the plate in such a way that it can be partly destroyed without losing the total image, but with loss of 'quality'.

(5) The multiple-pathway redundancy theory of Rose (1976:258) which reconciles the above theories. He emphasizes that it is quite acceptable that more parts of the brain (limbic system, reptilian complex, left and right hemispheres and other subparts) are involved with the same activities and that there is a multiple mechanism of 'storage'.

8.4 Right and left brain. The dual system

During the last few years it has become increasingly clear that Man's mind and thus his learning process are not only influenced by the duality of the Old and New Brains but also by the fact that the two physically divided identical-looking halves of the Neo-Cortex are neither straight duplicates nor substitutes for each other (see Figure 33). The LB and RB are quite different in functional operation and control.

An early discovery showed the cross-over effect, that is left hand, left eye, and other left parts are controlled by the RB and vice versa. Later it turned out that the functions of the two halves are much more complicated, they can work in parallel, in series, alternately, overlappingly, partly as a stand by; they need each other, can dominate each other and the Old Brain, but the most important aspect is their flexible and sometimes stringent 'division of labour', each half doing what it can do best. Slight genetic predispositions of the LB and the RB at birth get magnified during life (Chomsky, 1968); they develop into semi-independent processing units with *different* specialities.

There are persons, so called 'Split-brain' personalities, in whom the connecting cord, the *Corpus Callosum*, is damaged or has been (partially) cut, or selectively anaesthetized for medical reasons. In animals particular parts have been removed. Extensive tests have given most interesting, mindshaking new insights into the different natures and functions of the two halves.

In 95 per cent of western educated persons, the *L*B handles their talking, reading, and writing. It has specialized in critical, intellectual, analytical thinking, in the processing and assessing of digital, quantitative data in a rational, sequential, logical, and controlling fashion. It applies what we call the 'scientific methods'. The LB contains the mathematical and verbal faculties, the semantic, grammatical, and syntactical aspects of language, it thinks in words, figures, and 'hard' facts. Damage of the LB is most likely to impair the victim's abilities of speaking, writing, counting, calculating, problem analyses, decision-making, planning, any of the reasoned forms of cognitive activities—the typical beta faculties.

The *R*B sees, hears, and 'evaluates' people, scenes, sounds etc. It is specialized in patterns and forms, in dialectic and holistic thinking, in receiving and handling analogical, qualitative data simultaneously and randomly, in recognition of faces, body postures, and gestures: 'A picture is worth a thousand words'. The RB handles all types of free associations in artistic, creative, intuitive thinking, time/space related perceptions, imaginations and serendipity, it creates and enjoys dance, sculpture, painting, music, metaphors, hypotheses, myths, etc. Its amazing ability of gestalt or 'pars-pro-toto' recognition (Watzlawick, 1978:27) enables Man to perceive patterns and complex totalities upon sensing only a few minor details, for example one scribble can suggest a complete picture, one spoken word may remind us of a friend or a whole culture, a smell may bring back the atmosphere of a particular town or the experience of love.

The idea that there are two modes of thinking is of course not new. For ages wise men have recognized the duality and complementarity of rationality and emotion, of intellect and psyche, etc. 'In early civilizations this was acknowledged in many forms of philosophical, religious, and psychological endeavours. It has been emphasized in physics and in metaphysics by many. What is new is a recognition that these modes operate physiologically as well as mentally and culturally' (Ornstein, 1977:84). And now the newest feature is that we are able to *measure*, for example via the neuro-electrical (alpha) brain waves, which of the two hemispheres is active, where and when (awake and asleep) and to what extent.

Gradually, a clear 'picture' is emerging of the typical differences between the natures of the two hemispheres. Let me succumb to my own LB need to tabulate neatly in characteristic key-words the results of research and tests of various scientists: Ornstein, 1972; Sagan, 1977; Bateson, 1978; Watzlawick, 1978; Restak, 1979; Blakeslee, 1980.

LB or left neo-cortex	*RB or right neo-cortex*
Rational, intellectual	Emotional, affectional
Logical, cartesian	Coincidental, intuitive
Analytic	Dialectic, synthetic
Quantity	Quality
Digital, either–or	Analogical, more or less
Sequential, steps	Parallel, simultaneously, global
Linear, vertical	Lateral (De Bono)
Time	Space
Knowing that	Knowing how and why
Verbal	Pre-, non-verbal
Words, figures, facts	Pictures, gestures, postures
Events, cause-effects	Context
Units, elements	Relations, holistic, gestalt
Closed, finite	Open, continuous
Zero, negative, positive	No zero, 'PO'
Objective, explicit	Subjective, implicit
Deliberate, conscious	Involuntary, subconscious
Propositional	Metaphorical
Sciences, technology	Arts and humanities
Execution of plans	Creation of ideas

This table simplifies and generalizes the differences. Remember that the two hemispheres are almost identical physiologically; their significant differences in operational mode and content in any individual are the result of the very personal history and the 'profiling' (see Section 1.7) by oneself and others during one's lifetime.

A clear example of LB dominance is described by Darwin in his autobiography with admirable insight:

> I have almost completely lost my appreciation for pictures and music. It seems as if my mind has become a sort of machine that processes large amounts of factual data into one general theory after the other. But why this led to the deterioration of that part of my brain that houses my artistic interests is something I cannot understand. I suppose that a person with a mind that is more strongly or better organized would not suffer such impoverishment; and if I could live my life again I would make it a habit to read a few poems and to listen to music at least once a week. Then those parts of my brain which have perished would perhaps have been kept alive by regular exercise . . . . (in Watzlawick, 1978:78)

I read an important message through these lines that Darwin believed it to be possible and recommendable for Man to foster and train both sides of his brain. That is exactly the same as Jung's advocacy of a dialogue with one's Inner Self in order to become or remain an integrated person (see Section 6.2).

Also De Bono (1976) described how creativity could be promoted through 'lateral thinking' before the research of the last years could support his arguments in terms of brain physiology. In summary: the LB and RB should talk to, support, and utilize each other.

Few people are aware which side is doing what, and whether one hemisphere is dominant or neglected. Since the LB is quick in reading, writing, and talking, it gives the verifiable impression that it alone can think! But the RB has its own trains of thought, it controls action, remembers things, decides, has emotions, all of which are however not readily observable or accessible through reflection. The RB grasps many factors simultaneously, its thinking is complex and intuitive, not consciously controllable. It produces instantaneous insights and creativity. Blakeslee (1980) calls the RB our 'Silent Partner'. And Einstein said: 'the written or spoken words do not seem to play any role in my mechanism of thought'.

There are skills which are typically to be learned with the LB, for example reading, arithmetic, and typing; others with the RB, for example sculpture and playing ball games. The latter can be taught only by watching, doing, emulating. It would be cumbersome, if not impossible, to determine analytically the ball's speed and trajectory and adjust for wind and other factors through logical reasoning during a game of tennis. The teaching of dancing and playing music may start with sequential logical instruction but the results will remain sterile without the qualities of the RB.

Today a farmer may control his chickens, their feedstock and egg production electronically (LB analyses and process), whereas the good shepherd would know *at a glance* when one sheep was missing from a large flock (instant RB recognition). Charlie Chaplin (in *Modern Times*) acted as a robot with itemized instructions for tightening nuts on bolts, thus making a mockery of human beings at conveyer belts.

Let me put in here a simple exercise for the reader. While reading this chapter it is most likely that your *L*B has been the most active part; you may now experience a switch-over to non-analytical, global *R*B activity by taking a look at Figure 34 and deciding whether these hands are right and/or left ones. The chances are, even if they were shown to you in a flash, that you recognized

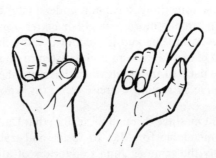

Figure 34   RB recognition of the hands

them directly with your *R*B. Only after logical reasoning with your *L*B would you be able to explain in words the justification for your 'spontaneous' recognition.

The thought processes of the RB are not readily controllable, we cannot force them or trace their ways, their memories. These RB insights have to come (often by themselves) through the *Corpus Callosum* to the conscious LB which may still have a hard job to verbalize them in logical sequence. If pressed hard the LB may dream up the reason.

8.5 The analogical digital modes of communication

The two modes of operation of the brain are more complex than just specializations of the right and left hemisphere. The biologically same 'grey mass' of the LB and RB can operate *physically* in fundamentally different ways. The contact points of the interlinking neurons called the synapses can, like simple on/off switches be either connected or disconnected by neural signals from the sensory organs in a fashion comparable with the electro-magnetic activation of the nodes of a computer's memory cell. These 'yes or no', '1 or 0', 'open or closed' situations are called binary digital information. The *left* brain works predominantly in the *digital* mode of operation.

Neuro signals can also create potentials of different strengths or cause the secretion of tiny amounts of biochemical substances (for example enkephalins, endorphins), the magnitude, concentration, or speed of reaction of which are proportional to cause or effect. That enables the brain to symbolize and process information through *proportional* representation. This is the *analogical* mode of operation. The human body works with many analogical messages: neural potentials, secretions of the glands (for example hormones), concentration of adrenalin in the blood, etc. Man's Old Brain works almost exclusively in this way.

Some fifteen years ago it was an important issue whether the New Brain has essentially an analogical or a digital mechanism. Bateson now explains (1979:111):

> In a vast majority of instances, the neuron either fires or does not fire; and if this was the end of the story, the system would be purely digital and binary. But it is possible to make digital neurons assume the *appearance* of being analogic systems. This is done by the simple device of multiplying the pathways so that a given cluster of pathways might consist of hundreds of neurons of which a certain percentage would be firing, thus giving an apparently graded response. In addition, the individual neuron is modified by hormonal and other environmental conditions around it that may alter its threshold in a truly quantitative manner.

Thanks to the thousands of millions of neurons (and each one can be connected to some thousands of others), any part of the brain can thus operate in the analogical mode. As this is fundamental to the life process of most living creatures, analogical processing has existed since the oldest phases of the evolution. It is the RB which seems to prefer the use of multiple pathways, this 'specializing' in memorizing and recognizing the multitude of complex patterns of faces, scenes, events, etc.

Indeed, communication started with analogical symbols, sounds, and gestures. Primitive picture-writing around 3000 BC on rocks and tablets is visual images and symbol language. The times of day and season were recorded through the analogical shift of the shadow of the sun. The Roman figures, especially I, II, III retained an analogical form. Analphabetes vote through colours and other symbols. Simple people prefer picture books. Refer also to the *Naked Ape* (Morris, 1967).

The digital mode of information is simpler, more precise, but more abstract. It is a more 'recent' invention in the history of the evolution, and brilliantly exploited and applied by Man's LB. Its major 'brainchildren' are the linguistic abilities, science, and technology. The modern digital clock has no relation with the sun any more, it flips-over discrete symbols (arbitrarily chosen) for days, dates, hours, minutes, and seconds. Computers process all types of information, including pictures/movies, via *digital* data called bits.

During the last century Man's learning has developed particularly in logical analyses of reasoning and processing of digital symbols. Mathematics, physics, and technology lend themselves to digital recording. This knowledge is easy to accumulate and copy and thus readily transferable to the next generation. The information explosion is increasingly digital. Expanding libraries of books, microfilms, and computer discs are proof of this. Or is it the other way around: information is exploding since it became digital? My recent visit to demonstrations with desktop-integrated computer word-processors convinced me that the end of info-technology is not even in sight.

Yet human communication is more than a convention, more than a pure codification of digital symbols. Our RB thrives on the 'music behind the words' in the form of gestures, pitch of voices, aphorisms, metaphors, and many other ways of adding quality to speech and writing. We can communicate without words, without having to say it digitally. Connotations enrich denotations, for instance the no-smoking signs in public transport. Advertisers try to be creative in this respect. Practically all non-verbal communication is in analogical form. There is a proliferation of books on body language. Silent Charlie Chaplin could move people of many cultures to tears.

Some abstract concepts can be processed only in words. For instance: 'He is ambitious' or 'I did not want to say anything', are very difficult to communicate in analogical form. There is no 'negative' in analogical language, no symbols for 'if–then' or 'either–or'. On the other hand there are perceptions and ideas that are difficult, even impossible to express exclusively in the digital mode. For instance, the beauty of a scene, the feelings during personal encounter, an interior motive to do something. 'One picture is worth a thousand words': the police apply this in the technique of 'photo-fit'.

With people whose language we do not know and with animals we have to communicate exclusively in analogical form. It is not the digital word 'sit' that makes a dog sit but the habitualized analogical intonation of his owner. I understand the notice 'sit' with my LB in many notations, even when logically misformed, say as ' ti2 '. Animals do not, unless the notice itself is 'Skinner-ized' through shape and colour. Man uses form, intonation, or any analogical symbol to draw extra, higher level constructs (meaning) from it; he recognizes and handles content *and* context.

To be more precise, Man draws additional learning from how the two modes of communication are mixed. The LB is mainly used for the factual, objective, logical, rational, verbal *content* of the message and the RB for the relational, qualitative, analogical *context* and for 'consulting' the (emotional) limbic system and reptilian complex. Many context signals (for example the sender being confident or nervous or whatever) are communicated unconsciously and/or perceived subconsciously. It is the subconscious interplay between LB and RB through the *Corpus Callosum* that determines what extra meaning is added to the memory, wherever it is located physically.

8.6 The dual system in sex and education

The recent research on mental differences between the sexes (a history of biased bias) is also, focused on the differences in the working of the brain. The obvious difference in volume, some 10–14 per cent more of it in men that in women, is directly related to body size and does not account for any systematic difference in intelligence or mental strength.

The brains of men and women are *un*like in a more complex, fundamental way, that is in the operation and in the co-operation of the various parts. Research has shown (Blakeslee, 1980) that chromosomes and hormones are responsible, before and after birth, for a masculinization or feminization of the brain functions. In short and simple terms this results in:

Women (more/better)	*Men* (more/better)
Early maturation	Catching up later
Intuition (RB)	Visual, spatial abilities (RB)
Verbally disposed (LB)	Analytical problem-solving (LB)
Memory for words, figures	(Stutters, dyslexia)
Symbol recognition	Mathematical insights
Sensitive tactile/other senses	Acting tougher/rougher
Alert to social cues, e.g. reading facial expressions and emotional elements in communication	Oriented to environment Curious about things, their working
Sense of territoriality	Directed outwardly, exploring
Nursing, maintaining, submissive	Competing, building, dominating
Attentive to detail	Short reaction time

148

Women (continued)	Men (continued)
Manual dexterity	Creativity
No towring genius	Specialized talents
Neo-brain = pair of generalists	Neo-brain = pair of specialists

It is not simply a matter of whether either LB or RB is more developed or dominant in men or women. The most important point is that the two hemispheres are more differentiated and specialized in men due to their slower maturation in infancy and adolescence. In girls the LB and RB develop more quickly, are more integrated and diffused via the *Corpus Callosum*.

Understandably this recent research is giving fresh, yet different fuel to the cause of feminism. And it has revived, in all its former intensity, the wrangle over whether nurture or nature plays the greater part. The obscuring fact is that the differences between the members of the same sex are invariably far greater than the average differences between the sexes; the valid generalization never applies, like weight, to all men or women. And their development is indeed most strongly influenced by the fact that they are treated as boys or girls from their birth onwards. Nevertheless it is now established that in addition to the obvious differences (in size, anatomy, sexual function there are fundamental genetic differences between men and women in the operational make up of their brains. There is some evidence that these differences are narrowing over evolutionary time.

Western education has moved there and more towards verbal tuition, the emphasis is very much on training the *LB*. Lectures, textbooks, and multiple-choice exams train and test LB capacities. All educational and academic institutes favour a 'scholarly' development at the expense of the (uncontrollable, soft, woolly) RB characteristics. This already starts with and sometimes dominates elementary education.

Ornstein (1972:85), Rogers (1969), Freire (1977), De Bono (1976) and Blakeslee (1980:52–75), to name a few, are gravely concerned about this imbalance. They call it the 'Left-brain take over of education'. After the fourth grade the students have almost exclusively been developed analytically, verbally. Many highly educated intellectuals let their RB atrophy by trying to use their LB for totally inappropriate tasks. (Remember Darwin's guilt feelings!) Even present-day musical education often neglects the natural, essential RB listening and creative talents in favour of LB analysis and technical performance.

Continuous use of only one hemisphere leads to mental fatigue; that is why people like to do completely different things in their spare time. Frequent change over, and fresh combinations give the best learning results. A simple example in this respect is the insight that $(a+b)^2 = a^2 + 2ab + b^2$ through a visual presentation. Then ask students to discover for themselves the formula for $(a-b)^2$. Young children are unspoilt in the use of both hemispheres, their eidetic memory is very good. Ideally this should be deliberately kept alive.

An exclusive RB approach, as was the case in the early history of mankind,

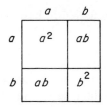

Figure 35   Visual presentation of a formula

does not lead to much progress either. Intuition and feelings have their limitations, they can fool us. They often need careful checking. Students who continue to guess the answers get into trouble; that is why schools discourage it. But RB abilities remain equally essential in modern times, especially for managers who are confronted with so many gaps in data, changes, in the environment, and time constraints. They sorely need their gut feel and well-developed intuition. Fortunate are those whose talents in this respect have not been strangled, but nursed in high school and university.

Helping highly verbal LB-trained adults to use their RB and do some lateral thinking is well nigh impossible. Not believing or trusting their own non-verbal consciousness, they cannot 'let it happen'. We should not expect to be able to redress this with an oriental way of life. Granted, eastern philosophers have indeed developed mental practices to silence (literally) rational verbal reasoning in order to tap elusive, complex insights, feelings, and creatively. Chinese Toa, Indian Yoga, and Japanese Zen foster completely different ways of thinking, doing, and being, but they are just as extreme and one-sided in the use of only one hemisphere and in the denial of the other, the LB.

The application of chips, tiny computers, and processors in toys and tools will demand an increasing proficiency in handling digital data. Youngsters seem to love it. Therefore we can expect a continued challenge and an instrumental extension of Man's LB. Educational institutions are scrambling to gear up for it.

Fortunately electronic technology is developing in the direction where it remains possible to organize truly dual learning: digitally and spatially, verbally and pictorially. Visual aids (RB) are becoming cheaper and easier to use, so are the recent home computers, video-games and rotating design displays on TV screens. These develop the students' insights into how digital variables influence complex phenomena like the bouncing of balls, the trajectory of spaceships, and the form and beauty of buildings and cars.

The question as to which is the more important for managing ourselves and the world, the RB or the LB, is a complex one and beyond this book. But from what I have studied and experienced so far, I conclude that we have to make a deliberate effort to develop and apply the RB better. 'More critical thinking, without creative and intuitive insights, without the search for new patterns, is sterile and doomed. To solve complex problems in changing circumstances requires the activity of both cerebral hemispheres: the path to the future lies through the *Corpus Callosum*' (Sagan, 1977:181).

'With a recognition of the physiological basis of the dual specializations of consciousness, we may be able to redress the balance in science and psychology' (Ornstein, 1972:85). But

> a real reform of the education system will not occur until the individual teachers learn to understand the true nature of the brain. A tutor who habitually thinks verbally himself simply cannot feed the students a course on intuitive thinking: how can he keep the attention of both the LB and the RB? . . . . The real problem is that the basic thinking of the entire educational establishment must be changed before real results can be expected. (Blakeslee, 1980:58, 59)

So? This requires a deliberate holistic development of all brain functions (see Section 8.9).

8.7 Homo discriminator

After paying all this attention to the make-up of the brain, to its subprocesses of storing, changing and processing of information, we have to address the important questions: How does the brain get *activated*? When and why does it notice something? What constitutes the threshold of perception? What triggers our energy behind it?

Bateson formulates these questions with a quasi-scientific fable: 'if we can get a frog to sit quietly in a saucepan of cold water, and if the temperature of the water is raised *very* slowly and smoothly so that there is no moment of *marked* increase, the frog will not notice, he will not jump. He may get boiled' (1979:98). Bateson suggests that the human species sits in the saucepan of its environment with slowly increasing pollution and slowly deteriorating education. Will we ever notice? Who will jump?

There is no learning without the ability to discriminate. Babies take for granted their own mothers' face and voice and milk and (have to) learn to appreciate what is different: other faces and voices, cows' milk and curry.

We always compare what we see, hear, eat, and feel with what we have personally seen, heard, eaten, and felt before in other places and situations. 'Comparison may be odious' but Man hardly does anything else. He goes on comparing, ranking, discriminating between things, persons, events, ideas, fantasies, until he dies. When things appear to be the same, people get bored and seek out new things. There is a fundamental need to be 'entertained', aroused, shocked.

I realize that many authors use rather different concepts for this same phenomena. Perls's gestalt theory: figures that *stand out* from the background; Kelly's *bipolar* construct (Section 7.5); my own categories of *contrasts* (Section 7.6); Festinger's cognitive *dissonants*; Berne's scripts: acting on (dis)*similarities* with past experience; Popper's search for *falsification* instead of confirmation; 'Discovery commences with the awareness of *anomaly*'

(Kuhn, in Phillips, 1973:104); 'Thinking in terms of *opposites* is natural to the human species' (Osgood *et al.*, 1965:327); 'Data becomes significant only to the extent that it assumes *new*, non-obvious meaning to a person' (Beer, 1975); 'One always has a model, a theory, an expectation with which the actual thing, person or event is appraised in comparison' (Zijderveld, 1975:300); and many more like: 'learning is changing', 'life is renewal', and, last but not least, the short definition by Bateson (1979:99): *'Information consists of differences that make a difference'*.

These are all variations on the same theme of Man's fundamental need and ability to discriminate. It is his neuro-biological 'mechanism' that enables him to sense differences in sound, sight, smell, etc. What are pleasure, pain, fear, curiosity? Simple abstract names for very complex patterns of differences and intensities. All prime movers of our biological and mental processes are triggered by differences and contrasts. Therefore the human species can be characterized by: *Homo Discriminator*.

The triggering discriminations are far from objectively mechanistic, they are very individualistic. Information and 'news' are, like beauty, only of value in the eye of the beholder. The process is:

(a) Selective. In emergencies we are not aware of wounds, we feel no pain. We can focus on one face, tune-in on one voice in a room full of people and noise.

(b) Subjective. 'Two men look out through the same bars: one sees the mud, and one the stars.' There is the well-known Persian story of how differently an elephant can be perceived by blind people (in Brakel, 1979:7). Any object is 'an object-to-me not through direct perceptual sense but in terms of its psycho-social significance' (Hutton, 1979:3). Wittgenstein philosophizes about the multiple perception of a triangle (Phillips, 1973:131).

(c) Subconscious. Whereas our mental focus searches explicitly for anomalies (problem recognition) or scans deliberately for alternatives (planning), in digital or analog form, comparisons also just happen involuntarily, semi-consciously, intuitively, or through instinctive reflexes.

(d) Gestalt. Man cannot stand unfinished business. Life must make sense. Hence the inclination to complete pictures, to form 'gestalts', to see more, for example, in inkblots and clouds, than is physically there, to fantasize (refer witness stories), to draw biased conclusions and make rash decisions.

(e) Creative. New ideas are triggered by fantasies, by leaps and bounds: 'Eureka!'

Recognizing the above categories still does not explain *how* the brain gets activate, and even less how we can start and accelerate the learning process. There are several reasons why we cannot put our finger on it. For one, the set of neurons which account for the phenomena of arousal are very difficult to locate. They are physically mixed with other strings of nerves. They run as a tiny network through the brain stem up as far as the thalamus and are called the 'ascending reticular activity system' (Rose, 1976:296). This reticular system seems to have a process/ability of screening the sensory signals that travel up the brain stem. When they contain information which is potentially worthy of consideration (but how is this decided upon?), neurons are fired which alert the entire brain or selected parts to 'take note of what is coming'. It thus works as a filter and as an amplifier. However, it is still not known what directs the filter and amplifier. (As with nuclear physics, there are always new queries behind the findings.)

It is a fact that monkeys have been made to respond more quickly and learn faster through electrodes implanted in the reticular. Drugs like pemoline, amphetamine, benzedrine, etc. have been tested in Russia and the USA for arousing or quietening down psychiatric patients and hyperactive children. The recently discovered enkephalins and endorphins (protein-like substances of relatively simple structure) can profoundly affect mood and temperament. This type of drug can activate the brain not only via the reticular system but also via the pain and pleasure centres of the OB or via selected parts of the LB and RB and/or indirectly via the glands in the body. Not knowing where and what these drugs are actually affecting, controls have been set up to detect possible after- and side-effects. The interpretation of all these ongoing experiments is often conflicting and far from conclusive.

Man's identity lies in his brain. No wonder brain research is a hot, sensitive issue. Most countries have put limitations on experiments with electric shocks, with awareness-widening drugs (e.g LSD), learning pills and other stimulants. But carefully directed experiments will continue and may result in a breakthrough for which the human mind may not be ready.

8.8 Turning on and turning off the brain

So, the brain cannot (yet) understand its own working! And we are not yet able to manage its activating mechanism. What does this mean for the everyday practice of those for whom motivating is a profession? The advertising business and politicians try to turn on, often none too subtly, all kinds of 'hidden' persuasive factors. Do they just rely on their natural talent of attracting people's attention, of inducing them to buy or do something?

The fact that discrimination and perception are very personal, selective, subjective, subconscious, etc., refer previous section, means that there are more ways of getting individuals to learn than can be described here. It confronts us educators with the question whether stimulating students just remains a very personal 'art'.

I have given this issue a good deal of thought and I have tried to systematize my experience. And yet, I regret not to be able to formulate straight 'dos and don'ts', or criteria for the competence of the trainer in this respect. The fact that ethics and cultural values play a role and can override effectiveness makes this a rather complicated and very personal subject. I shall come into the open with a few thoughts in the last section of the book.

Here let us limit ourselves to three aspects: (a) the nature of the general relationship between the efforts of the educator/trainer and the resulting learning of the student, (b) the principle issue of how far the educator's responsibility goes, and (c) the importance of relaxation.

The extent to which the *external* motivators activate the *internal* functions of the student's brain can be generalized by the well-known conventional bell-shaped curve shown in Figure 36. This characteristic curve is borrowed from Hunts and Hilton (1973:111) and was originally described, I believe, by Yerkes and Dodson in 1908! Though simple, I like this generalized relation much better than Skinner's black-box model. It shows that the facilitator may expect a threshold (1) below which there is little response, then a rapidly increasing effect (2), mainly depending on the innate ability and energy of the student, then a plateau (3) where the effect is maximal. More external pressure or stimulation will not help. Any more talk or effort by the educator will be counterproductive. The effectiveness will decrease (4).

The actual relationship (form and quantity) is unique for each situation, viz. for each individual, subject, objective, time of the day, etc. This clearly shows that it is not possible to arrange for the most effective optimal learning by all students at the same time (e.g. points a and b in Figure 36). The individual optima can be far apart. In addition, time has different effects on saturation and tiredness, which are difficult to quantify. The tension may be too high or too prolonged for some of the students. I sometimes ask course participants: 'Where do you think you are on the effectiveness curve at this moment?'

I shall not discuss the competence criteria for organizing and creating the best stimuli. I refer to the commendable work done by the Manpower Service Commission, London, in formulating 'common areas of know-how' and the 'areas of specific knowledge and skills' for *Training the Trainers*. (Manpower Services Commission, no date.) I would rather pose the principal question of the nature and the extent of educators' responsibility. Here is the same question in five forms: can and should the responsibility of the facilitator include:

— the inner workings of the black-box, or should he be content with whatever the response mechanism happens to be?
— the shape of the relations curve, or should he try to change it, for instance leading student B from point b to c?
— (in Bateson's terms) creating differences that make significant differences for those addressed?
— (counter to the popular saying), only 'taking the horse to the water', or also 'making the drinking attractive and effective'?
— methods and means that are causing (some) pain.

The effectiveness of many *extrinsic* motivators are changing and diminishing (e.g. the carrots and sticks and 'duty' to study). This is not disquieting in itself,

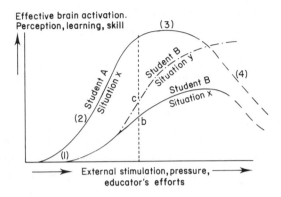

Figure 36   Effectiveness of brain activation

they are not important in themselves. The aim is to activate the very individualistic *intrinsic* factors. Therefore it is the task of the educator/trainer to find ways and means to act as a *catalyst*. Cross-culturally, it is not easy to know and appeal to the learners' real motivation. It is rather sensitive to raise their collateral energy. Can one ever be confident that the learning events will be 'good' for them?

One would say that educators and trainers have always been responsible for finding and formulating training needs, viz. whether and what the horses should drink. But it has been proved over and over again that it is the person of the tutor/trainer who makes or breaks a particular programme, that it requires an enormous amount of work and mental energy for him to keep latching in, from moment to moment, to the curiosity, interest and motivation of the students in such a way that they can and will continue to learn after the contrived event. This qualitative attribute, this catalytic ability, is essential for educators/trainers at home and abroad. Though better recognized now, it is seldom given the practical attention in the 'training and trainers' courses that it deserves and needs.

A few words about turning off the brain: *de*-activating is the result of habituation, addiction, rigidity, routine, and ageing. It is quite normal to get accustomed to signals/noises, to develop gradually higher thresholds for repeated stimuli, to get bored; adults can only be surprised once, novelties stop to make a difference. A lecturer who stops talking may wake us up!

A healthy turning off process is essential for the *husbandry* of our consciousness. Daily life would be impossible if we had to give attention to everything, or if we noticed differences in every situation. Our mental focus must, or sheer necessity, be efficient and *manage by exception*.

Therefore, learning is not only promoted by being alerted, but also by a gradual transfer to an activity-routine that *bypasses* the conscious. This frees the mental focus for new and unexpected matter. Much, if not most of what we know and do must be husbanded into the unconscious; some of it has to be *un*learned later through conscious effort.

Finally, the tight form of alertness *gets in the way* of improving the coordination of the brain and body. This is experienced in daily life when our mind and memory is narrowed by being too tense or under stress. This is the signal that one is overdoing it. The educator or students themselves may be trying too hard. At times the mind has to be relaxed and clear to let all parts of the brain and body get freely in touch again.

Refer to the discussion on the complementarity between the LB and RB in Sections 8.4–8.6 (example: Gallwey's *The Inner Game of Tennis*). I also like the fable of the centipede: after being asked how he managed to move his hundred legs so neatly in sequence, he became conscious of it, stumbled, tried harder, and could not walk any more until he forgot about it again.

8.9 Resemblance between model and brain. Some conclusions

What conclusions can we draw from this chapter? What tie-in can we make with the learning model? The brain is an amazingly powerful, complex organ. Its functions are more manifold and interwoven than originally envisaged. Its memory and processing capacities are phenomenal. We honestly do not know what the limits will be. Surprisingly little is understood about its working, even less about how we can manage the activation of the brain to make it more effective. Because of the risks involved, brain research is restricted and slow. Yet, it will lead (soon?) to further insights, a breakthrough is possible.

Man is what his brain is! A person's cognitive and psychological characteristics, his mind and identity, are physically located in and determined by his brain. A close resemblance between the physical and operational characteristics of the main parts is evident. Therefore, its main operational functions can be summarized by redrawing the schematic picture of the triune brain of Figure 33 in the operational form of Figure 37.

With respect to learning and development it is obvious that the old brain (limbic system and reptilian complex) is the least accessible, least controllable, and least changeable core of the person. As discussed in Chapters 5 and 6, this is the unconscious genetic Inner Self.

The outer layer is directly accessible from the environment by others and completely controllable by the mental focus of the person himself. He is aware of and able to process what he senses, thinks, plans, and does. This (self-) conscious layer of learning and development is for all practical purposes identifiable with the operational activities and abilities of the LB.

The layer in between provides the transitions and connections. Its functions are not directly controllable, traceable, or changeable, but we know from practice that they are partly accessible and influenceable under certain conditions. In this intermediate layer learning and development takes place subconsciously and intuitively through sensing, thinking, planning, and doing. This represents very closely the operational characteristics of the RB.

In the global terms of evolution, the neo-brain grew as a distinctly new organ over the LS and RC, with the LB undergoing a 'recent' development.

156

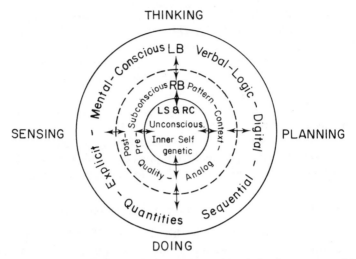

THINKING

SENSING

PLANNING

DOING

Figure 37   Schematic comparison between the personal development model and the operational functions of the triune brain

development processes in the personal development model resemble operationally the Old Brain—Right Brain—Left Brain respectively, with consciousness the highest in the outer (LB) layer.

To account for the operational controlling 'mechanisms' of the processes, the model employs the concepts of 'mental focus' and 'mental barriers'. Their functions, described in Chapter 3, can now be understood in brain terms as the selective discriminators and the turning-on, turning-off controls. Bringing all features together in one picture, the complete Process Model for Personal Development can now be shown as given in Appendix 12.

Writing this chapter has convinced me that motivating and helping students to develop themselves remains a very complex affair. On the other hand I am excited because of the possibilities of small or even larger breakthroughs in Man's potential to develop further, for instance by the fact that the limits of the human brain have not yet become apparent. On the contrary, realizing how much improvement we have witnessed in recent times in the physical fitness, appearance, and performance of the human body (for example in sports), we may expect the multiple functions of the brain to benefit equally well from optimum nutrition and effective mental stimulation. The existing scope for a more holistic utilization of the human brain, individually and as a species, even excluding the potential of 'artificial intelligence', is larger than we can handle.

8.10   Brain's population: the selfish memes

Now I would like to make a short and a somewhat whimsical detour, though an interesting one I hope, to show the relation between the last two chapters, that is between personal constructs and the brain.

A person's continuously changing constructs, his system of thoughts, opinions, and memories is more than a network; they are a lively lot. They should be visualized as a thriving, interacting, growing community of ideas, values, concepts, theories, etc.: brains are populated by *memes*.

Meme itself is a meme, that is a concept. It has a strong analogy to the word 'gene', the unit of heredity. This can be best explained by referring to Dawkins' book *The Selfish Gene* (1978) in which Darwin's evolution theory is rephrased in a remarkable way. Dawkins propounds a natural selection theory in which the genetic DNA molecules called 'genes' are considered (metaphorically) as active agents which work purposefully for their own survival. Since they have no consciousness they have no foresight, and therefore they are always competing savagely 'here and now'. They replicate themselves selfishly and exploit all living matter, animal and man alike, as their throwaway survival machines. A chicken is merely an egg's way of producing more eggs!

Dawkins' account of how the genes have replicated and differentiated and dominated this planet ruthlessly for the last 300 million years is a witty, speculative, yet scientifically based treatise. His last, eleventh chapter interested me most. He launches a new idea about the secondary evolution of the brain. Relatively late, during the last hour of Sagan's compressed calendar (Sagan, 1977:13–17), the genetic evolution produced the neo-brain that became conscious of things and self, thus creating intelligent speech and the accumulation of knowledge and ideas. A new, independent source of replication emerged: the unit of cultural transmission: the meme.

Dawkins sees speech and self-awareness, language, arts, sciences, actually the whole of civilization as a new *non-genetic* evolution, that is a non-genetic transmission and replication of opinions, values, literature, tunes, fashions, ways of doing and making things. He quotes 1978:204 Popper and others as having pointed out this analogy between the first genetic evolution and subsequent scientific/technological development.

A meme is defined as an idea, as any entity of thought, a construct in Kelly's terms (1955), which is capable of replicating itself, of being transferred from one brain to other brains. Memes compete with rival memes for attention, acceptance, survival, and further replication. Just as genes propagate themselves by spreading sperm to fertilize eggs to survive through new offspring, so memes spawn their seeds by word of mouth, by books, magazines, newspapers, and the modern media to propagate themselves through fertilization and survival in the brains of other individuals.

Memes should be regarded as living structures, not just metaphorically but technically.

When you plant a fertile meme in my mind, you literally utilize my brain, turning it into a vehicle for the meme's propagation in much the way that a virus may parasitize the mechanism of a host cell. And this is not just a way of talking. The meme for say, 'belief in life after death' is actually duplicated physically, millions of times over, as a thought-structure in the nervous systems of individual men the world over. (Dawkins, 1978:207)

Dawkins puts forward the fundamental principle that all life, whatever that may be, evolves throughout the universe by the differential survival of replicating entities. This new independent source of replication produces meme-populations that are surviving in stable groups of co-adapted meme-complexes (say: architecture, theology, music, finance, nationalism, technology, and so on). They evolve in the same way as mutually assisting, co-adapting gene-complexes. The *Encyclopaedia Britannica* is the largest available bank of meme seeds: 43 million words on 10,000 entries by 4000 scholars.

Actually, says Dawkins, this new kind of replicator is staring us in the face: the peculiarity of memes is that they replicate and evolve at a much faster rate than the genes and their longevity can be higher as well. Of the man Socrates there may not be any gene alive any more in the world of today, . . . but who cares? His meme-complexes and those of Moses (the Ten Commandments), of Jesus and Mohammed (praise be upon them), of Copernicus, Shakespeare, and Einstein, are still going strong. Once the genes had provided their survival machines with brains, once they produced a thinking, talking, human being, the memes could take over. 'All that is necessary is that the brain should be capable of imitation and emulation: memes will then evolve which exploit this capability to the full' (Dawkins, 1978:215).

I may skip Dawkins' more elaborate argumentation and justification, but I should mention the example in which genes and memes are not reinforcing each other, that is that a gene for celibacy is doomed to failure whereas the meme for celibacy is still successful in the meme pool.

It is worthwhile to compare this meme-concept with Kelly's theory of personal constructs. I find it more stimulating to imagine a community of living, interacting memes in people's brains than to visualize our constructs as a network of thoughts, recorded and updated in our memory system. What does the reader think of my meme that regards a repertory grid as a black and white still photograph of some contemporary members of someone's meme colony?

Whereas Dawkins states on the last page of his book that he 'is not going to argue the case of altruism one way or the other, nor to speculate over the possible memic evolution . . . .', I cannot resist the temptation to draw the analogy and differences between genes and memes a little further.

If a particular gene-pool is too small, the species of genetic traits will die out. In analogy: sound memes of gifted persons have died out and will die out through lack of offspring if they cannot find enough people (of sufficient intelligence?) for whom the meme is relevant. Also, closing a country off with an 'iron curtain', censuring, confining, and expelling dissidents, may all lead to memetic death of valuable construct families.

It is obvious that Man on this planet earth is now far more diverse memetically than genetically and that the memetic evolution is more dynamic and seems to progress at a faster pace than the genetic one. The advance in communication technology is facilitating a high incidence of intercourse and an enormous amount of cross-fertilization between memes the world over. The population explosion of memes is several times bigger than the explosion of genes.

Historically the fight for survival of the genes increased when the species populating the earth had to compete for resources; thus I can imagine that the fight between the memes is increasing now that so many memes (ideas and theories) are crossing hitherto established boundaries to compete with rival memes of different cultures, religions, etc. Incompatible memes have difficulty in co-existing in peace. Cultural upheavals are caused by popular and assertive memes (for example jeans and Islam), they seek cross-fertilization, expansion, and domination.

I see three intriguing trends. Firstly, during this century education is gradually reaching many more millions of people. This is inevitably resulting in people thinking for themselves, not just accepting the opinions of others. Own-grown memes (internalized values and concepts) are stronger and have a higher survival rate, especially in the brains of people on which the genes are losing their grip (for example in developed and post-industrial societies). It has become socially less acceptable that memes should be implanted forcefully. For instance: indoctrination, which I would call memetic rape, and brain-washing — memetic murder — belong to the meme-family of 'illegitimates'. In terms of this book: 'learning to learn' and 'self-organized development' are memes of a higher order in their evolution than training and education.

Secondly, genes are losing their power over the memes; the magic formula of the sorcerer's apprentice (Goethe) did its work in producing an increasing flood of memes without the genes knowing the formula to stop them. There are all the signs that the reverse is happening already, that is that the memes are capable of influencing and even of changing and dominating the genes. No fewer than 1200 genes have already been registered, they are tied down by the memes' need for better classification. Genes beware! Genetic engineering is already operational! It seems frightening that there are memes that know how to change and clone genes.

Thirdly, whereas genes are *un*conscious, blind replicators which are unable to forgo their short-term selfish interest, memes are just as selfish and competitive, but they can employ Man's unique mental feature: his capacity of hindsight and foresight. Every time that Man learns through planning, doing, and evaluation why and how a long-term principle may work better than a short-term one, a new meme is born that starts its fight for long-term survival against any shorter-sighted one. The sheer selfishness of memes assures that those survive which are proved fit and can ride out refutations (Popper) better than other memes. The memes with the power of survival, fecundity, and longevity will gradually evolve further into mutually supporting meme-complexes (ideas, principles, theories) which are capable of weathering the harsh tests of real life. Will the 'Good' memes survive the continuous onslaught of all Devil's advocates? Or (and that may be the same!) will the longest surviving memes be crowned the 'Community of Truths'?

9

Man's O-A-U Levels

The 'Interlude' of this book integrates my own experience with what several authors have said about the fundamental relatedness of Man's psychological and intellectual abilities. One more chapter must be added. Having started with Man's *inborn* faculties (Chapter 5), we are now concerned with his *learned* abilities. It is essential for any educator, trainer, or consultant to be able to recognize the present level of abilities and to envisage and plan for what the next level could/should be. Therefore it is important to consider now how to distinguish and measure levels of attainment in learning and development.

Instead of 'Levels of Attainment' I titled this chapter 'Man's O-A-U levels' in analogy to the X-Y-Z dimensions of Chapter 5 and in symbolical association with the well-known O- and A-levels of the British educational system, while U stands for *un*classified. I shall follow the same pattern of bringing together what various sources have said about this subject and then integrate them with some ideas of my own.

In daily life all sorts of criteria are in use to indicate acquired and required standards. Babies should regain their birthweight around the tenth day; the first tooth, step, menstruation, etc., all have their benchmarked dates. We administer IQ tests and exams, require youngsters to reach O- and A-levels at a certain age, diplomas of scouting and swimming are framed, bachelor and master and doctor degrees are testimonials of academic wisdom, jobs are ranked in hierarchical levels of responsibility, seniority, and/or authority. In short: we cannot escape from categorizing the human resources in levels of potential and acquired abilities.

I am *not* interested here in levels expressed in terms of 'more-of-the-same', for instance whether someone knows 2000 or 15,000 words of a foreign language, whether someone can type 20 or 40 words per minute. My focus of curiosity is understanding what aspect or quality has to be added to reach a higher level of learning and development.

The early Chinese already knew that life itself is more than 'more-of-the-same'. They distinguished three natural bio-psychological levels of development in every person's life: 0–20 is the period to learn, 20–40 the period to perform (build, expand, fight, etc.) and 40–60 the period to become wise. Similar life-stages, with recognizable characteristic transitions (crises or passages) between them, have been distinguished by Erickson, Sheehy (1976), Lievegoed (1979) and Vaillant (1977). The NPI group of Management trainer-consultants apply similar growth-phases to the development of organizations (Lievegoed, 1973).

I hope that the reader remembers Dale and Payne's ideas (in Section 5.2) about the dimensions and levels of development. Let me quote a few sentences. Any particular dimension is made up by smooth growth ranges, which are interrupted at some points by thresholds and barriers. At these points rearrangements or repatterning need to take place before growth can continue. There is no substantial progress without excitement, pain, or other emotional involvement. Indeed, the concept of development comprises the fact of life: the death of some elements allows the creation and integration of new principles.

9.1 Levels of competence and maturity

Having found it useful to compile and compare Man's X-Y-Z dimensions in Chapter 5, Figure 20, I was curious to see how a similar comparison of levels of development of a number of authors would look. The tabulation of Figure 38 contains those who claim to have studied levels of the competence and maturity of managers. Although some similarities can be perceived (for example differentiation, integration of Kolb, Lievegoed, and Sperry) the great variety in terms is most striking. Would it be possible to bring these together under a few common denominators?

An approach to simplification is to realize that most qualifications in the tabulation of Figure 38 are combinations of competence and maturity. Some levels directly refer to *competence* like novice, skilled, and mastery by Dale and Payne. These are quantitative *and* qualitative degrees of explicit, practical attainment of expertise in a particular activity, subject, or field. On the other hand there are pure levels of *maturity*, like those of Harrison and Loevinger, that define the degree and balance of a person's total ego-development.

Indeed, it is a reality in organization that in some situations, and mostly in lower positions, competence is more relevant and more important than maturity, and vice versa. They are independent because a great disparity between the two may exist, up into the highest regions: people can be competent for complex tasks while still immature, and people may be wise though not particularly competent for a specific task. People of the same level of maturity need not have similar competence. And the other way around, persons with a similar level of competence may not be equally mature.

It was Socrates, I believe, who noticed from one of the earliest investigations of people's satisfaction at work, that higher maturity adds quality to professional competence. Interviewing marble-cutters in the quarries of Athens some 2000 years ago, he distinguished four categories: those who cut just for bread and wine; those who wanted to raise a family; those who proved they were the best cutters in town; and those who found delight in helping to build the new temple. These levels of 'attitude to work' fit very well Maslow's well-known hierarchy of development levels.

Loevinger has tried to verify this scientifically with six empirically derived major stages of maturity with four to five transitional positions in between. She claims (Pfeiffer and Jones, 1978:192–204) that her 'sentence-completion-test' yields a total score of a person's maturity in a similarly objective way as IQ tests are supposed to be a pure yardstick for a person's intellectual ability. The practical application of her work, for instance in a large refinery in Curacao, has proved that it is not easy to increase the level of performance by increasing only the level of maturity.

I shall now try to convince the reader that the aspects of competence and maturity can be illustrated in the cyclic learning/development model. A new science grows through the following phases: first we become aware of a phenomenon and start recording it, then we analyse, describe, and hopefully understand it, and only then are we able to predict and influence it. Or in general, the major steps in mastering a subject are:

(1) Knowing *that* = noticing, observing, sensing, perceiving, recording, etc.
(2) Knowing *why* = analysing, cataloguing, describing, understanding it.
(3) Knowing *how* = predictive knowledge, ability to plan, organize, and influence it.
(4) Managing = making it happen, directing, monitoring, adjusting, re-designing, re-creating, then going through phases 1, 2, 3, 4 two or more times round.

The similarity with the learning stages: Sensing — Thinking — Planning — Doing, and around again, is quite obvious. We only speak of a person as professionally competent if he is an educated observer, *and* understands what he is doing, *and* is able to plan and organize applications, *and* is experienced in their execution. In other words the cyclic learning process (a) represents levels of competence; (b) illustrates that each successive level (stage) is complementary (not just more of the same); and (c) assumes that the stages are mutually reinforcing each other (see the holistic and other principles of Section 4.8).

In a similar way it can be shown that maturity is the *radial* component in the model. Maturity depends on the degree to which the non-directly accessible qualities of the Inner Self are being developed congruently and the degree to which these are integratingly employed at the stages of Sensing — Thinking — Planning — Doing. Maturity is operationally manifested by the manner in which mental barriers (Window — Skin — Gate — Rubicon) are being utilized by the primary and secondary processes for a healthy regulation of the person's mental focus.

The reader may have noticed already that Muller's ranking method of the overall potential of managers (see Section 5.1) is missing from the table of Figure 38. The reason is that his method does not work with defined levels of competence and maturity but defines the HAIR qualities as *potential* in terms of the *radial powers* (see Figure 22). The actual attainment, that is a person's career and promotion, is then equated with his competence and performance in particular job *levels*.

Sources	Level 1	Level 2	Level 3
Dale and Payne (refer Section 5.2)	Existence	Relatedness	Growth
	Novice	Skilled	Mastery
	Powerless	Got it together	Authenticity
	Inertia	Acting out	Self-enactment
Kolb	Acquisition	Specialization	Integration
Pedler	Memorize	Understand	Apply, transfer
Neth. Pedag. Institute	Physical	Social	Cultural
Lievegoed	Pioneering	Differentiation	Integration
Steiner	Behaltung	Gestaltung	Empfaltung
Ten Siethoff	Operate	Maintain	Create
Humanistic Psychology	Human existence	Hman relations	Human resources
Maslow	Survival and security	Belonging and esteem	Self-actualizing and transcending
Harrison	Dependent	Counter-dependent	Interdependent
Sperry	Directed	Differentiated	Collaboration
Emery and Trist. System: environment is	Redundancy of parts	Redundancy of function	System is learning
	placid	disturbed reactive	turbulent
M. Emery. Systems seek	targets	purposes	ideals
Management by knowing how to	survival/crises	strength/objectives	synergy
	play the game	change the rules	change the game
Loevinger (level of maturity)	Impulsive and self-protective	Conformist and conscientious	Autonomous and integrated

Figure 38   Levels of development

This is the moment to define the difference between learning and development in terms of the model: learning can be expressed in competence and may be limited to the explicit, cyclic tertiary process; development combines competence and maturity, it must comprise also the secondary and primary processes through radial integration.

Three important questions come to my mind. When is a consultant, facilitator, tutor responsible not only for learning but also for development? If he is, how to promote the interaction between the primary and secondary and tertiary processes in the individual? When a person/student has to progress to higher levels of development, would the trainer/consultant have to change the nature of the learning process? Looking at the tabulation of Figure 38 I certainly can imagine that it would be much harder for most teachers, consultants, etc. to operate on those higher levels (fostering authenticity, self-enactment, interdependence, collaboration, synergy, and so on).

Few authors are very specific about it. But Maslow spent the greater part of his life trying to understand what helped people rise to the high levels of personal development. He distinguished empirically a series of levels which are significant. They are connected hierarchically, which means that they are to be attained successively and cumulatively. With respect to the primary, secondary, and tertiary processes, Maslow concluded that personal growth means a gradual shift from instinctive, biological drives (= survival needs under old-brain control) towards motivations of the total mind, that is self-actualization and transcendence. (I shall describe these further on.)

This means that for development to progress, the *two-way radial* interaction must increase, that means that outer direction (= control by environmental factors) has to shift to inner direction, and the subconscious parts of the brain have to play a more substantial interactive role.

9.2 Levels of awareness

Amongst the 1000 or more institutes in the State of California that offer training programmes for 'personal growth', many advertise with catchphrases containing the word 'awareness' or 'self-awareness'. They claim to make us aware that awareness is a critical aspect. But is there a causal relationship? Is awareness the same as consciousness? Can it be raised and trained to expedite the development process in the direction of higher levels? Can we distinguish and define un-, sub-, pre-, post-, and self-consciousness? And how do they function with respect to learning and personal development? It has been really disappointing that the books I have read so far on this subject, even those with brain, mind, or consciousness in the title (Jung, 1958; Ornstein, 1972; Rose, 1976; Sagan, 1977; Bateson, 1978 and 1979; Dennett, 1979; Blakeslee, 1980; Hampden-Turner, 1981) clarify this issue so little. Perhaps it is too complex and too elusive.

I consider it worthwhile to describe the various forms of awareness as I now see them. I shall try to do this in concise, everyday terms. I am aware of the dangers of simplification; any reduction can be refuted by the real complex thing. Nevertheless, I shall put my brains to work on sequential description and formulating definitions, because I have learned already that such forced left-brain–right-brain interaction breeds understanding.

9.2.1 The instinctual level

This is the level of zero awareness at which all innate, genetic, hereditary factors and processes of the old brain operate. Midgley (see Section 6.3) classifies these totally involuntary processes as the 'closed instincts'. These 'wired-in' reflexes are neuro-anatomical (for example the knee-jerk), biological (digestion), psycho-biological (hormone production), and other instinctual reactions to pain, danger, pleasure, etc. It is popularly regarded as a miracle if such a basic life factor can be temporarily suspended, for example by fakirs, magicians, or priests.

9.2.2 The unconscious level

To avoid a common confusion, we are not talking about lack of alertness or about the effects of sleep and drugs brought about by the reticular system of the brain as discussed in Section 8.8: turning on and turning off the brain. I am now describing the *permanently* unconscious parts of the brain, also called the field of depth-psychology. Three groups are distinguished:

(1) The *semi-hereditary* processes which are not completely closed-instinctual, that is the ones which can be influenced *in*directly or on a longer time scale. Examples are: fundamental health and vigour; aptitudes, dispositions, and talents; processes like blushing and dreaming; sexual preferences.
(2) The *conditioned* habits and beliefs and behaviour (some with genetic roots) which have become so ingrained, for example early in life, that they are hard to distinguish from hereditary traits. Examples are: attitudes and postures copied from or conditioned by parents; claustrophobia; acculturated male/female values; dispositions for particular climates and staple foods; appreciation of certain people, events, art. I consider Jung's collective unconscious to belong to this group.
(3) The *repressed* experiences. This is the 'Freudian view of the unconscious as the cellar to which fearful, painful experiences have been consigned, deliberately or involuntarily, by a process of repression' (Bateson, 1978:108).

These permanent unconscious parts are the *in*accessible core of the person's Inner Self. As Bateson says (1978:112): 'The algorithms of the unconscious are doubly inaccessible. It is not only that the conscious mind has poor access to this material, but also the fact that when such access is achieved, e.g. in dreams, art, poetry, religion, intoxication and the like, there is still a formidable problem of translation' into the language of our conscious thoughts. The term *primary* process was originated by Freud to indicate that the effects that these hereditary and unconscious factors have in one's life are beyond Man's control.

It is most difficult to deal with the primary process in training and consultancy. One never knows, and it is unpredictable, to what extent a person's character is rooted in it. When I come across someone who displays deep disturbances or in whom I suspect derangements of the involuntary nervous system, I always feel that I cannot and should not do much without the professional help of a psychologist or psychiatrist.

Here lie the ambiguity and danger, I think, of some forms of sensitivity training. Participants (and trainers) with (slight) psychological disorders are often attracted to this particularly sensitive form of training. The emotions of participants can then easily be stirred to deeper levels than the trainer can handle professionally.

9.2.3 The subconscious level

The subconscious is the grey area of awareness. To indicate that our mental focus could or should work on this level but cannot reach it (yet) we say for intance: 'I am unaware of this', 'I cannot remember', 'I should know this', or 'Let me think'. I see the subconscious as a repository for engrams (= brain imprints, that is perception of things, events, creatures, ideas, actions) which are on their way down from the conscious to the unconscious and also for engrams coming up from the unconscious to the conscious. It is an *antechamber* with two doors or rather two hatches. It is essential to distinguish two main groups.

First is the *post*-conscious that contains all engrams which have been conscious *before*, but which have subsided into the subconscious. There are two subgroups: all those memories that are 'gathering dust', and those engrams assigned to the antechamber for efficiency, that is all that has been learned so well that our mental focus need not be bothered any more. A substantial part of this post-conscious archive can be recalled when required. Some of it needs more effort, tricks, or 'hooks', such as mnemonic devices or hypnosis. We are often surprised ourselves that so many memories can be triggered back into the conscious by smells, tunes, faces, voices, photographs, or some other intermediary.

The other is the *pre*-conscious, which entails all engrams of which the person is not yet aware and *has never been* conscious of. This group is also much larger than we normally think. It consists of two subgroups with subtle yet important differences from the post-conscious ones. First comes the subgroup of skills and thoughts of which a person was not aware at the time of acquisition. A large amount of learned understanding and behaviour starts at birth without the baby being aware of the many constructs it is continuously construing from all that happens in the world around it. Only gradually will it convert these *pre*-concious, dormant constructs into conscious ones, perhaps not until much later in life. An adult also has learned manifold things without knowing that he knows, or without being able to apply them deliberately.

Secondly there is the group of *pre*-conscious constructs (such as values, opinions) which are being *deduced* from subconsciously sensed information and from rearranging existing experiences. These may not yet have been made explicit to ourselves and are therefore inaccessible. I do not refer to instinctive motives but to intuitive insights, and actions for which we may not be able to give a reason. Sometimes we need more experience to give a considered opinion. Other times thoughts have to be nursed and prodded before it dawns on us . . . . The pre-conscious takes time: 'It only occurred to me later that . . . .'

In short the pre-conscious entails the learning in genesis, the 'memes-in-incubation'. Importantly, it is the birthplace of the more abstract hypotheses, of complex constructs, of higher learning (see Section 9.4).

In general, most of the *post*-conscious matter will have been acquired through reading or listening and can be expected to be of *LB* nature (verbal, rational, digital, etc.). In contrast, much of the evaluative, qualifying, *pre*-conscious matter is born out of recognition and discrimination of patterns and contexts. Associations and relations have to be nursed, insights come in a flash: 'Eureka!'. This is typical *RB* activity.

In conclusion, Man's *sub*conscious houses his *secondary* learning process. It connects the subconscious skills with *post*-conscious knowledge and vague *pre*-conscious notions. Our mental focus should 'let interactions happen' more often and foster interbrain contacts more and deliberately, as it is potentially a large treasure house for new, usable learning. We should make the RB support the LB and vice versa, to pick up valuable connections and translate them into conscious thought constructs.

9.2.4 The conscious level

As said before, I have not been able to find much of substance with regard to a concise description or explanation of consciousness. Even the *Encyclopaedia Britannica* is uncharacteristically brief and gives only the different views on the concept. Bateson is clear but not much of a help: 'With regard to consciousness, the matter is obscure . . . . Note that the processes of perception are not conscious but its products may be conscious . . . . I do not know of any material really connecting the phenomena of consciousness to simpler phenomena and have not attempted to do so in the present work' (1979:128). Or somewhat sarcastically: 'Nobody, to my knowledge, knows anything about the conscious process. But it is ordinarily assumed that everybody knows all about it, so I shall not attempt to describe it in any detail . . . .' (1979:112). The reader would not be happy if I abstained likewise, therefore let me describe three definitions which have meaning for me.

The first one is by Hofstadter (1979:388): 'Awareness is the monitoring of brain activity by a subsystem of the brain itself . . . . this resembles the sensation which we all know and call consciousness'. With this definition 'it is plausible that a computer programme with this kind of structure would make statements about itself similar to those which people make about themselves . . .'

Such an explanation on the direct physical level is also advanced by Rose (1976:31): 'Consciousness is a consequence of the evolution of a particular level of complexity and degree of interaction among the nerve cells (neurons) of the celebral cortex'. And 'it is not a thing but a process expressing the relationship between the mind/brain and its environment' (1976:339).

The second is based on Hofstadter's chapter on free will (1979:711): 'Consciousness is the property of a system that can generate alternatives and make choices'. This view is of particular interest to learning and development because my fundamental ethic (of education) is that the options have to increase. As said under the liberating principle of Section 4.8, development is in the direction of greater choice, to a condition with a higher degree of freedom.

The third one is from myself: 'Consciousness consists of those brain functions (process) and of those engrams (content) which a person can make use of whenever he wants or sees fit'. If expressed as: 'Consciousness is the awareness of alternatives' then the connection with the two other definitions is obvious. I like that phrase because (a) it is congruent with the learning/development model and (b) it means that Man is *not* automatic in his thoughts and behaviour. Skinnerism does not hold. Our mental focus, biased and subjective as it may be, goes continuously through the stages, prospectively and retrospectively, and *chooses* all the time. It has the freedom deliberately to follow other options, now or tomorrow. Consciousness can span all times and places, Man can dwell on past events for pleasure or problem-solving, or live in the future, 'anticipating events by construing their replication' (Kelly).

Management literature is focused too exclusively on this conscious way of thinking and behaving. Some forget that consciousness includes the option to focus on our subconscious in order to bring some pre- and post-conscious learning, thoughts, and values to light. It also includes the option *not* to focus, but to drift and let the primary and secondary processes do work and influence our awareness. Or have I already crossed the boundary to the next and next-after-next level?

9.2.5   The self-conscious level

The unique quality of the human brain is that it can become aware of its awareness: 'Cognito ergo sum' (Descartes). That fact seems to be a popular LB discovery nowadays to judge from the many words with the prefix 'self', like self-awareness, self-help, self-development, self-organized learning, self-profiling, self-interest, self-validating, self-survey, self-management. All these concepts assume the person to be able to reflect on himself, to do unto himself, and to evaluate himself by himself. As with the infinite regress in the hall of mirrors one can think about oneself thinking about oneself thinking about . . . .

All these self-such-and-such modes do not necessarily lead to self-development in the sense of this book. Self-awareness can be restraining and can degenerate into a stale situation of no development at all, when a person becomes too preoccupied with one part of himself, in a similar crippling way to that centipede who could not walk any more as soon as he tried to explain how he was moving so many legs. As discussed in Section 1.7, self-profiling and self-validating can easily lead to limited and one-sided development. Higgin (1973:99) exposes such an unhealthy centrality of ego-consciousness in western society, the 'me-first' syndrome.

Healthy self-consciousness requires Man to stand back from himself and observe, appraise, and be critical of himself as if he were someone else who knows and cares about the actor. However, according to Bateson (1978:101): 'Man's behaviour can be corrupted by self-deceit. Through self-consciousness Man can lose the naïveté, the simplicity, the "grace" which animals still have'.

The essential point for my subject is that Man's genetic ability of self-consciousness enables him to make *his own learning process the object of his learning*. That constitutes, as we shall see further in Section 9.4.3, the essential step via self-directed learning to personal development.

9.2.6 The transcendent level

It is possible to reach a level of awareness which feels like stepping out of oneself, transcending above oneself. It is a total, open, simultaneous awareness of one's thinking and one's body, as a unique total being: a so-called 'peak-experience'. Few authors of management literature mention it and still fewer describe what it is. It was Maslow who took the subject out of the exclusive domain of psychology and (eastern) religion and experimented with this state of mind. He explains it in *The Further Reaches of Human Nature* (1972:269–79) as a natural, healthy, and attractive activity for any human being, managers not excluded.

What a person experiences at this transcendent level is a combination of the unconscious, subconscious and self-conscious, whilst at the same time transcending them. One has a sense of happiness, a serene form of ecstasy and exultation, the past, the present, and the future seem to unite. One has to suspend judgement, let go control over mind and body and transcend the self as ego into a unity with children, spouse, sea, landscape, or whatever. Basic needs and weaknesses are no barriers. One's perception is relaxed, wider, of a different nature, transcending adversaries and conflicts of views and ideas into new meaning and significance. Friedlander described ancestor 'Exi' in similar existentialistic qualities and values (see Section 5.3).

During these peak experiences it happens that one surprises oneself in being able to do more or better than one thought one could, it comes, without really trying. Deliberate effort would destroy the spell, one has to experience the activity without any reservation. Persons who at times have such wonderful experiences have difficulty explaining (in left-brain fashion) why they feel so unique at these moments, why they are so inexplicably better as a brave leader, as a pianist, as a tennis-player (Gallwey, 1974). The person has 'feelings of letting things happen, of sheer enjoyment, of hope fulfilled, of being pleased with one's own courage and abilities' (Bach, 1973).

From his studies Maslow recognized some thirty forms of transcendence. He found several common characteristics in those who had peak experiences regularly: for instance, they valued these moments as creative high spots in life; they readily understood parables, paradoxes, artistic activities; were responsive to beauty, justice, personal encounters and other 'meta-values' (Maslow's term). It is well known that opium can induce similar experiences, or modern mind-broadening drugs like LSD. But they are addictive and make a person *less* aware of reality. Instead of giving happy or beneficial insights, these can flip over into nasty and dangerous 'trips'. (I have not experimented with any form of pot so far.)

The strictly scientific Hofstadter calls self-transcendence a modern myth. It is precisely the main point of his latest book (1979:477-9) that no system can jump out of itself; it is an illusion that Man could *not* obey the law of physics, that he could violate the biological instructions of the human system. Hofstadter makes the distinction between transcending oneself and *perceiving* oneself in all sorts of ways. 'There is a lesser ambition which it is possible to achieve: that is, one can certainly jump from a subsystem of one's brain into a wider subsystem . . . . As I see it [Zen] the hope is that by gradually deepening one's self-awareness, by gradually widening the scope of the system . . . may come enlightenment.'

The reason why I describe this level in some more detail is that peak experiences, though not common, are very important. In terms of the learning and development model, it is the supreme opportunity for *radial* communication, all levels of awareness are connected and the primary, secondary, and tertiary brain processes can interact directly.

I experience such occasions myself as particularly effective and lasting, sometimes as a breakthrough in my development. Normally this transcendent interawareness lasts only a few seconds, other times several minutes, but seldom longer than an hour. Once experienced these moments will occur more often, not when one is torn and set against oneself, but only when one's state of mind and psyche are at peace, open, quiet, and relaxed and when there is no mental barrier between one's Inner and Conscious Self.

Because it will be difficult to believe, I must state explicitly that I have found approximately as many transcenders among business men, industrialists, managers, educators, political people as I have among the professional religious, the poets, intellectuals, musicians and others who are supposed to be transcenders . . . . Most industrialists will carefully conceal their idealism, their meta-motivations and their transcendent experiences under a mask of toughness, realism, selfishness and all sorts of other words . . . . Their more real meta-motivations are often not repressed but only suppressed. I have sometimes found it quite easy to break through the protective surface by direct confrontations and questions. (Maslow, 1972:295)

9.2.7 Summary

Our minds can operate on various levels of awareness. A first step in fuller utilization is to be able to recognize these levels, allow them to occur, facilitate them.

(1) Instinctual level. Closed instincts and genetic reflexes regulate the basic functions of brain and body.
(2) Unconscious level. Semi-hereditary processes, semi-closed instincts; conditioned habits, beliefs, and repressed experiences, governing thoughts and behaviour.
(3) Subconscious level can be tapped:
    (a) post-consciously: dusted memories, routinized behaviour.
    (b) pre-consciously: learning in *statu nascendi*, intuition. Implicit (new) constructs; insights.
(4) Conscious level. Where our mental focus operates most of the time. Explicit constructs, retrievable engrams. Here and now, prospection and retrospection. Aware of alternatives, options.
(5) Self-conscious level. Mental focus reflects on Self. Awareness of one's awareness. Managing one's learning process: LTL. Self-managed development.
(6) Transcendent level. Relaxing, no deliberate focusing, or mental effort; planning, analyses, and judgement suspended. Experiencing unity of all parts of Self, with others; feeling one with larger, higher system. Transcending time, space, adversaries.

I have not (yet) found out, either theoretically or practically, whether the boundaries are gradual or sharp and discontinuous. When trying this out on myself, my mental focus turns instantly self-conscious, of course. But I have reason to believe from the brain chapter that the above levels are very useful but artificial distinctions; that they are *overlapping* and therefore can be contacted and used, sometimes forcefully (via a dialogue with oneself and LB–RB interchange) and sometimes by letting it happen.

9.3 Levels of hierarchy

There is one more way to characterize the levels of development, namely by the levels of hierarchical complexity of a person's construct system. The nature of the structure that binds people's constructs together in complex networks was discussed in Section 7.4; how to explore and externalize one's cognitive thoughts in Section 7.8; and the evolution of memes (that is the surviving collective ideas of mankind) in Section 8.10.

In this section I have to describe briefly the concept of hierarchy as a fundamental principle in life, with the help of Koestler's views and Russell's theory of logical typing, in order to explain in the next section what I consider an essential addition: the levels of awareness of learning. These are needed to formulate a strategy and practical approach to improve and accelerate the process of personal development.

First then a few quotes from Koestler (1978:289–304). When using the word hierarchy

> one often encounters a strong emotional resistance. For one thing, hierarchy is an ugly word, loaded with ecclesiastic and military associations, and conveys to some people the wrong impression of a rigid or authoritarian structure. But that is not at all what the term is meant to signify. Its correct symbol is not a rigid ladder but a living tree, a system branching into sub-systems, which branch into sub-systems of a lower order, and so on; a process activating sub-processes and so on.

> The hierarchic tree diagram may serve equally well to represent the branching out of the evolution of species—the tree of life; it serves to represent the step-wise differentiation of tissues in embryonic development; it may serve as a diagram of the parts-within-parts of organisms or galaxies, or of the phrase-generating machinery by the psycholinguist. It may represent the locomotor hierarchy of limbs, joints, individual muscles, and so down to fibres, or, in reverse direction, the filtering and processing of the sensory input in its ascent from periphery to centre. It could also be regarded as a model for the subject-index of the Library of Congress, and for the organization of knowledge in our memory-stores; as an organizational chart for government and business organizations; and so on.

> All complex structures and processes of a relatively stable character display hierarchic organization, and this applies regardless whether we

> are considering inanimate systems, living organisms, social organizations, or patterns of behaviour. Complex systems will evolve from simple systems much more rapidly if there are stable intermediate forms than if there are not.

> The evolutionary stability of these sub-assemblies is reflected by their remarkable degree of autonomy or self-government. Each of them—a piece of tissue or a whole heart—is capable of functioning *in vitro* as a quasi-independent whole, even though isolated from the organism or

transplanted into another organism. Wholes and parts in the absolute sense do not exist. What we find are intermediary structures on a series of levels in ascending order of complexity, each of which has two faces looking in opposite directions; the face turned towards the lower level is that of an autonomous whole, the one turned upward that of a dependent part. I propose the word 'holon' for these Janus-faced sub-assemblies.

Biological holons are self-regulating open-systems governed by a set of fixed rules which account for the holon's coherence, stability and its specific pattern of structure and function. A sub-skill or behavioural holon on the (n) level of the hierarchy has more degrees of freedom (a larger variety of alternative strategic choices) than a holon on the $(n-1)$ level.

A different approach to hierarchy was originated by Whitehead and Russell at the beginning of this century and published in 1910 as *Principia Mathematica*. Little could they foresee how fundamental their theory would turn out to be for many more sciences. Their basic assertion is that any thing, person, idea, or event is related to other things, persons, ideas, and events in a systematic way: everything is a member of at least one class, any class in turn is a member of at least one higher class. The classes are hierarchically connected with a step-wise *discontinuity* between each member and its class. For instance: 'Daisy'-cow-cattle-herbivores-mammals-vertebrates — is a series of hierarchically related members and classes of animals. No member can be the class, no class can be a member of its own, nor can a class be classified as a non-member. This theory proved to be valid not only for mathematics, but also for the sciences of logic, philosophy, linguistics, systems-theory and others.

In daily parlance not only nouns, but also adverbs and adjectives may represent a group or class, for instance: British, bright, brown, big, wet, philosophically, etc. Kelly (Chapter 7) expanded this principle by talking about bipolar constructs and implication networks, to allow for any association a person may care to have between words.

People are in general rather loose in the logical typing of their communication. Errors are frequently made by confusing the name with the thing itself, not realizing that one cannot eat the menu (card). The map is not the territory. The symbol is not the thing symbolized. This makes the connection with Section 8.5: the digital and analogical modes of communication. A message can only be understood correctly from perceiving two signals: one for the *content* and one for the *context*. Animals need the analogical context, they know whether the voices and gestures from other animals or people are meant seriously or as play, as threat or bluff, etc. Computers can only accept data if they are also told what to do with it.

Any elementary signal needs an extra message to classify it. Human beings always qualify what they communicate either consciously or subconsciously; they indicate somehow whether it is for real or for teasing, for phantasy or fun. Whether we are aware of it or not, we send and perceive two signals. We *cannot not* communicate (Watzlawick's first axiom).

Russell's theory of logical types implies that the context-signal is a 'meta-message' which is always of a higher level of abstraction than the content-signal. It is possible and logical to qualify again the context of the message with a 'meta-meta-message' to mark the context of the context(s), and so on in an increasing level of hierarchy and abstraction. For example: a person may act as if he plays a game of words, which means that it is not a play of words, he has an intention at a higher level.

Sections 9.1, 9.2, and 9.3 were to demonstrate that we can observe and diagnose the different levels on which the human being behaves, communicates, operates with his mind, thus learns and develops. This brings us to one of the major subjects of this book.

9.4   Levels of awareness of learning

Writing a book like this one is an example of personal development, because it requires a precise (re)structuring of my personal constructs to produce an integrated account of my experience with what I read and studied. This section is not much different in that I will use Bateson's framework of learning levels and describe their significance in terms of my own experience. What follows *is* different in that it presents my most recent and newest insights into the process of learning and development. These occurred to me when I made an extra subdivision in Bateson's levels of learning. By distinguishing *within* each level also the levels of awareness, it becomes visible how deliberate progress can be 'engineered' between levels. I shall illustrate this with the scheme of Figure 39.

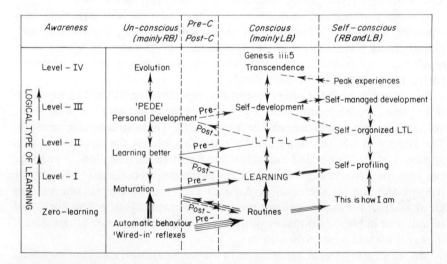

Figure 39   Staged-path to Self-development. Progress through RB- and LB-awareness of learning levels

Let me, ahead of the detailed reasoning below, illustrate the idea with one example. The reader may remember that LTL ('learning-to-learn', see Sections 1.1 and 1.2) is learning of the second order. This happens indeed on Bateson's 'learning-II' level. But it appears very important to me to distinguish whether this happens *un*consciously as an adaptive ability only (as in the higher animals) or as a pro-active skill (consciously or self-consciously) which only Man is capable of.

As indicated by arrows of step-wise progressing to higher levels in Figure 39, I shall postulate that learning and development can be accelerated by helping insights and ideas to germinate pre-consciously and by raising these deliberately to the conscious and self-conscious levels. I will leave it till Section 12.3 to relate this scheme with the personal development model with regard to energy, the mental focus, and concerted effort of the brain.

9.4.1 Zero learning

We speak of zero learning if the response is always the same, including no response, to the same stimuli. I distinguish three groups, depending on the level of awareness (see the bottom line of Figure 39).

The first group is the automatic behaviour which is totally determined by genetic factors; the responses are completely 'wired-in', or so conditioned in early life that they are fully automatic. (See Midgley's close-instincts in Section 6.3.) Unconscious learning-I takes place through maturation (see Figure 39).

The second is the large group of conscious routine behaviour, all learning that has been completed and/or stereotyped, and which can, if required, be 'husbanded' into the post-conscious. It includes habituation and all routine responses and behaviour of which we can become conscious if we want to. This heavy traffic between the conscious and subconscious is indicated in Figure 39 with heavy multilane arrows.

The third group can be called 'As I am', which is self-awareness and acceptance of whatever talents and imperfections one has without doing anything about it. 'Life' takes care of what is done with them.

It must be noted that the word 'learning' is misused in a zero-learning meaning. For instance: 'I have just learned that . . . [say] the plane has arrived', which only records a fact as such, but does not lead to a (progressive) change in understanding or behaviour. The similar event or the same data at a later time will only convey the same once-off information, the person will have 'learned' the same fact but not really have learned anything. Another way of expressing zero-learning (for those who learn from graphs) is any horizontal part in a learning diagram, for instance the interrupted line (*a*) and the *horizontal* parts of the normal learning curves (*c*) and (*e*) in Figure 40.

In real life zero-learning phenomena are seldom without accompanying effects. In the example above, when on the next occasion the person hears that 'that the plane has just arrived' he may perceive, (un)consciously, that the message is slightly different from last time. For instance he may 'learn' willy-nilly from the voice that another person is making the announcement. Or with another well-known example: one cannot kiss a girl for the first time twice.

9.4.2 Learning-1

This first-order learning is defined, in accordance with Russell's theory of logical typing, as the *class* of *changes* in zero learning. In Bateson's not so simple terms: learning-1 is 'characterized by a change in the specificity of response by correction of errors of choice within a set of alternatives' (1978:264).

This group is by far the most common type of learning: walking, talking, reading, typing, driving a car, and so on; it also includes (partial) *un*learning and gradual reconditioning. This type covers all cases in which a living organism responds differently at time t_{n+1} from time t_n. The change in knowledge, skill, or ability need not be an equal improvement at each subsequent event. A learning curve is not a linear relation, it is specific for the subject matter, the learner, the conditions, etc. (see Figure 40). It may be a steep one—learning quickly (curve *b*)—or a flatter one (curve *d*) or an S-shaped growth curve (curve *c*), when there is little result initially, and ultimately.

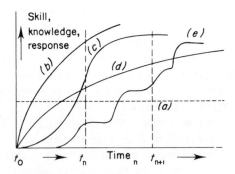

Figure 40   Zero- and first-order learning

The rate of learning, that is the shape of the curves, depends on the subject, person, conditions, motivation, etc. Its dependence on the degree of *stimulation* and other factors was discussed in Section 8.8, Figure 36. Most learning curves flatten off gradually after a certain amount of repetition and time. When such a plateau in learning is reached and further accumulation of experience has no further effect on the skill, learning-1 has regressed to a routine at the *zero*-learning level; the mental focus transfers the control of the activities to the post-conscious.

An essential premise for a learning-1 process (for any curve in Figure 40) is the notion of the *same, repeatable context*. In order to improve an ability, the learner must recognize the context of the stimulus as being the same at time t_{n+1} as at t_n. If the context is not recognized there would be no learning, just guessing; responses would be either at random, or instinctual, or none at all. That is why learning-I is defined as *changes* in *specificity* of constructs and/or skills *within* a recognized *set* of alternatives. It is a prerequisite to be able to recognize the context markers correctly, to perceive the relevant mode-identifying signals, to hear the music behind the words. These context markers may be verbal or non-verbal, digital or analogue (see Section 8.5).

It is possible to disturb any learner, even to drive him crazy by making the context unclear or ambivalent. For example, animals have broken down under continuous pressure to choose between a circle and an oval when the latter was made to look like a circle as well. People can avert this situation by reverting to tossing a coin, by braking out of the bind. Bateson has developed a theory for 'double-bind' situations (1978:178, 268): he describes neuroses and schizophrenia in terms of the learner's inability to deal with the 'logical typing' of context in communication. To function healthily Man must have very substantial skills in recognizing 'situations'.

Recognition of context need not be at the conscious level. In children especially, as in animals, much is at the unconscious and perhaps instinctual level. Using Midgley's open-instinct category, there are learning-I phenomena *within* a contextual instinct, like the hunting abilities of cats. Is this confined to retrospective response, or does it hold also for prospective application (for examle the migration of birds, instructing the young)? People learn many things within a culturally structured context of which they are not aware. Because most of this natural, subconscious learning-I happens during growing-up, like walking and talking, I have called this the 'Maturation' category in the scheme of Figure 39. The plain term 'learning' is reserved for the conscious column, that is for when a person can discriminate and apply context marking *consciously* to and from persons and things. It is only a small step for a human being to realize self-consciously when he is learning, but an essential step to seek out learning-I and profile himself in the manner described in Section 1.7. He may then become the self-conscious learner on his way to the next level, that is to learning-to-learn, or regress to zero learning marked: 'that is how I am'.

9.4.3 Learning-II

Second-order learning is the ability to make deliberate changes in the processes of learning-I. Whereas L-I can be qualified as 'more-of-the-same', L-II means doing it differently, changing the familiar pattern. In terms of learning curves, see Figure 41: learning-II is defined as not following one curve or another, but as the ability to see more alternatives and choose an appropriate one from amongst the many, and to change over if desirable or required. Figure 41 shows the example with line p_1 that someone learns a skill in context A (say in a classroom) and has to apply it later in a more difficult context B (say in real

178

life); the learning process is then different and he may experience a fall back or a step-jump in learning. This can happen again later in context *C*. By changing methods or tutor one may find a way of learning quicker (line *q*).

In mathematical terms: the learner is able or forced to see that the existing equation is not valid and is able to accept or change the parameter for learning to continue. In the terms of Bateson (1978:264): 'Learning-II is a corrective change in the *set* of alternatives from which choice is made, or it is a change in how the sequence of experience is punctuated'.

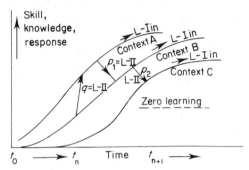

Figure 41   First- and second-order learning

Most important for learning-II is the human ability to discriminate on an abstract level. Referring to Section 8.7, *Homo Discriminator* always qualifies what happens. He considers that Mr X is ambitious, aggressive, or playful; that mountains are wild, peaceful, or desolate; events are funny, dangerous, or boring; computers are reliable, tricky, or very smart, etc. As explained in Section 9.3, such constructs express a particular pattern, class, or qualification and thus a second or higher logical type.

Bateson and Watzlawick call this discrimination 'punctuation', see the definition of L-II above. It means that people may perceive the same data, event, or situation differently, subjectively. They may attach a special meaning to the message depending upon their point of view. Like perceiving a picture in a cloud or inkblot, it is neither correct nor incorrect. It has much to do with a person's set of beliefs, values, norms, superordinate constructs, etc. The flip-over from conjuncted to disjuncted contrasts (Section 7.6.10 is a typical punctuation phenomenon. Practical examples were discussed with the model of teamwork in Section 7.7.

This punctuation is often necessary for sheer self-clarification. But it may reflect the phenomena of cultural bias, self-fulfilling prophecies, etc. Self-validation, which can be defined as hanging on to self-preferred gestalt, is in fact a resistance to L-II. In the extreme, self-validation can become self-deceit. For intance: a spinster may believe that 'all men are the same . . . .' A laboratory rat may believe that he has trained the researcher in providing food as soon as he, the rat, presses the lever!

Level-II learning is not straightforward, one may be fooled or fool oneself.

There is a flood of literature from counsellors, psychiatrists, and educators about people having difficulty with their own and other peoples' interpretation of meta-messages. Man can manipulate them, he can lie without words.

Bateson calls all learning-II 'deutero-learning', that is the same as 'learning-to-learn'. But I propose to be more precise. I shall again distinguish different levels of awareness with*in* L-II (see Figure 39).

Man has a natural genetic capability of bettering his learning which is *unconscious* in the same way as some animals can learn to learn better (horses, dogs, monkeys, dolphins, etc.) without becoming aware of it. Most of Man's L-II capacity is *pre*-conscious because learning starts in childhood: basic values from relationships, subconscious interpretations of non-verbal contexts like intonations, postures, eye contacts, etc., from parents and teachers, and the cultural norms from the societal group. Therefore, the way in which an adult punctuates information and events is closely related to his history of maturation. That is why subconscious skills and constructs are often confused with basic personality traits. They may be called 'cultural heritage' or the 'emperor's clothes', dependent on the punctuation.

I am afraid that, without help, few people are able to realize how and when they learn and which cues trigger off their spontaneous and intuitive thoughts and behaviour. They have to rely on the interaction between their subconscious and conscious constructs and between their secondary and tertiary skills (see the model in Appendix 12), without the benefit of conscious control.

Fortunately, we are often *compelled* to realize and verbalize our pre-conscious L-II qualifications. In daily life, and especially at work, people often force us to express the feelings behind our conclusions and question the reason for our plans—all in an understandable and acceptable manner please! As a Philips manager told me: 'The staff council often oblige me to explain myself in *their* terms. That seems a nuisance but my ideas have improved by doing so'.

Therefore a critical prerequisite to developing to a higher level is the step to *conscious L-II*, that is the ability to probe one's pre-conscious to lift underlying feelings and talents to the conscious, to become aware of the meaning of one's experiences and convert them into communicable constructs. This can be promoted through a rigorous dialogue with one's 'Inner Self' (Jung), or through a self-directed grid analysis (Kelly), an eliciting guide for feedback (Juch), or just through a meaningful encounter with a significant Other (the staff council). In the context of Mangham's work (1978:107): 'Rethinking and rewriting one's own life script is a second-order change'.

After my 'experimental' definition of learning-to-learn in Section 1.1, we can now be more precise in allocating the term 'LTL' in the scheme of Figure 39 to the *conscious* effort of improving a person's learning. This is different from and more than Revans' concept of 'Action Learning' (1971) because the latter (need not, but) can be limited to variety in learning-I and to 'more-of-the same'.

The final step on this L-II level is becoming *self-conscious* of one's own learning. That means organizing one's activities with the explicit purpose of becoming wiser. This entails hypothesis—planning—doing—evaluating— reformulating one's own learning activities. Or, in terms of my model, self-conscious L-II requires knowledge of one's learning style, strengths and weaknesses of abilities to Sense, Think, Plan, and Do, and understanding the functions of the mental barriers (Window, Skin, Gate, and Rubicon) as the regulators of healthy personal development.

As an extra illustration this should be compared with what Argyris and Schon (1974) have studied and published extensively about the necessity for managers and organizations to rise above L-I in planning and decision-making. They propose the concepts of Model-I and Model-II, or single-loop and double-loop learning. Argyris defines (1977:119) Model-I managers as those who behave routinely in compulsive, defensive, and repetitive ways. They are unaware of the propositions they use and are prisoners of their own theories; they are out to win, to emphasize the intellectual aspects, and to suppress their own and others' feelings. This description, though consistent with our Learning-I, is rather negative. It excludes conscious and self-conscious L-II learning.

Argyris' Model-II managers ask the right questions, allow statements to be challenged, propositions to be tested and changed; they look for the underlying and more fundamental causes, suggest creative solutions and new ways of doing things. This is more than L-II. Indeed, Argyris defines his Double-loop learning rather highly, he includes radical changes in a person's 'theory-in-use', for instance a change in paradigm. No wonder that less than 5 per cent of his test persons were found to operate on Model-II level.

Since it would not be fair to put the remaining 95 per cent under L-I, I conclude two things: (i) Argyris' double-loop learning and Model-II are closer to level-III (three!) learning, see next section; and (ii) there is a big hiatus between Argyris' Models-I and -II. In my opinion many people and most managers are stagnating precisely in and around L-II due to the difficulty of making her step to the third level, as I shall now explain.

9.4.4 Learning-III

If L-II is learning about learning, (that is understanding and managing the contexts of L-I) then, again according to the theory of logical typing, L-III should be understanding L-II and managing the contexts of those contexts. In Bateson's terms (1978:264): 'L-III is changing the process of L-II, e.g. a corrective *change in the system of sets* of alternatives from which choice is made'. In terms of learning curves (Figure 41), L-III replaces the known and expected set of curves by a completely different set in a way which is not yet established, say, by sets of curves which include another dimension. In terms of Hofstadter: L-III is jumping out of a subsystem into a larger one.

In the context of this book, L-III could be called 'learning to learn to learn', which I would rather define as Personal Development. Development not according to a blueprint but according to capabilities and circumstances, going through passages and crises into new dimensions and domains. That this requires maturity and self-confidence is obvious from the characteristics that Argyris attributes to managers on this level (see the preceding section). Not holding on to acquired L-II abilities is no mean feat, the person is willing to face openly rational and emotional contradictions, he has to display and receive trust, experience 'cultural shocks', etc., knowing that he may have to change his way of looking at things quite radically and replace his pattern of beliefs, values, and paradigms. Gestalt theory describes L-III phenomena. And creative breakthroughs are typical for this level.

Let me again distinguish different levels of consciousness within this L-III. Referring to the scheme of Figure 39. I define the *sub*conscous L-III mode of attitude and behaviour as the *natural* way of personal development. This type of person is active and open, is enthusiastic and searches out new ways, takes risks, is not afraid of pressures or setbacks, enjoys life, etc.; he does all this 'without really trying' and his own personal development is a healthy 'spin-off'. I hope that this reminds the reader of young 'Pede', the promising adolescent whom I added to Friedlander's parable (Section 5.3).

Conscious level-III is the next step in development. It means that a person is aware of what personal development is; that is self-development in the explicit and specific meaning of the various authors I discussed earlier: Rogers' fully-functioning, Jung's Individuation, Maslow's self-actualization, Koestler's self-regulating open hierarchic system, etc.

Self-conscious L-III level is more than an awareness of personal development, it is a development of Self by Self, a holistic consciousness of Self in and with one's environment. I consider Maslow's study of people's characteristics, experiences, and feelings at this level most enlightening, not only because he describes the actual conditions, circumstances, and motivation, but also because he destroys the myth that only philosophers, religious people, and oriental mystics reflect on self to experience moments of insight, truth, and beauty (see the last paragraph of Section 9.2.6).

Maslow's major contribution can be indicated in the scheme of Figure 39. He lifted the healthy personal development from the subconscious into the conscious by establishing that Self-actualization is an obtainable objective, not least for managers. And he forced himself and others to become aware of how all parts of the mind and body interact so that the process and results can be communicated to and shared with other persons.

Few persons ever reach the third level consciously. I see three main reasons for this. Firstly, many people never get out of the mental framework of *survival* and *economics*. Even if they have enough they opt for a life in easy comfortable routine and stay at zero learning (Fromm, 1978). Generally accepted procedures and short-term efficiency are powerful factors to operate at L-I, doing things better with least effort. Only a small portion of humanity can afford the time and effort (they think) to rise above the common and explore and consciously enjoy the world at L-II level.

Secondly, an understandable barrier that prevents people (and managers for that matter) from progressing from L-II to L-III learning is Man's inclination to self-validation and fear of losing his ego. A manager needs guts to risk temporal unsettlement by letting himself be vulnerable during an open review of objectives, values, and personal style. For instance those who say or think: 'I cannot accept this new idea or other way of doing things, it would change my whole life' are 'prisoners of their own theories' (Argyris, 1977:119). A person striving for L-III no longer views his Inner Self as a given fixed personality, because L-III implies a profound questioning and redefinition of the Self. That is uncomfortable, even frightening for most of us. Quoting a Zen master: 'to become accustomed to anything is a terrible thing'.

Last, but not least, I have more than a hunch that both the left *and* the right brain need to be *well*-developed and well-exercised in *support* of each other. In order to progress step-wise through L-I and L-II towards L-III, Man has to be able to utilize all levels of awareness, his right brain just as expertly as his left brain. Accepting the holistic approach to development as a sound principle does not mean that many of us are experienced in 'living it' overnight.

My conclusion from analysing the difficult step from L-II to L-III is that we, educators, tutors, consultants, can facilitate this by:

(i) making people/managers aware of all factors on L-II;
(ii) helping them to experiment with their own learning-to-learn style, on the basis of the Personal Development Model;
(iii) using different resources, being open for others' points of view, creating room for creativity, and cross-cultural empathy, all of which should be stimulated and practiced;
(iv) creating reasonably safe opportunities and being supportive.

Mastering this step (L-II to L-III) is where the present generation can achieve the greatest advance: liberating ourselves from habitual thinking, using the LB to express ourselves better and using the RB more to understand others and grasp the new. It is here, at this boundary of L-II and L-III, that I hope this book and my model may contribute most.

9.4.5   Learning IV

Strictly logically and in analogy with the above definitions, fourth-order learning would be the ability to change Learning-III. It is difficult though to imagine what this is. And thinking about it is rather speculative. For instance, would L-IV be a completely different form of development? Or a switch to other forms of life, elsewhere in the cosmos? Would it explain telepathy, parapsychology, spiritualism, life after death, etc.?

Bateson argues (1978:264, 277–9) that L-IV probably does not occur in any living organism on this planet. But as many philosophers have reasoned before me, there must be an ulterior motive behind what happens, one higher level to account for unexplainable phenomena. Therefore I suggest that we expect L-IV to exist somewhere, because if evolution has brought the human species to the abilities of L-III, then I envisage that the evolutionary drive itself, that is 'Nature', is capable of L-IV.

The upper limit in the level of awareness and learning of any living organism is biologically determined by the combined potential of its genes. Any change in the organism proves the fact that it has the capability to do so whether genetically programmed, accidentally changed, or 'learned' over millions of years. I rephrase Midgley's statement (see Section 6.3) on the 'Nature or nurture' question: 'At what logical levels can learning take place and when is genetics the final determinant?'

Observed at my modest level at this point of the ongoing evolutionary process: flatworms cannot go beyond unconscious L-I (adapt to and use of the environment unknowingly); mammals can achieve 'Learning' (*conscious* L-I) and some are capable of *un*conscious L-II as well (see the levels and categories in Figure 39). Man is clearly capable of LTL and personal development (conscious and subconscious L-III). A few achieve, or should I say enjoy, conscious and self-conscious L-III. From this I deduce that Man is unconscious and willy-nilly in evolution phylogenetically (as a species). That is why I have marked 'Evolution' in the unconscious L-IV column of the scheme of Figure 39 on page 174.

Unconscious L-IV means that Man's Selfish Genes have been driving him incessantly to improve his L-III capability, that is leading him to higher levels of development. This in turn became 'tangible' in the production of more ambitious Memes. This started with searching the surroundings of his cave, via ruling the waves, to exploring the cosmos; all the time pushing back the limits of genetic constraints. As a result it seems that the evolutionary process is being taken over by Man's 'Selfish *M*emes' which are now capable of tinkering directly with their masters, the genes. Memes on genetic engineering are past the inception stage and have already proved viable and operational (see *Scientific American*, September 1981). How long will it take them to master L-IV, thus changing the human species profoundly? Does this make us guilty or not guilty of: 'trying to be as God?' (Genesis iii:5).

9.4.6 Summary of levels in simple terms

Zero learning: Same response to stimuli, no change in knowledge, insight or skill. Routine behaviour.

Learning-I: Improving responses to stimuli, increasing repertoire of knowledge, clearer insights, better skills, but of the same kind.

Learning-II: Responding in appropriate ways to *changes* in context of stimuli. Handling meta-messages, improving learning abilities, learning-to-learn. Developing a style, identity.

184

Learning-III: Responding in completely new ways, distinguishing changes in the context of the *set* of contexts, handling meta-meta-messages. Improving learning *capa*bilities, that is self-development to the extent of conversion and changing one's character, identity. Creativity.

Learning-IV: is in Nature: the ongoing evolution of the human species, which made Man capable of conscious L-III.

PART IV

Andante with Camel

10

Planning an Application

Back to praxis! Before I could finish writing this book, I was asked to plan, organize, and execute a series of management-training activities in the Sultanate of Oman, mainly for the Shell-managed 'Petroleum Development Oman, LLC' (PDO for short), and also for some high officials in the government. That gave me the *experimentum cricis* to show that sabbatical years are worthwhile in terms of getting 'ideas more grounded and practice more founded'.

The title of this IVth part 'Andante' means that after the long expounding Interlude, we have to move on; 'with camel' means: moving on in a manner appropriate to the culture of the new work environment. The chapter title is obvious, it refers to the cyclic development model: after conceptual 'thinking' and creative ideas, the next stage should be 'planning' for action. Hence, this chapter will be a design in terms of the above principles. It is not *the* application but *an* application, because it is impossible to test out all the ideas that I have voiced in the preceding chapters. Some important suggestions that could not yet be tried out, but are worth recording, will be discussed in Chapter 12.

The general atmosphere and circumstances at work have to be described. But to keep it short, the focus will be on 'Stages and Levels', on the use of the learning models and on the application of the principles of personal learning and self-development as presented in the earlier chapters.

10.1 Re-entry and strategy

How did I go about the re-entry in practice and the re-entry in Oman? There were the usual interesting issues between client and consultant of understanding and accepting each others' expectations, but the fact of being welcomed back to Oman indicated that I had sufficient credit and trust from an earlier assignment to 'negotiate' my position and work programme openly.

I was expected to organize and run a fairly intensive series of off-site management-training activities. I was also expected to advise on the development of the Omani staff. A special attraction for me was the 'gentlemen's agreement' that allowed me to devote part of my time and effort to consultancy and training of senior Omani officials in the Ministry of Finance and, if so required, in other government ministries. Although I had my reservations about being called a 'Management Trainer' I accepted this as my official title mainly because it is simple and clear. There were no routine duties and no department to run,.so that I would have the actual freedom of a consultant.

I planned a matrix approach of three activities and three interests:

(1) Working in turn on three fronts: (i) consultancy within PDO with individuals and groups on any managerial, organizational subject; (ii) a series of off-site training activities for PDO staff; and (iii) consultancy training for the government. My initial aim was to spend about 25–50–25 per cent of my time on (i), (ii) and (iii) respectively.

(2) My points of interest when working on these fronts would be (i) to stimulate the *personal* development of staff *in* and *with* the organization; (ii) the cultural and cross-cultural aspects of managing and co-operation; and (iii) the advancement of Omani participation.

I intended to distinguish clearly between *content* and *process*. With respect to the content, that is the subject matter of the work, I would not be directive at all, I would accept whatever presented itself as the topic or problem. That is obvious for open-ended consultancy anyway. With respect to the topics for the training activities, I planned to take about two months to find out from management and from staff what they considered to be general issues in working together and what were seen as opportunities for improvement. These would then determine the main subjects and main thrust for the training activities.

What to do with respect to the process was clear from the start: I would follow the ideas and principles of this book about how to guide the development of individuals, Omani and others, especially those with energy and capacity. I planned to design a new self-scoring learning-style questionnaire based on my new model and a planning guide for self-development, and to provide good resources (articles, books, films, cassettes, specially prepared handouts, etc.). More systematically, I could use the training activities to raise participants' awareness about their own development, letting them explore the opportunities of improving their competence in their functions and in the situation of their jobs.

I was sure that I could expect a great diversity in the nature and degree of motivation with respect to the idea of self-development: PDO staff varies from practical oil-field people to highly specialized scientists; some government officials have little formal education and others have degrees from middle-eastern and western universities.

10.2 Informal discussion groups

As is normal, I met and interviewed most department and section heads and I did the rounds through the offices at the coast and through the oilfields in the interior to familiarize myself with the people, organizations, and operations. It soon became clear that PDO was a different organization and in a different mood compared with two years earlier. The higher oil price and successful exploration had brought about a high level of activity. There was a general atmosphere of expansion and urgency and a feeling of being understaffed for the many projects in hand. There was the concern of the more senior staff that the quality of the work was suffering; the younger staff complained about the lack of procedures and communication; and the Omanis said that little real effort was put into their training and development. I felt that the different groups hoped that I would find a magic formula for reducing the negative side-effects of an otherwise appreciated expansion.

It was fortunate that in my first discussion with him, the Managing Director had already agreed to organize a series of informal discussions with staff from various levels. Each group would consist of eight to ten persons from various departments, plus the Managing Director, the Administration/Personnel Manager, and myself. They would come together at the MD's house from 3–6 p.m. for tea, a drink, and a 'fire-side' chat.

The objectives of management were to sound out the feelings and views of the staff, to clarify policies and decisions, and to strengthen the appreciation between departments. The objectives for the participants were to get background information, to hear future plans, to voice concerns and ideas on PDO's organization and operation, and to be confronted by the different views from staff of different departments, levels, and nationalities. It would give me the necessary mixed forum to probe further the current salient topics and a sounding board for what should be tackled in the envisaged training activities.

It turned out that my objectives were served very well. Three issues came out loud and clear:

(1) Understaffing and/or overambitious targets. Discussions focused on getting qualified staff, how targets should be set realistically, getting more clerical-administrative support to free specialists from menial tasks, etc.

(2) Deficiencies in horizontal planning and co-operation, not only between departments and functions but also between sections. Who co-ordinated the grey areas between the service and operating departments, between design, construction, operation, and maintenance sections? More dedicated Project Groups? More procedures and standard instructions? (All the typical issues of an organization growing double in size.)

(3) The need for more effort to be put into recruiting, training, and career development of Omanis. Making PDO a more Omani company.

After some six weeks I had gained enough information and insight to distil the subjects, the objectives, and a framework for the intended training activities. The following is, in short, what I presented to the Management Team for their approval.

10.3 Proposed workshops

Since planning and horizontal (cross-sectional and interdepartmental) co-operation seem to be the major areas for improvement, let us organize a series of 'workshops' where staff from the different departments—those who could/should deal with each other directly—discuss and work on issues that are relevant to them. That means that the participant-groups should be horizontal slices through the organization. In order that operational staff can participate, these workshops should not last a full week, but yet should be long enough for them to get to know each other and to bring up matters that do not normally come out in day-to-day work. Hence the proposal of three-day workshops in an off-site hotel. For a substantial impact the majority of the staff should participate successively in 20–30 groups of 12 participants each over a period of 12–18 months.

Expectations should be kept realistic. Workshops at whatever level can easily produce platitudes and lists of complaints that ought to be put right by bosses and other persons not present. To prevent this, let us formulate clearly which constraints are likely to be imposed on PDO for some time (for instance: more projects than can be handled, shortage of experienced staff, and the obligation to develop Omanis rather quickly). In short, the leading motive for the workshops should be: 'What can we participants do to plan and co-operate better under the given circumstances and expected constraints?

In addition to Planning and Co-operation, it was agreed to include the subjects 'Matrix- and Project-organization', 'Interpersonal Skills' and 'Personal Planning'. These would give me the explicit opportunities to encourage the participants (a) to look at their own style of working and learning, (b) to assume (joint) responsibility not only for the success of the workshop, but (c) also for the follow-up action and extension of their own competence on the job.

To maintain the link with management and to provide an opportunity to discuss worthwhile matters that were beyond participants' authority, it was agreed that one or two managers should join the workshop around lunchtime on the third day for discussing suggestions and/or questions identified and prepared for that purpose on days one and two.

Quite some effort would have to be put into getting the right composition of each group. The twelve participants should be multinational (mainly British, Dutch, and Omani) and at the same time be a cross-departmental mix of professional, administrative, and operational field staff. Participation would be voluntary, but once agreed, last-minute cancellations would only be accepted if authorized by the participant's line manager.

The Managing Director sent a personal circular to all Senior Staff: 'With the arrival of Bert Juch we can now again organize a larger series of training/ development activities for most of our Senior Staff'. (There follows the purpose, objectives, procedures, etc. of the workshop.) . . . 'Realizing the investment of time, money, and effort in such an activity, we expect all participants to co-operate fully to derive optimum benefit for PDO and for themselves. PDO management team will also attend such a workshop early next year . . .' I was pleased with this public commitment of the management team to the training activity, in particular that they would appraise the 'formula' themselves and work an extra full day on their own problems and issues.

This was the global planning and setting. Something more specific has to be said about the building-in of the learning-to-learn principle, that is to say of the application of personal development in these workshops.

10.4 Building in personal development

I make a point of meeting each participant in his office or at his workplace, three weeks or so before the workshop, to invite him to attend, explain the background and objectives (see Appendix 1), and give him an outline of the programme, etc. A few questions (would he/she like to come, whether the subjects seem relevant, what earlier experience he/she has within such work-sessions, etc.) will normally bring out expectations and reservations. Thus, I get an idea of the person, his job, and expectation. I encourage him to do some thinking beforehand along the questions of Appendix 11, including what he hopes to get out of the workshop for his job and himself.

The first few hours of the workshop are crucial in striking the right chord. It is very important to establish an informality and freedom in which it feels quite natural to contribute and to learn, the earlier the better. The atmosphere must be relaxed and open, but not too permissive, as this may be threatening to some. I realize, every time, how important and unique this delicate evocative process is.

I try to get the process really going with the following: (see also Sections 1.3 and 1.4):

(1) Assembling informally around the tea and coffee trolley, first name introduction and free seating (and free moving!).
(2) Restating the background of the workshop and the purpose of going beyond 'obvious' problems and constraints.
(3) Doing the 'Personal Introduction' as a serious exercise in communica-tions.: 'I am . . . ., my job is . . . ., my personal expectations are . . . ., to be formulated in such a way that it is (a) clear and interesting to those around the table, (b) of use for working together here and later on the job, and (c) concise, a maximum of five minutes. Personal expectations are listed on flipcharts and questions can be asked. I exemplify this, if no one else volunteers.
(4) Raising awareness that *how* we work here is just as important as *what* we discuss. I invite joint responsibility for procedures, for breaks, for trying out new things, for decisions to move on, for the quality of interpersonal communication, and for own learning. The degree of my

challenge is determined by the response; I can do this cautiously or quite incisively, for instance by eliciting in brainstorming fashion what participants see as the process objectives (see Appendix 1).

(5) Raising participants' awareness of their individual learning-profiles with a self-scoring inventory. I designed a new Learning-Profile Exercise to go with my new model, taking advantage of my earlier experience (see Chapters 1, 2, and 3), and found the most successful one by trying out several versions. This new LPE is described in Appendices 13 and 14. The latest version of the exercise sheets is attached as Appendices 15 and 16.

(6) Presenting the *Personal Development Model*. Time, depth, and degree of differentiation and completeness depend on the questions and discussion. For instance, in sequence of elaboration:

(i) only the four stages, see Figure 8 on page 31;
(ii) the four stages and the four barriers, see Figure 9 on page 40;
(iii) typical prominent examples, see Appendices 6 and 7;
(iv) the complete model, see Appendix 12;
(v) plus the levels of awareness of learning, Figure 39, and Section 9.4.6.

Their presentation can best be interlarded with questions about relevance to life and/or work, see Appendix 4.

The above six agenda items normally take the whole morning. During the rest of day one and day two, the programme contains no special process-subject, but the process is stimulated continuously by 'living' the LTL principles and building up responsibility for what goes on:

(7) The advancement of the process is put to the test late in the afternoon of day two and in the morning of the third day with exercises in diagnosing relationships and interpersonal skills (see Appendices 8 and 9) and in giving/receiving feedback.

(8) The maturity of the process is also put to the test by how the group prepare themselves for the meeting and lunch with the visiting manager. The (potential) usefulness of such a discussion is debated. Participants have to organize themselves and put flesh to the bones of a few proposals and/or questions.

(9) After lunch with the manager(s), I reopen the personal-development subject with questions like: 'Should we manage our own careers?'; 'How useful are the procedures and practices around the yearly staff reports?' (see Section 5.1); 'What opportunities are offered by the organization for you to increase your marketable skills?'; 'What are your short-term and long-term goals in life?'. To promote concrete personal planning of at least a *few action points* which can realistically be implemented when back on the job, I offer a two-page guide that spells out what one could do within one's own organizational situation (see Appendix 17).

(10) To stimulate further initiatives in participants to work on their own development, time is made available to browse through articles, pamphlets, training manuals, and books related to the subjects of these workshops. These are continuously on display for this purpose during the three days. Participants can borrow, copy, or order them. I am around actively, for information and comments on this material and for suggestions on further study.

Every trainer knows all too well that at the end of any off-site meeting, lip-service comes easy, but generating real commitment for application is a most difficult task. Increased awareness is not enough, good intentions are only a step out of the 'gate' in the right direction, but crossing the 'Rubicon' on the job is the big hurdle. I must say that I still do not know whether I am pushing hard enough. The fact is that I have not been all that successful in building that bridge between thinking, intentions, and doing. My experience with a few hundred staff members is that half of them can verbalize what they are aiming for, some 30 per cent of the participants have serious intentions, but less than 10 per cent work systematically with an action plan for their own development.

10.5 Participants' observations

It is not my idea to evaluate here the experience and results of the thirty or more workshops in terms not directly related with the subject of this book. However, I will not withhold a few points which were most frequently mentioned by the participants:

(1) The major advantage of this type of 'workshop' is that practical issues which are common and relevant to participants are better formulated, dealt with, and/or presented to management.

(2) Understanding of what goes on in other departments is of much greater interest and importance than envisaged before sitting together.

(3) Individuals experience for themselves how their personal styles and individual contributory skills compare with those of colleagues.

(4) Exchanging opinions and experience about various organizational policies and structures is very valuable; scientists and specialists prefer more freedom and horizontal-, matrix-, and project-type organizations, whereas operational field staff prefer, often as a necessity, the clarity and directness of the single command line. Such differences in appreciation are not always accepted as healthy and normal, but recognition improves horizontal planning and co-operation throughout the organization.

(5) Omanis expect to learn more particular techniques. They consider that they have most to contribute in the small syndicate groups. Cross-cultural issues are important but not always the most prominent.

(6) The management team experienced the workshop 'formula' positively: 'We should have done this earlier'. Their points for action include regular follow-up workshops, once every six months.

194

(7) The relatively good relations between management and staff were further improved by these activities. However, there remains a rift of some significance in appreciation (or is it trust?): management very much want staff to be involved, to speak up, to take responsibility, but they think that staff often take it too easy and have to be controlled. Staff genuinely want to be involved and take responsibility; they believe, however, that there is reticence on the part of management, inclined as they are to withhold sensitive information, decision-power, and prerogatives. Never the twain shall meet?

11

Another Application

The Sultanate of Oman struggles, like many developing countries, with a shortage of professionally trained personnel. The Civil Service is in general manned by young Omanis with a natural flair for government business, but only a few have more than a minimum of formal knowledge and experience of what administrative management entails.

Through the Board of PDO, the Ministries of Petroleum and Finance have a major influence on PDO's projects and operation and also on personnel policies and the level of training activities. Their ministers are thus well aware of what is internationally available in the field of management training. It is, however, very difficult for their own growing and overloaded ministries to find ways and means and time to train their (middle) managers off and on the job.

A training Institute for Public Administration has been created. Its programmes are mainly concerned with administrative financial methods and with procedures and techniques of public administration. The man-management side of running a government gets scant attention.

11.1 Management seminars for government officers

To fill this need, the management of PDO was willing to offer PDO's resources and facilities on a modest scale to the ministries with which there were regular business contacts. This provided me with an excellent opportunity to experience how a self-development process could catch on in an all-Omani culture.

In my discussion with one of the ministers, he said that he would like to see his directors delegate more, show more initiative in putting forward proposals, and more co-ordination with colleague directors. He would like to reduce the downward flow of orders and increase the upward flow of suggestions and comments. Subsequently I had discussions with several directors to acquaint myself with their work and problems. The directors in charge of personnel planning, training, internal audit, and computers especially had additional views on what was required. They also stressed that it would not be easy to take a group of key persons away from work for a few days.

It was agreed that PDO would organize and run some full five-day (non-residential) management courses for directors, deputy directors and section heads, in fact for all who had a reasonable command of English. Although the course subjects should be the conventional ones—for instance, managers' tasks and responsibilities, management by objectives (planning), motivation, delegation, problem-solving and decision-making, making proposals, interviewing, running a meeting—the training should not be conventional from the Omani point of view with respect to atmosphere and process. Participants would be encouraged to contribute, to discuss their concerns and problems, and to work in small teams on proposals as they saw fit. Open discussions, trying out new things, showing initiative, were seen as more important than increasing knowledge. That is why the term 'Seminar' was to be used.

As the subject content would be rather basic, I would be able to pay most attention to the process. Although the cultural ambience, the emphasis and depth, would be different, I could use a strategy similar to the workshops described above, that is dealing with the objectives, process, introduction, and learning during the greater part of the first day, living LTL during the week, and back to explicit self-organized development on the last day.

A follow-up of these seminars was considered essential. I would work with whoever expressed the wish to develop further his or her individual management style. Starting from the current tasks, we would try to expand their competence and scope of work while retaining congruence with the cultural and ethical values of their staff.

11.2 Participants' observations

The evaluation of these seminars for government officials could easily fill a full chapter in itself. The objective is, however, to compare their learning process with that of the expatriate participants of the workshops. This is done in Chapter 12, but here are first a few observations of general interest that characterize these Omani seminars:

(1) The participants were very keen and active. It was acceptable to me and appreciated by the participants that when discussions became rather intensive, they could switch over from English to Arabic.
(2) There was recurring tension between me and the participants. In the Omani culture seminar leaders are considered to be the experts and thus expected to do the talking and the teaching and always have ready answers. But the (agreed) objective was that the participants would come forward with their own ideas and contributions. It was crucial that all participants should recognize before the end of the course that this is the same key problem in the boss–subordinate relation in their Omani work situation. That is: how to foster confidence/initiative to increase the upward flow of comments and proposals.

(3) Several seminar activities and ways of doing things were completely new to most of them. Some had never conducted or planned an interview, some were discussion leaders for the first time ever. Towards the end of each seminar there were lively team-discussions, presentations were made, and flip charts were used, etc.

(4) The learning-profile exercise and learning model were eye-openers. To avoid infringing their privacy in any way or giving the feeling that they were being tested covertly, I did not feel free to take scores, not even anonymously.

(5) Most agreed that their styles were rather intuitive and implicit with little conscious attention to systematic analyses and/or explicit planning. Their learning during the seminars was very much inductive and retro-spective (see Section 4.4), that is recognizing (sometimes in others) what they had done or thought before. Prospective learning through planning or analysing alternatives was seldom evident (see further Section 12.1). Therefore they needed appreciably more training in the basic techniques for problem analyses and decision-making.

(6) A research study by the Middle East Industrial Relations Counsellors (MEIRC), Beirut 1976, classifies the 'Motivation of National Employees in the Arab World' in terms of: T = being *t*reated well, P = being *p*aid well, and U = one's capacity being *u*sed well. Participants' consensus was that T is indeed most essential, not least for lower employees, and that P may well take a second place. Only higher staff find U most important. Training and development *in* the work situation is a completely new concept in the Arab world.

(7) A success was the introduction of and discussion about a 'developmental leadership style' which is, in short, a gradual and systematic increase of delegation to develop a subordinate. That was typically seen as a desirable style for their boss to adopt to facilitate their developing on the job, but it was somewhat risky for they *themselves* to encourage their subordinates to take initiative and be pro-active. 'This style is what the country needs'!

(8) It was not (yet) possible to arrange an open discussion with their top management on the last day. But long lists of individual action points were drawn up. These indicate clearly that there are many follow-up jobs for any management consultant, both for on-the-job projects and for leading one-day work sessions on specific topics.

PART V

The Coda

In the cyclic model for personal development, there is always a following stage. It is the same in this book: after the 'doing' in Chapters 1 and 2, the 'thinking' in Chapters 3 to 9, the 'planning, doing, and observing' in Chapters 10 and 11, some reflective 'thinking' and new hypotheses are to follow. The process must be kept going with new ideas for testing and application in the next period of 'doing', *ad infinitum*.

On the other hand, I must conclude the book. This last chapter will be like a coda, a quick concluding piece of music, which the reader can best enjoy if he/she is familiar with what has been presented in the preceding pieces and if this has attuned him/her to hearing new themes.

12

A Few New Thoughts

It is all right for new ideas to be bold, simplified, and somewhat exaggerated. Therefore the following thoughts are only roughly formulated, with all the possibilities of further specification, confirmation, or refutation through more experience.

12.1 On the cultural differences

The principal differences in the learning that took place in the workshops and in the seminars were strongly influenced by the cultural difference of the participants. The basic mode of learning for an Arab child, whether at home, at a Qur'an school, or through government education, is (still) predominantly 'listen-repeat', that is rote-learning (see the instruction specialization in Section 4.5.4). Objectives and methods are determined by the teacher, he does the talking and instruction. Pupils are hardly ever encouraged to ask why or how. But their memory is excellently trained.

No wonder that the Omani participants at the seminars expected a lot of learning-I, preferably through straightforward instruction by me. They wanted to catch up as much as possible with the available knowledge and techniques of management. The step to learning-II (context) always had to be made by me, for instance by discussing why or how a concept or technique had been used elsewhere and could/should be applied by themselves.

If Kelly's fundamental postulate: 'A person's psychological (learning) processes are channelized by the way he anticipates events' applies to the Arab culture then it is mainly subconsciously, intuitively. Few have been trained in setting objectives, rational planning, scanning and assessing alternatives, potential problems, etc. Deductive learning through explicit forward planning is rather foreign to their philosophy in life. Their learning during the seminars was mainly inductive learning-I.

That was very different in the PDO workshops (see the comparison in Figure 42). These were set up so that the (predominantly expatriate) participants could hear and compare what their colleagues had to say and did in other departments. The focus was on comparing opinions, experiences, and the peculiarities of each others' functions. There was a lot of learning-II, that is learning about contexts. Actually, although many books were on display, very few were interested in learning-I; they did not expect to learn particular techniques but *about* particular usage of techniques within PDO.

Despite the opportunities and efforts from my side, I don't think that many reached learning-III level in either the seminars or the workshops. There was evidence of an occasional eye-opener and a few profound changes in the way of looking at things. I hope that there was more L-III than was disclosed to me!

With respect to the learning stages, these were clearly apparent in the workshops. Participants' mental focus moved from sensing to analysing, to thinking ahead, planning and organizing (for instance the meeting with the manager). However, the related superordinate values and the unconscious processes were not talked about. I tried to raise these into awareness. In the seminars the learning stages were far less prominent, or skipped completely in favour of intuitive decisions and ready acceptance of *faits accomplis*. Courtesy, modesty, and other quality factors of the Inner Self tended to moderate critical analyses (for example of the seminar itself). Initiative and creative behaviour are not so much required for L-I.

With respect to the use of the brain, I personally was quite aware of having to use my RB intensively in the seminars to perceive and understand how the Omanis perceived and understood what was presented and what was going on. Since the participants wanted to pick up existing methods and techniques, *they* had to exercise their LB more than they were used to. I often insisted on more logical and analytical reasoning, I hope in a way that was supportive of and in congruence with their RB. The whole idea was that they should not just emulate the rational, analytical management techniques of the West, but appraise them in the context of their own culture, and adapt or change or reject them if not suitable (that is: understanding L-I within L-II).

This was again very different in the PDO workshops. There was too much reliance on and reference to logic and quantification. The LB dominated. Participants were struggling with qualitative appraisal, subjective relationships, contexts, pattern recognition, value judgements, and so on. There I had to plead continuously for empathic listening for the ideas (meaning) behind the words, for understanding of other persons' views, grasping the larger picture, etc. In other words: the workshops required the participants to use their RB capacities. Those who did, and/or had natural talents, often hesitated in going public with their values, feelings, etc., and found it difficult to express in verbal logic the constructs and opinions that were clear to themselves as a 'picture' in the RB. One reason why the Omanis felt relatively more confident in the small syndicate groups was apparently due to the well-known fact that participants listen and understand each others' views better in small groups, and conversely, that one has to be well trained to make one's point clear and logical and acceptable in a larger group.

It is difficult to ascertain how much L-II took place in the workshops. I think quite a bit, but most of it may have remained subconscious. Some persons are not really interested in other people's context and experiences.

	WORKSHOPS	SEMINARS
Participants	Mainly W. Europeans	Omanis only
Aimed to develop:	L-II and RB	L-I and LB
How much learning-I?	Plenty already	Keen to get much more
How much learning-II?	Growing, becoming conscious	Sufficient, but imperceptible
How much learning-III?	Incidental	Kept privately
Learning stages	All four explicit	Sensing and planning had to be exercised
Processes: Tertiary	Strong	Weak
Secondary	Weak	Strong
Spare development capacity?	Not sure how much	Majority had plenty
Development opportunities	Many	Some
Utilizing them	A few	Some
Managing self-learning?	Disappointingly few	A promising few
Seminar leader used mainly his most effort to foster	LB + RB on L-II and L-III; LTL, awareness of L-II, L-III transfer responsibility	RB on L-I and L-II; Reconciling L-I with L-II

Figure 42   Comparing characteristics of workshops and seminars

204

Some are prepared to listen and mature further in this way. The few persons who make conscious efforts are quite apparent; they ask questions, they want to know what and how others see and do certain things. Those are, in my experience, the ones who stand out and have the best career potential.

Simplifying the above further: just learning a new method or technique is L-I. A lot of it is required in the worlds of technology and business. For most of it we exercise the LB more than the RB. But broadening our outlook, understanding different contexts is L-II. Seeing colleagues' points of view is not a LB but a RB ability. Relying exclusively on LB and L-I makes it impossible to understand other people's ways of thinking and operating. If planning and co-operation with colleagues is our business then we have to exercise our RB and level-II learning.

The educational system of the West is giving us little exercise in this respect. Teachers push their own subject in depth and in isolation from other subjects. They compel pupils to work individually (without helping each other) for a grading system based on tests that require more LB than RB. The dominance of L-I learning causes a deficiency in training of the RB and almost total absence of holistic brain and L-III development.

Comparing the characteristics between the expatriate and Omani group leads me to two conclusions. Firstly, the neglect of L-II and L-III in western society and educational institutes may have led to or aggravated the individualistic 'Me first' culture. In order to get more synergistic co-operation between people in organizations and society, a substantial increase in RB training and higher level (II and III) skills would be required. Secondly, there is a need for developing countries to catch up on L-I and LB learning but they should not fall into the trap of doing this in isolation from contexts and culture. Whatever techniques and skills they want to adopt, there should not be a straight L-I emulation of the West. It should rather be a reassessment and an adaptation through using their naturally stronger RB approach, that means staying in touch and enriching their own culture.

12.2 On awareness and self-development

I have already mentioned that I am rather disappointed with the results of my intentions and deliberate efforts to promote self-organized learning and development. In the workshops and seminars there are carefully prepared handouts to assist whoever wants to go further into the subject; a large selection of books, articles, pamphlets on relevant subjects is on display; information on further training/education is available or can be asked for. When consulting in the work situation I make suggestions for further experience, for contacting people who know, and so on.

In the beginning I was really surprised that so few participants took advantage of this. Only one or two in ten make a deliberate effort to survey the resources, try out the opportunities, etc. Even attractive workbooks like the *Manager's Guide to Self-development* (Pedler *et al.*, 1978) and *Planning your*

Future (Ford and Lippitt, 1976) were not in the high demand I had expected. To get participants to sit down and plan their personal follow-up and formulate a few concrete action steps to be put into practice when back on the job, I had to push them more than I liked. Why is this so?

Argyris' work (1977) had warned me. He is rather pessimistic about managers willing and able to acquire what he calls Model-II behaviour. This led me to think through a number of reasons why it is difficult to progress up to learning-III level (see Section 9.4.4). I tried to bring this to bear in my praxis of encouraging managers and staff to become more active self-developers. Yet the results remained below expectation. Therefore, I had to review my views even further and came close to Hague's (1979:2–3).

Firstly, the catchphrase 'self-development' is grossly and glibly overused in recent (management) literature. Books and articles create unrealistic expectations and suggest that it is possible for almost everybody to be able to manage their own career just by deciding to embark on self-development. This is not the case. Good intentions are not enough. Whether self-development is at all possible depends on whether the person has spare capacity *and* spare energy as well. And even then, continuously and flexibly pursuing a programme of self-development against the odds of daily life is not easy. A strong motivation and great perseverance are required to overcome delays and setbacks in perceivable results.

I have learned to spot persons with spare capacity and energy from their relaxed attentive behaviour; they are the ones who ask questions in workshops and seminars and contribute pro-actively. I help them to get a better insight into their own learning style, to discover their spare strengths and dormant talents, and to make a plan to get more scope and try their wings. And make sure that they are not becoming dependent on my assistance.

Secondly, in developing countries there is plenty of untapped human capacity. Genuine cases of rapid career development are numerous; these happy, visible examples motivate many less able persons, even if only through dissatisfaction with their own lower status. Expectations can easily be raised and raised too high. Hence one may expect much scope for self-development in Oman. In fact, when the hope is to catch up in one generation's time, self-development must be considered as a likely method to achieve this. However, when it comes to planning and practicalities, self-organized learning is (too) foreign to the established education and social patterns in the Omani (Arab) culture.

Thirdly, many of the western expatriate staff are just too busy. Little time is (made) available to think and plan, there is not much spare energy. Some show signs of stress in their work. Though managing one's own career appears attractive enough, many consider it unrealistic to think that their own priorities can be pursued or that it will be possible to integrate their own interests with those of the company. And let me not forget to mention the general human reluctance to acknowledge that one's attitude and skills could be improved and that people often *under*estimate their own potential.

Fourthly, good intentions and some energy, crystallized in a personal plan, form a laudable start, but it may still not be good enough for a self-driven development process. That needs more than systematic learning by doing—sensing—thinking—planning. The western educational system has trained our LB and provided a solid L-I base, but it has been deficient in exercising the RB and conscious L-II abilities. Personal development is impossible for someone (however wide his L-I base) who has no experience of seeing L-II contexts in RB fashion. People who are entrenched in their professional views, who are not experienced in open appraisal of different opinions, who have difficulty in perceiving completely different cultures or value systems, who take no risks, cannot possibly 'just do some self-development'. Even high-powered managers (with wide-spanning views and ambitious 'helicopter quality' at the time of their ascent) may actually be on, or have fallen back on to, the 'more of the same' level. They may not be able to lift themselves by their bootstraps out of the prison of their established theories and practices.

I conclude with Hague (1979) that having a facilitating consultant *cum* trainer in a purposive enterprise is not good enough. Many middle managers and staff need more forthright assistance from a counselling tutor/coach. His task and professional art is to help them over little thresholds and guide them in developing themselves through utilizing opportunities in their work situation and through crises in their private lives (see Section 1.7, my article of 1979, and the books of Hague, 1979 and Evans and Bartolome, 1980). That is why I designed the Planning Guide (Appendix 17) on purpose and unabashedly, as the most directive of my handouts.

My point is that, except for the self-making few, most students, managers, and staff, if they want to rise to conscious, self-sustaining development, will need more guidance into learning-to-learn experience and through the levels of development in order to discover and combine holistically all the talents of body and mind.

The road to Personal- and Self-development is not a parkway, it is a rocky, long-winding, and adventurous path. Figure 39 may be compared with climbing a mountain. One needs (a guide and) energy and skill and resources. One has to build camps on successively higher levels, make sidesteps and look out for alternative roads, means, and companions. Who wants to leave the hurly-burly behind, rise above the crowded lowlands and pass through the clouds? Are sunlit uplands and peak experiences awaiting? Is this all worthwhile? 'For in much wisdom is much grief, and he that increaseth knowledge, increaseth sorrow' (Ecclesiastes i:18).

12.3 On the cyclic model for personal development

Through the above considerations I have come full circle to my original query: 'Can and should the learning and development of Man be accelerated?' Personal development is a system of interconnected circular causal processes (see the model of Appendix 12). Cybernetics teaches us how such processes can be regulated, accelerated, or slowed down. The process will escalate, may even run wild, if stimuli are continuously reinforced positively while carried through the circuit; when *un*controlled it is potentially an explosive situation. If on the other hand the damping and controlling mechanisms are too selective or are cutting out too much, then the system gets isolated and runs below its (growing) capacity. To prevent a system from either dying down or running wild, from oscillating too much and from settling on too low or too high a level, it is essential that all available regulators react properly to stimuli and disturbances and are adjusted carefully.

The model of personal development simplifies Man's primary, secondary, and tertiary (cybernetic) processes in order to grasp their workings. Any stimulus (any perceived 'difference that makes a difference') will be processed through the conscious or sub- or unconscious stages of sensing, thinking, planning, and doing. The new information will update constructs, refine skills, change behaviour and create self-sustaining reactions if it has triggered collateral energy. The 'mechanics' of regulating the input, throughput, and output (the amount of traffic on the three roundabouts of the model) are the mental focus, operating consciously, and the four mental barriers (window, skin, gate, and Rubicon) which operate mainly sub- and unconsciously. These devices are necessarily discriminate and selective, they screen, throttle, or amplify. Their function is to keep Man in healthy mental balance, prevent *under*load, and protect him against neurotic *over*load.

Can we honestly ask people to 'accelerate' psychologically and physically, to be more effective, to take mental risks? Are not most people already fully stretched in their daily lives? To what extent is their system loaded up with red herrings, unreal problems, and unproductive worries? In western-type organizations the psychosomatic stress is bigger than the purely physical. To what extent can people be enticed to remove filters, blinkers, and other self-restrictive barriers in order to increase the input, throughput, and output of their learning and development? Or should it be the other way around: urge mankind to slow down?

I assume that most of the staff I encountered had spare capacity, but who knows how much for how long? If the capacity of the brain is boundless can we count on a limitless human capacity for further development? Or should the individual first clarify and husband his personal situation, making time and energy free to think, plan, and do as suggested in the Planning Guide of Appendix 17?

To summarize, I propose for further consideration, four general steps in accelerating/improving personal development:

(1) Familiarize educators, students, and managers with the stages of the cyclic process model, with the levels of learning and development, and with the related principles of learning-to-learn.
(2) Make learning-to-learn a major objective of education and in teaching/ training practices. Review priorities of content and process, eliminate

historic ballast and correct imbalances in effort on the various aspects of mind (and body).

(3) Apply this personally. That is: clear and debottleneck one's own system. Compare goals and talents with present abilities. Evaluate internal synergistic interaction between the three processes. Make an action programme for further professional and personal development.

(4) Review one's interactive skills and improve the usefulness of one's environment, physically and psychologically. Cover the wide range from life-companions to career, from quality of work to effectiveness of learning material.

This is more than enough to keep us, learners and educators, busy for some time to come.

12.4   On me as a facilitator-trainer

Compared with five years ago when I started to work on the subject of this book, I certainly have improved as a consultant and management trainer. I cannot say, however, that I am much more relaxed when consulting or running discussion groups, workshops, or seminars. My interventions and contributions may be more grounded and founded, but every time I am still somewhat apprehensive. The better I have thought through the day's objectives (of consultancy or training) and the less I need to worry about peripheral arrangements (facilities, equipment, material) the more available is my attention and energy for the individual or group.

Regarding my professional development, I have to think and work more on the following aspects:

(1) I am inclined to run a 'smoother ship' than is optimal for learning. A certain level of excitement, anxiety, and other emotions is essential for lasting learning and breakthroughs in development. I know that participants judge me on 'how I live what I preach' in *my* handling of surprises, disturbances, setbacks, etc. Therefore I ought to tolerate more challenge and disputes, permit more changes in programme and structures, learn to live with more suspended ambiguity and anxiety, leave more business open-ended for 'tomorrow'.

(2) Since the emphasis is shifting towards process and resource facilitation, this requires a concurrent shift in style and attitude. More than ever, the facilitator/trainer should hold back his hobby horses, his personal views, and preferred style of approach. He should not do his own thing. Yet his personal influence remains all-important. It becomes more difficult to educate through self-discovery, to decide when to confront and/or be directive, when to intervene and cut short on 'time-consuming mistakes'. The basic problem is that one and the same situation can never be dealt with again in a different way.

(3) Fostering self-organized learning and self-managed development requires a great variety of supporting modes and techniques of learning and excellently organized (cheap) resources. These should be different for L-I, L-II, and L-III, for RB and LB and combinations thereof. Ideally, resources and application should cater for the motivation and disposition of individuals and groups, and be differentiated for different cultures. I shall have to know better when and how to use the more sophisticated technology (video-packages, computer-assisted learning, etc.).

(4) Primary aims. What rates higher: achievement or enjoyment, practical results or longer term development? Who or what gets my first loyalty? The individual, the group, the organization, or what particular value in society? (a teaser in developing countries). Sometimes choosing is important or unavoidable, but normally experience determines my dialectic balance, that is if one beneficiary shows progress, I proceed further; if not, I move somewhat towards another 'mission'.

(5) My task. Students, staff, and managers are served best if I do not try to change them but get them instead to realize their own preferences and spare capabilities. Holding judgement on their style and performance at low key, I have *them* evaluate their own (longer term) effectiveness in actual co-operation with others. In summary, I see it as my task to identify and coach those managers and employees who have the ability of and accept responsibility for organizing their own ongoing development and to create an organizational climate which fosters concerted performance and mutual benefit.

(6) The ultimate right. Who am I to have the right to coach, to intervene, to hold up a mirror, to take off the soothing blinkers? Mostly I have the excuse that I am being asked to. Other times I am aware of the inherent professional risk that some will conclude that I am not making them happy or making things better. This paradox holds for me: I am least vulnerable when I am open to criticism.

(7) Touch of humility. Educators should be modest. Wisdom cannot be spoon-fed and development does not result from classroom training (alone). Most learning is picked up at home, at play, and from non-contrived situations at work. Overteaching and perfectionism are also counter-effective in education. A tutor/coach should be able to let go, and make himself redundant.

Applied to this book, I hope that the ideas and memes on personal development will fertilize the RB and LB of many readers on Levels I, II, and III. As all memes, they are subject to confirmation or refutation when put to the test wherever and by whoever. Time will show which propositions and practices survive and prosper.

So I end the deliberations.
April–December, 1981.
Ras al Hamra, Oman.

Bert Juch

Appendix 1

Discussion Paper for
PDO's Man-Management Training

1. *Overall Aim:*
   To improve PDO's effectiveness, through increasing its Senior Staff's managerial confidence and competence.

2. *Content Objectives.* Participants:
   (a) To take stock of their personal attitudes, skills, and behaviour at work.
   (b) To experience and understand how these affect communication and co-operation, and how their contributions are perceived by others.
   (c) To advance their motivation and competence for thinking and working together in effective work teams.

3. *Process Objectives.* To facilitate and create:
   (a) A supportive climate conducive to open discussions and personal learning.
   (b) Learning by planning and doing, by sensing and understanding why, individually and through group exercises.
   (c) Joint responsibility for activities and results.
   (d) A total process that is stimulating to apply the self-learning and team-building of the participants in their *work* situation.

4. *Participants are asked to:*
   (a) Contribute in accordance with ability.
   (b) Be honest and open in communication.
   (c) Confront in a constructive way.
   (d) Acknowledge that people are different.
   (e) Give 'room' and support to those who need some.
   (f) Co-operate, and share responsibility for group work.

5. *Participants are entitled to:*
   (a) Opportunities for experiments and development.
   (b) Fair share of time, attention, feedback.
   (c) Support from others.
   (d) Personal opinions, preferences, and choices as long as other people's freedom is not trespassed.
   (e) Determine their personal limit of disclosure and need for privacy.
   The total package to be simple, practical, interesting, catching, stretching.

Appendix 2

Facilitator's suggestions for the 'Panel Session'

Supervisory Management Courses

A. *Objectives*
Overall: To improve PDO's effectiveness through open and candid discussions between supervisors and top management.
Specifically:
(1) Management to provide background information (which may be difficult to communicate in writing).
(2) Supervisors to put forward ideas and suggestions to improve the organization's performance.
(3) Exchange views and feelings difficult to quantify such as opinions about policies and practices.
(4) Increase the commitment of supervisors to management's decisions.
(5) Increase management's credibility with supervisors.
(6) Broaden the horizons (helicopter quality) of the course participants by involving them with the ideas and plans of senior management.

B. *Process*
Course participants are divided into syndicates and asked to formulate two or three constructive questions/propositions for the Panel. These should relate to:
(a) The work, organization, or future of PDO.
(b) Responsibilities and authority of supervisors.
(c) Concerns and problems of a *general* nature.

The best three questions from all the syndicates combined are then selected by the participants and put in writing to the Panel members who receive them twenty-four hours in advance.

C. *Aims behind this pre-work:* to help the supervisors to:
(a) Think about and communicate on intra- and interdepartmental problems and issues.
(b) Analyse data, quote examples, etc.
(c) Use their own judgement and decision-making abilities in the selection and formulation of the questions/proposals.
(d) Anticipate arguments in a constructive two-way discussion.

D. *Suggestions for the Members of the Management Team:*

  (1) Arrive prepared and relaxed.

  (2) Introduce yourselves to the course participants during the pre-Panel drinks and luncheon.

  (3) Try to understand the concerns *behind* the students' questions and arguments. Exercise empathy.

  (4) Avoid defensiveness and/or dominance. This could result in distorted information or silence on the part of the participants.

  (5) Start to respond to points you agree with and build up to the point you want to make.

  (6) Keep the contributions from the management team in reasonable balance.

  (7) Establish credibility with the course participants in a way that you can support/sustain later in day-to-day operation.

Appendix 3

Instructions and Scoring Sheet of Kolb's LSI Test

Instructions

There are nine sets of four words listed below. Rank order the words in each set by assigning a 4 to the word which best characterizes your learning style, a 3 to the word which next best characterizes your learning style, a 2 to the next most characteristic word, and a 1 to the word which is least characteristic of you as a learner.

You may find it hard to choose the words that best charcterize your learning style. Nevertheless, keep in mind that there are no right or wrong answers—all the choices are equally acceptable. The aim of the inventory is to describe how you learn, not to evaluate your learning ability.

Be sure to assign a different rank number to each of the four words in each set; do not make ties.

1. __discriminating	__tentative	__involved	__practical
2. __receptive	__relevant	__analytical	__impartial
3. __feeling	__watching	__thinking	__doing
4. __accepting	__risk-taker	__evaluative	__aware
5. __intuitive	__productive	__logical	__questioning
6. __abstract	__observing	__concrete	__active
7. __present-oriented	__reflecting	__future-oriented	__pragmatic
8. __experience	__observation	__conceptualization	__experimentation
9. __intense	__reserved	__rational	__responsible

Scoring

The four columns of words correspond to the four learning style scales: CE, RO, AC, and AE. To compute your scale scores, write your rank numbers in the boxes below only for the designated items. For example, in the third column (AC), you would fill in the rank numbers you have assigned to items 2, 3, 4, 5, 8, and 9. Compute your scale scores by adding the rank numbers for each set of boxes.

Score items:
2 3 4 5 7 8
□□□□□□
CE = _____

Score items:
1 3 6 7 8 9
□□□□□□
RO = _____

Score items:
2 3 4 5 8 9
□□□□□□
AC = _____

Score items:
1 3 6 7 8 9
□□□□□□
AE = _____

To compute the two combination scores, subtract <u>CE</u> from <u>AC</u> and subtract <u>RO</u> from <u>AE</u>. Preserve negative signs if they appear.

$$AC-CE: \overset{AC}{\square} - \overset{CE}{\square} = \text{\_\_\_\_}$$

$$AE-RO: \overset{AE}{\square} - \overset{RO}{\square} = \text{\_\_\_\_}$$

Appendix 4

Your Learning Profile

A. *Some Notes*

(1) No profile is good or bad, whether shaped symmetrically or prominently high in one or more sectors.

(2) Each individual has his own pattern which only he himself can explain in terms of his talents, preferences, dislikes, energy, and interests.

(3) People are 'born *and* made', that is: most profiles can be explained partly by inborn traits and partly by history, circumstances, and constraints. People can become conditioned by their jobs and/or profile themselves.

(4) Profiles often change during life. Different periods and situations may require a different emphasis on being assertive, sensitive, or thoughtful, on the need for planning, organizing, or being busy, etc. Most people become more reflective later in life.

(5) Awareness of one's style is an essential prerequisite to organizing one's own (career) development.

B. *Some Questions/Suggestions for Consideration/Discussion*

(1) Do you recognize, can you explain your own profile? Why yes or why not?

(2) Does it have any significance for your work? Is it supportive of, or in conflict with the requirements of your job?

(3) Does the present profile represent all your talents and capabilities, or not (yet)?

(4) Would strengthening of one of the stages/skill groups be desirable?

(5) Would it be worthwhile to reduce the restrictive effect of any of the mental barriers?

(6) Can you imagine and accept that persons close to you (for example in your work) have different profiles? Can you act compatibly with and be useful to them?

(7) Are your conscious and subconscious processes supporting each other?

Appendix 5

Different and Complementary Ways of Distinguishing Stages in the Learning Process Cycle

Year	Author	Subject	Stage 'A' Sensing (Observing)	Stage 'B' Thinking	Stage 'C' Addressing (Planning)	Stage 'D' Doing
1980	Juch	This thesis	(dis)conformation — revision — anticipation — investment — encounter			
1955	Kelly	Personal Construct Theory	feedback, evaluation	integrate, map	possibilities, decision	autonomous investment
1966	H. Turner	Human experience	beeldvorming	oordeelvorming	besluitvorming	doen
1970	Neth. P. Institute	Group decision making	attention	cognitive development	expectations	surprise
1969	Charlesworth	in Pedler, 1969:31	reflective observation	abstract concepts	active experiments	concrete experiences
1971	Kolb	Experiential learning	waarnemen	oordelen	plan maken	executie
1973	Euwe	Strategic chess	attending	intending	committing	implementing
1975	Ramsden	Action motivation	generalize	discover	invent	produce
1977	Argyris	Double-loop learning	review	purpose	strategy	outcome
1976	H. Augstein	Self-organized learning	communication	thinking	project	encounter
1976	Rowan	Research paradigm	control	purpose, aim	planning	implementing
1977	Ansoff	Strategic decision-making	effects	purposes	strategies	actions
1977	Torbert	Collaborative inquiry	biological	psychic	sociological	physical
1978	Raming	Co-ordinative model	observing	interpreting	rehearsing	acting
1978	Mangham	Dramatic interaction	evaluation	diagnosis	goal-setting	action
1978	Pedler	Mgt. guide self-development	data	theory	advice	activities
1978	Boydell	Resources for mgt. dev.	awareness	concepts	tools	practice
1978	Hague	Facilitators' course				
1980	Morris	Learning process	review progress	interpreting	project-planning	active achievement

Appendix 6

The Fifteen Major Categories of Learning Styles

Sub-category	Main stages of activities and skills				Prototype	Others
	DOING operational	OBSERVING sensory	THINKING cognitive	PLANNING contactual		
Outstanding in one stage	O				Executive	performer, pusher, doer
		O			Photographer[a]	researcher, inquirer, reader
			O		Mediator	contemplater, thinker, brooder
				O	Inventor[a]	deviser, contriver
Strong in two stages	S	S			Supervisor	instructor, mechanic, executor
		S	S		Scientist[a]	philosopher, theorist, introvert
	S		S		Planner[a]	teacher, preacher, consultant
	S			S	Entrepreneur[a]	activist, implementer, extravert
			S	S	Lone wolf	intuitive performer, specialist
		S		S	Intermediary	negotiator, diplomat
Weak in one stage	W				Bureaucrat	staff officer, politican
		W			Deductionist	futurist, idealist (no feedback)
			W		Operator[a]	self-made, down to earth
				W	Inductionist	adhocrat, fatalist, analyst
—	All four balanced				Integrator	manager? facilitator? (faceless)

[a] Depicted in Appendix 7.

Sub-subcategories exist when two or three abilities are not equally strong or weak, or when the nature of the mental barrier(s) is different. These differentiations lead to the individual learning *styles* (see Figure 1 and Appendix 7). Groups, organizations, and cultures can also be perceived as exhibiting the above categories of styles.

Appendix 7

SOME PROMINENT FUNCTIONAL LEARNING STYLES

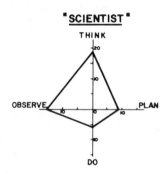

"SCIENTIST"

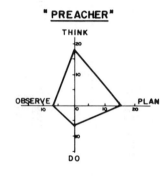

"PREACHER"

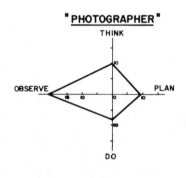

"PHOTOGRAPHER"

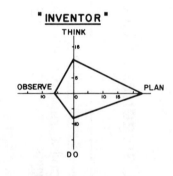

"INVENTOR"

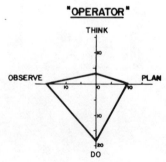

"OPERATOR"

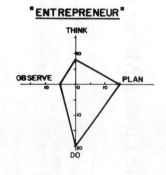

"ENTREPRENEUR"

Appendix 8

Self-Survey

Interpersonal skills for horizontal co-operation

This self-scoring survey can assist you in finding out what your strengths and weaknesses are in presenting yourself, your ideas and requests, and how you are getting on with colleagues and other persons in work situations where co-operation is essential.

Take sufficient time to rate yourself thoughtfully. Be honest and rather critical; do not hesitate to mark yourself low or high.

Low   High
0 2 4 6 8 10

(1) I take the initiative in making contacts.

(2) I am a good face-to-face communicator,

(3) and I listen well

(4) My written notes and reports are clear and concise.

(5) I get things done with/through others.

(6) They accept my influence based on my
    order (position)
    expertise (experience)
    reasoning (arguments)
    personality.

(7) I understand and accept myself.

(8) I give and receive information voluntarily.

(9) I am willing to let myself be known.

(10) I can 'stand fools around me'.

(11) I acknowledge contributions of others and I support and build on their ideas/proposals.

(12) I can say 'no' and explain why.

(13) I take comments about my behaviour seriously, without becoming defensive.

(14) I give advice/feedback to others such that it is accepted/appreciated.

(15) I can laugh about myself.

(16) I do delegate, give mandate, put trust in others.

219

220

Low					High	
0	2	4	6	8	10	(17) I handle challenge and confrontation without being irritated,

_____ (18) and can question and criticize others without discouraging or putting them down.

_____ (19) I organize and contribute to meetings effectively.

_____ (20) I accept others as being different and potentially compatible.

_____ (21) I have no difficulty in assuming an active and leading role without becoming dominant.

_____ (22) I remain 'cool' under pressure in emergencies.

0 2 4 6 8 10

Appendix 9

Giving Feedback about Interpersonal Skills

This questionnaire is meant to help you formulate the *impressions* you have about the interpersonal skills of your colleague Mr/Mrs ....

Do not guess what his/her personality is or what his/her intentions might be.

Think of the impressions he/she made on you in actual situations; he/she will get most benefit from your feedback if you can mention the occasions objectively as if these had been filmed or recorded. The clarifications and the discussion with him/her are more important than the scores.

Be as generous with favourable impressions as with less favourable ones, do not hesitate to mark him/her low or high.

Low					High	
0	2	4	6	8	10	(1) Taking the initiative in making contacts.
						(2) Being a good face-to-face communicator,
						(3) and listening well.
						(4) Writing clear and concise notes and reports.
						(5) Getting things done with/through others.
						(6) They accept his influence based on his
						order (position)
						expertise (experience)
						reasoning (argument)
						personality (likeability)
						(7) Understanding and accepting himself.
						(8) Giving and receiving information voluntarily.
						(9) Willing to let himself be known.
						(10) Being able to 'stand fools around'.
						(11) Acknowledging contributions of others and supporting their ideas/proposals.
						(12) Being able to say *'no'* and explain why.
						(13) Taking comments about his behaviour seriously without becoming defensive.
						(14) Giving advice/feedback to others such that it is accepted/appreciated.
						(15) Being able to laugh about himself.

222

```
Low                High
0   2   4   6   8   10   (16) Delegating, giving mandate, putting trust in others.
_____ (17) Handling challenge and confrontation without
                              being irritated.
_____ (18) Questioning and criticizing others without dis-
                              couraging or putting them down.
_____ (19) Organizing and contributing to meetings effectively.
_____ (20) Accepting others as being different and potentially
                              compatible.
_____ (21) Having no difficulty in assuming an active and
                              leading role without becoming dominant.
_____ (22) Remaining 'cool' under pressure, in emergencies.
0   2   4   6   8   10
```

Appendix 10

Personal Construct Theory

(a) *Fundamental Postulate:* A person's processes are psychologically channelized by the ways in which he anticipates events.
(b) *Construction Corollary:* A person anticipates events by construing their replications.
(c) *Individuality Corollary:* Persons differ from each other in their construction of events.
(d) *Organization Corollary:* Each person characteristically evolves, for his convenience in anticipating events, a construction system embracing ordinal relationships between constructs.
(e) *Dichotomy Corollary:* A person's construction system is composed of a finite number of dichotomous constructs.
(f) *Choice Corollary:* A person chooses for himself that alternative in a dichotomised construct through which he anticipates the greater possibility for extension and definition of his system.
(g) *Range Corollary:* A construct is convenient for the anticipation of finite range of events only.
(h) *Experience Corollary:* A person's construction system varies as he successively construes the replications of events.
(i) *Modulation Corollary:* The variation in a person's construction system is limited by the permeability of the constructs within whose ranges of convenience the variants lie.
(j) *Fragmentation Corollary:* A person may successively employ a variety of construction subsystems which are inferentially incompatible with each other.
(k) *Commonality Corollary:* To the extent that one person employs a construction of experience which is similar to that employed by another, his psychological processes are similar to those of the other person.
(l) *Sociality Corollary:* To the extent that one person construes the construction processes of another he may play a role in a social process involving the other person.

Glossary of terms

Formal aspects of constructs
Range of Convenience. A construct's range of convenience comprises all those things to which the user would find its application useful.

Focus of Convenience. A construct's focus of convenience comprises those particular things to which the user would find its application maximally useful. These are the elements upon which the construct is likely to have been formed originally.

Elements. The things or events which are abstracted by a person's use of a construct are called elements. In some systems these are called objects.

Context. The context of a construct comprises those elements among which the user ordinarily discriminates by means of the construct. It is somewhat more restricted than the range of convenience, since it refers to the circumstances in which the construct emerges for practical use, and not necessarily to all the circumstances in which a person might eventually use the construct. It is somewhat more extensive than the focus of convenience, since the construct may often appear in circumstances where its application is not optimal.

Pole. Each construct discriminates between two poles, one at each end of its dichotomy. The elements abstracted are like each other at each pole with respect to the construct and are unlike the elements at the other pole.

Contrast. The relationship between the two poles of a construct is one of contrast.

Likeness End. When referring specifically to elements at one pole of a construct, one may use the term 'likeness end' to designate that pole.

Contrast End. When referring specifically to elements at one pole of a construct, one may use the term 'contrast end' to designate the opposite pole.

Emergence. The emergent pole of a construct is that one which embraces most of the immediately perceived context.

Implicitness. The implicit pole of a construct is that one which embraces contrasting context. It contrasts with the emergent pole. Frequently the person has no available symbol or name for it; it is symbolized only implicitly by the emergent term.

Symbol. An element in the context of a construct which represents not only itself but also the construct by which it is abstracted by the user is called the construct's symbol.

Permeability. A construct is permeable if it admits newly perceived elements to its context. It is impermeable if it rejects elements on the basis of their newness.

Constructs classified according to the nature of their control over their elements

Preemptive Construct. A construct which preempts its elements for membership in its own realm exclusively is called a preemptive construct. This is the 'nothing but' type of construction — 'If this is a ball it is nothing but a ball.'

Constellatory Construct. A construct which fixes the other realm memberships of its elements is called a constellatory construct. This is stereotyped or typological thinking.

Propositional Construct. A construct which carries no implications regarding the other realm memberships of its elements is a propositional construct. This is uncontaminated construction.

General diagnostic constructs
Preverbal Constructs. A preverbal construct is one which continues to be used, even though it has no consistent word symbol. It may or may not have been devised before the client had command of speech symbolism.
Submergence. The submerged pole of a construct is the one which is less available for application to events.
Suspension. A suspended element is one which is omitted from the context of a construct as a result of revision of the client's construct system.
Level of Cognitive Awareness. The level of cognitive awareness ranges from high to low. A high-level construct is one which is readily expressed in socially effective symbols; whose alternatives are both readily accessible; which falls well within the range of convenience of the client's major constructions; and which is not suspended by its superordinating constructs.
Dilation. Dilation occurs when a person broadens his perceptual field in order to reorganize it on a more comprehensive level. It does not, in itself, include the comprehensive reconstruction of those elements.
Constriction. Constriction occurs when a person narrows his perceptual field in order to minimize apparent incompatibilities.
Comprehensive Constructs. A comprehensive construct is one which subsumes a wide variety of events.
Incidental Constructs. An incidental construct is one which subsumes a narrow variety of events.
Superordinate Constructs. A superordinate construct is one which includes another as one of the elements in its context.
Subordinate Constructs. A subordinate construct is one which is included as an element in the context of another.
Regnant Constructs. A regnant construct is a kind of superordinate construct which assigns each of its elements to a category on an all-or-none basis, as in classical logic. It tends to be non-abstractive.
Core Constructs. A core construct is one which governs the client's maintenance processes.
Peripheral Constructs. A peripheral construct is one which can be altered without serious modification of the core structure.
Tight Constructs. A tight construct is one which leads to unvarying predictions.
Loose Constructs. A loose construct is one leading to varying predictions, but which retains its identity.

Constructs relating to transition
Threat. Threat is the awareness of an imminent comprehensive change in one's core structures.
Fear. Fear is the awareness of an imminent incidental change in one's core structures.
Anxiety. Anxiety is the awareness that the events with which one is confronted lie mostly outside the range of convenience of his construct system.
Guilt. Guilt is the awareness of dislodgment of the self from one's core role structure.

Aggressiveness. Aggressiveness is the active elaboration of one's perceptual field.

Hostility. Hostility is the continued effort to extort validational evidence in favour of a type of social prediction which has already been recognized as a failure.

C-P-C Cycle. The C-P-C Cycle is a sequence of construction involving, in succession, circumspection, preemption, and control, and leading to a choice precipitating the person into a particular situation.

Impulsivity. Impulsivity is a characteristic foreshortening of the C-P-C Cycle.

Creativity Cycle. The Creativity Cycle is one which starts with loosened construction and terminates with tightened and validated construction.

Appendix 11

General Information
Planning and Co-operation Workshop

A series of off-site training activities are being held with the following objectives:

(1) To extend participants' skills of planning and co-operation under the conditions and constraints of PDO's operations.
(2) To appreciate and improve the planning activities and control procedures in the various departments and sections of PDO.
(3) To understand the advantages and disadvantages of various organizational forms (project groups, task forces, matrix organizations, committees, meetings).
(4) To increase participants' abilities to work effectively with colleagues of various nationalities and experience.
(5) To generate ideas to help participants continue to develop themselves and to improve PDO's performance when back in their jobs.

An outline of the programme is attached. The idea is to use it flexibly and keep it practical.

Each group will consist of twelve participants from different departments. This composition will hopefully generate plenty of points for discussion. Please spend some time beforehand thinking about the various subjects, for example considering the following questions:

(1) What aspects of your work are of interest to the other participants?
(2) Do you, or your section/department, apply any planning technique or practice that may be of use to others? What type of control do you need?
(3) Should we involve each other more and earlier? How could we improve on this?
(4) What are your positive or negative experiences with teams, project groups, matrix organizations, and/or meetings? What would you like to discuss with your colleagues? Any suggestions for improvement?

(5) Getting co-operation from other sections/departments is not easy without 'putting pressure on'. What is *your* most effective style of influencing colleagues?

And last but not least:

(6) What would you like to get out of this workshop for your job and for yourself?

Bert Juch

Appendix 12

The Process Model for Personal Development

The conscious tertiary process consists of learning activities grouped in 4 stages separated by 4 mental barriers. The learning results are 4 groups of skills plus a system of cognitive constructs, all of which extend into the subconscious process which connects them. Their common root is the unconscious Inner-Self, the primary process.

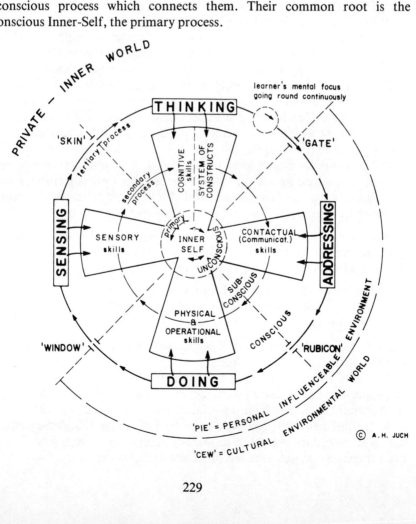

Appendix 13

The New Learning Profile Exercise

Having developed a new process model for Personal Development (see Appendix 12), it was necessary to design a new Learning Profile Exercise (LPE) to go with it. After trying out several versions, the following design was accepted:

(1) Twelve terms are used for each stage, see Appendix 14.
(2) The terms (words and expressions) have been carefully chosen from the experimental collection suggested by course participants and other authors, presented in Figures 4 and 7. Terms that were not clear at first reading or considered ambiguous by the users were deleted or changed.
(3) In the actual learning profile questionnaire, see Appendix 15, the terms are not arranged in groups that represent the four stages (as in Appendix 14), but randomly *mixed* in *three* columns. In this way the forced-choice method of assigning per set a simple 2 and 1 and 0 is easy and the test-person will not recognize the 'key'.
(4) The scores have then to be transferred to a second sheet (see Appendix 16) and added up for each stage. For some persons a pictorial kite-type diagram can be more meaningful. Plot the totals in the diagram and connect them as a kite-type profile (examples in Appendix 7).

One issue is often raised, especially by higher level staff: 'What is the question exactly referring to?' Indeed, one should adopt one out of two or three possible frames of mind when assigning the scores:

(i) deficiencies: 'This is what I learn most from'; or,
(ii) acquired abilities: 'This is the way I operate best'; or,
(iii) ideal profile: 'This is how I would like to be'.

The user has to select the frame of mind most meaningful to him. It is possible to make all three profiles of oneself.

This LPE can be used best in conjunction with questions like those of Appendix 4 and be explained by the process model for Personal Development, see Appendix 12, and with the text of Chapters 3 and 4 and page 192.

So far this new LPE has been done by more than 500 participants. The indicated procedure proved to be equally acceptable to managers, scientists, and supervisors, as well as to less numerate participants.

Appendix 14

Learning Profile:
Key to Composing Expressions

THINKING
A   creating ideas
E   rational arguments
L   thinking ahead
P   analysing problems
R   setting objectives
X   defining policies
c   discovering (aha! insight)
j   theorizing about . . .
k   reflective thinking
p   adjusting my opinions
t   analytical, logical mind
y   with my own 'head'

PLANNING
B   selling ideas
F   explaining, motivating
G   making arrangements
M   organizing events
N   working out ideas
S   negotiating projects
U   designing things
b   forecasting, programming
d   proposing, advising
g   raising expectations
r   making personal contacts
z   supervising others

DOING
C   applying ideas
J   being active, being busy
Q   realizing projects
W   making, maintaining things
Y   showing, exemplifying
a   experimenting
e   testing, trying out
l   doing, maintaining things
n   practical experience
s   implementing decisions
u   realistic, practical mind
x   doing things with my own hands

SENSING
D   listening
H   reading, studying
K   monitoring events
O   noticing the results
T   being attentive
Z   being aware, receptive
f   questioning, investigating
h   evaluating data, events
m   watching, emulating others
o   reviewing performance
q   finding facts, documentation
w   an inquiring mind

© A. H. Juch

Appendix 15
Learning Profile Questionnaire

This questionnaire is designed to *highlight* your *style* of learning, *not* to test your abilities. Therefore, there are no right or wrong answers.

Rank-order each horizontal set of expressions. First compare A, B, and C as follows: Choose the expression which *best* characterizes your present way of learning and write 2 in front of it. Then put a 0 (zero) in front of the expression or word which is *least* typical for you, and assign 1 point to the expression with in-between importance to you. Then do the same (assigning a 2, 0, and 1) for the next set D, E, and F, and so on until x, y, and z.

Keep yourself in *either* of the following frames of mind: I learn most from: (delete one)
                                                            I am most competent in:

A	creating ideas	B	'selling' ideas	C	applying ideas
D	listening, reading	E	rational arguments	F	explaining, motivating
G	making arrangements	H	reading, studying	J	being active, being busy
K	monitoring events	L	thinking ahead	M	organizing events
N	working out ideas	O	noticing results	P	analysing problems
Q	realizing projects	R	setting objectives	S	negotiating projects
T	being attentive	U	designing things	W	actually making things
X	defining policies	Y	showing, exemplifying	Z	being aware, receptive
a	experimenting	b	forecasting, programming	c	discovering (aha! insight)
d	proposing, advising	e	testing, trying-out	f	questioning, investigating
g	raising expectations	h	evaluating data, events	j	theorizing about . . .
k	reflective thinking	l	doing, maintaining things	m	watching, observing others
through n	practical experience	o	reviewing performance	p	adjusting my opinions
through q	finding facts	r	making personal contacts	s	implementing decisions
with my t	analytical, logical mind	u	realistic, practical mind	w	inquiring mind
with my x	own hands	y	own head	z	by supervising other persons

© A. H. Juch

Please transfer the assigned points to the next appendix, the 'Scoring-sheet'.

232

Appendix 16

Learning Profile Scoring Sheet

THINKING	_PLANNING_	_DOING_	_SENSING_
A	B	C	D
E	F	J	H
L	G	Q	K
R	M	W	O
P	N	Y	T
X	S	a	Z
c	U	e	f
j	b	l	h
k	d	n	m
p	g	s	o
t	r	u	q
y	z	x	w
────	────	────	────

(add up to 48)

Totals:

Plot these totals in the diagram below and connect them as a kite-profile.

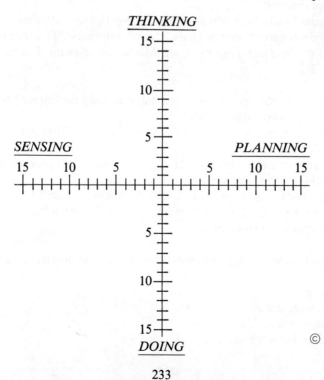

THINKING

SENSING

PLANNING

DOING

© A. H. Juch

233

Appendix 17

Planning Guide for Personal Development with/in the Organization

(Self-organized career development and improvements on the job)

A. *Priorities and Efficiency.* Most common constraint or complaint is: 'How to find the time?'. Will it be worthwhile to invest my scarce time in rethinking, planning, organizing my own career/life?

There is no more time!   TIME = PRIORITY

Actions to free time:

(1) Rethink your priorities.

(2) Review the schedules of your days, your weekly activities, your leisure time.

(3) Reduce time on . . . .

(4) Cut your losses. Set realistic targets for worthwhile activities.

(5) Maybe reorganize personal habits and indulgences. 'Time management' (books: *The Time Trap* by R. A. Mackenzie, *Getting Things Done* by E. C. Bliss).

B. *Learning.* Only effective if you know and manage your learning style (refer test and model of Appendices 12–16).

(1) Want to strengthen any particular group of skills? Thinking—Planning —Doing and/or Sensing?

(2) Talk and/or work with Mr/Ms . . . . (He/she knows, or is good at something you want to learn).

(3) Read a book, magazine, article . . . . a week/a month.

(4) Ask for feedback (how am I doing . . . . ?) from a friend, colleague, subordinate, and/or boss.

C. *Experience*: Most organizations offer plenty of opportunities to get more experience.

(1) Do more . . . .

(2) Participate in . . . .

(3) Volunteer to . . . .

(4) Stand-in for some one . . . .

234

D. *New things.* Nothing ventured is something lost.
   (1) Get information about . . . .
   (2) Ask questions more frequently . . . .
   (3) Investigate . . . .
   (4) Try out . . . .

E. *Relations.* It is impossible to do much of the above in isolation. Effective, synergetic relations at home, with friends, colleagues, boss and/or subordinates are essential so that your efforts are not frustrated but are appreciated and supported, by at least one trustful caring person.

   How good are your interpersonal skills? Take some time to work through Appendices 8 and 9.

F. *Life goals.* Last but not least. Better still: do this first. Since the importance of your interests, values, and motivations is likely to change appreciably during your lifetime, a regular (yearly) review is worthwhile.

   You may use: (Refer library and hand-outs).
   (1) Short questionnaire on job satisfaction.
   (2) Article: 'Should you manage your own career?', by C. B. Handy.
   (3) Article and 1–2 hour exercise by G. Lippitt, *Training & Developmental Journal*, June 1979.
   (4) Article 'Self-development within the organization', by A. H. Juch in *MEAD*, 10 1979.
   (5) Books by Lievegoed, Sheehy, Vaillant, Evans, etc.

The above intentions can be further specified, sharpened up, and *worked out* into an *action plan* with the field force analyses techniques.

References

Ackoff, R. L. (1974). *Redesigning the Future*, Wiley, Chichester.
Ackoff, R. L. and Emery, F. E. (1972). *On Purposeful Systems*, Tavistock, London.
Argyris, C. (1977). 'Double-loop learning in organizations', *HBR* September–October, 115–25.
Argyris, C., and Schon, D. (1974). *Theory in Practice*, Jossey-Bass, San Francisco.
Bach, R. (1973). *Jonathan Livingstone Seagull*, Pan Books, london.
Bannister, D. (ed.) (1970). *Perspectives in Personal Construct Theory*, Academic Press, London.
Bannister, D. (ed.) (1977): *New Perspective in Personal Construct Theory*, Academic Press, London.
Bannister, D., and Fransella, F. (1977). *Inquiring Man*, Penguin, Harmondsworth.
Bateson, G. (1973, 1978). *Steps to an Ecology of Mind*, Paladin, Granada St. Albans.
Bateson, G. (1979). *Mind and Nature*, Wildwood House, London.
Beck, J., and Cox, C. (eds) (1980). *Advances in Management Education*, Wiley, Chichester.
Becker, E. 61973). *The Denial of Death*. The Free Press, New York.
Beer, S. (1975). *Platform for Change*, Wiley, Chichester.
Beinum, I. L. van (1973). 'Elements and problems of the learning process', Third International Small Business Seminar, September, Zürich.
Berne, E. (1972). *What Do You Say After You Say Hello?* Bantam Books, London.
Blake, R. R., and Mouton, J. S. (1978). *The New Managerial Grid*, Gulf, Houston.
Blakeslee, T. R. (1980). *The Right Brain*, Macmillan, London.
Bonarius, J. C. J. (1979). 'Reptest interaktie techniek', Paper Pg-76-12-EX. School of Psychology, Utrecht, Holland.
Boot, R., and Boxer, Ph. (1980). 'Reflective learning', in Beck, J., and Cox, C. (eds). (1980), *Advances in Management Education*, Wiley, Chichester, pp.23–51.
Boydell, T. (1976). 'Experimential Learning', Manchester Monograph no. 5, University of Manchester.
Brakel, A. (1979). *'Equal is not equal'*, doctoral thesis in Dutch with a six-page summary in English. Erasmus Universiteit, Rotterdam, published by Krips Repro, Meppel, Holland.
Briggs, K. C., and Briggs, Myers I. (1943, 1976). 'Myers–Briggs type indicator', Form F (questionnaire) Consulting Psych. Press, Pablo Alto.
Brown, M. E. (1977). *Het Geheugen* (original title: *Memory Matters*), Elmar, Rijswijk, Holland.
Buber, M. (1943, 1971). *De Vraag Naar de Mens*, Bijleveld, Utrecht.
Burgoyne, J. G. (1975). 'Learning theories and design assumptions in management development programmes', Management Teacher Development Unit, University of Lancaster.
Burgoyne, J. G., Boydell, T., and Pedler, M. J. (1978). 'Self-development' (theory and application for practioners), ATM Occasional Paper.
Buzan, T. (1977). *Use your Head*, BBC Publication, London.

Castaneda, C. (1973). *The Lessons of Don Juan*, Simon & Schuster, New York.
Chomsky, N. (1968). *Language and Mind*, Harcourt, Brace & World, New York.
Clark, P. A. (1972). *Action Research and Organizational Change*, Harper & Row, London.
Dale, A. and Payne, R. (1976). 'Consulting interventions using structured instruments', Seminar Paper, European Institute for Advanced Studies in Management, Brussels.
Dawkins, R. (1978). *The Selfish Gene*, Paladin, Granada, St. Albans.
De Bono, E. (1976). *Practical Thinking*, Pelican, Harmondsworth.
De Bono, E. (1977). *Wordpower*, Pierrot Publishing, London
Dennett, D. C. (1979). *Brainstorms. Philosophical Essays on Mind and Psychology*, Harvester Press, Brighton.
Desatnick, R. L. and Bennett, M. L. (1977). *Human Resource Management in the Multinational Company*, Gower Press, Farnborough, UK.
Diesing, P. (1971). *Patterns of Discovery in the Social Sciences*, Routledge & Kegan Paul, London.
Ditfurth, H. V. (1976). *Der Geist kam nicht vom Himmel*, Campe Verlag, Hamburg.
Drucker, P. F. (1980). *Managing in Turbulent Times*, Heinemann, London.
Eden, C., Jones, S., and Sims, D. (1979). *Thinking in Organizations*, Macmillan, London.
Emery, F. E., and Trist, E. L. (1973, 1975). *Towards a Social Ecology*, Plenum Press, New York.
Eysenck, H. J., and Wilson, G. (1975). *Know your own Personality*, Penguin, Harmondsworth.
Evans, P., and Bartolome, F. (1980). *Must Success Cost so Much?* Grant McIntyre, London.
Festinger, L. (1964). *Conflict, Decision and Dissonance*, Tavistock, London.
Ford, G. A., and Lippitt, G. L. (1976). *Planning your Future*, University Associates, La Jolla, California.
Foy, N. (1981). *The Yin and Yang of Organizations*, Grant McIntyre, London.
Fransella, F. (ed.) (1977). *Personal Construct Psychology*, papers of Oxford seminar, The Royal Free Hospital, London.
Fransella, F., and Bannister, D. (1977). *A Manual for Repertory Grid Technique*, Academic Press, London.
Freedman, R. D., and Stumpf, S. A. (1980) 'Learning Style Theory: Less than meets the Eye', *Academy of Management Review*, **5**, no. 3, 445–7.
Freire, P. (1972). *Pedagogy of the Oppressed*, Penguin, Harmondsworth.
Freire, P., and Negt, O. (1975). In Hamman-Poldermans, *Methoden van Bewustwording*, H. Nelissen, Bloemendaal, Holland.
Friedlander, F. (1976). 'OD reaches adolescence: An exploration of its underlying values', *Journal of Applied Behavioural Science*, **12**, no. 1, 7–21.
Fromm, E. (1976, 1978). *To Have Or To Be*, Jonathan Cape, London.
Gallwey, W. T. (1974). *The Inner Game of Tennis*, Random House, New York.
Glaser, R. G., and Strauss, A. L. (1967). *The Discovery of Grounded Theory. Strategies for Qualitative Research*, Aldine Publishing, London.
Glasl, F. (ed.) (1975). *Organisatie Ontwikkeling in de Praktijk*, Elsevier, Amsterdam.
Goffman, E. (1971). *The Presentation of Self in Everyday Life*, Pelican, Harmondsworth.
Hague, H. (1979). *Helping Managers to Help Themselves*, Context, Oxford.
Hampden-Turner, C. M. (1966). 'An existential learning theory and the integration of T-group research', *JABS*, **2**, no.4.
Hampden-Turner, C. (1981). *Maps of the Mind. Charts and Concepts of the Mind and its Labyrinths*, Mitchell Beazley, London.
Harri-Augstein, E. S. (1976). *How to Become a Self-organized Learner*, Brunel University, London.

238

Harri-Augstein, E. S. (1978). *Learning to Learn. Conversational Uses of Grids*, Brunel University, London.

Harris, Th. A. (1973). *I am OK — You are OK*, Pan Books, London.

Harrison, R., and Hopkins, R. L. (1966). *The Design of Cross-cultural Learning* (with examples from the Peace Corps). NTL, Washington DC.

Herman, S. M., and Korenich, M. (1977). *Authentic Management* (a gestalt orientation to organizations and their development), Addison-Wesley, Reading, Mass.

Higgin, G. (1973) *Systems of Tomorrow*, Plume Press, London.

Hinkle, D. N. (1970). 'The game of personal constructs', in Bannister, D., *Perspectives in Personal Construct Theory*, Academic Press, London.

Hofstadter, D. R. (1979). *Gödel, Escher, Bach*, Harvester Press, Brighton.

Holland, R. (1970). 'Constructive innocent and reluctant existentialist', in Bannister, D., *Perspectives in Personal Construct Theory*, Academic Press, London.

Holland, R. (1977). *Self and Social Context*, Macmillan, London.

Hunts, S. and Hilton, J. (1973). *Individual Development and Social Experience*, George Allen & Unwin, London.

Hutton, G. (1969, 1972). *Thinking about Organizations*, Tavistock, London.

Hutton, G. (1972). 'Assertions, barriers and objects', *Journal Theory of Social Behaviour*, **2**, 1, 83–98.

Hutton, G. (1978). 'Thinking about systems, ideas and action', WP 78/12 CSOCD, University of Bath.

Jacobi, J. (1953). *Psychological Reflections* (an anthology of Jung), Pantheon Books, New York.

James, K. (1980). 'Development of senior managers', in Beck, J. and Cox, C. (eds), *Advances in Management Education*, Wiley, Chichester.

Juch, A. H. (1978). 'Some trends and developments in society. How organizations can interact', Symposium papers, School of Management, University of Bath.

Juch, A. H. (1979). 'Self-development within the organization', *MEAD*, **10**, no.1, 37–53.

Jung, C. G. (1958). *The Undiscovered Self*, Routledge & Kegan Paul, London.

Kelly, G. A. (1955). *The Psychology of Personal Constructs*, Vols 1 and 2, W. W. Norton, New York.

Kelly, G. A. (1963). *A Theory of Personality*, W. W. Norton, New York.

Kelly, G. A. (1970). In Bannister, DC. (ed.) *Perspectives in Personal Construct Theory*, Academic Press, London.

Kepner, C. H., and Tregoe, B. B. (1965). *The Rational Manager*, McGraw-Hill, New York.

Kesey, K. (1973). *One Flew Over the Cuckoo's Nest*, Pan Books, London.

Koestler, A. (1975). *The Ghost in the Machine*, Picador, Pan Books, London.

Koestler, A. (1978). *Janus*, Hutchinson, London (also Pan Books).

Kolb, D. A. (1976). *Learning Style Inventory. Technical Manual*, McBer & Company, Boston.

Kolb, D. A. (1979). 'Student learning styles and disciplinary learning environments: Diverse pathways to growth', in Chickering (ed.) *The Future American College*, Jossey-Bass, San Francisco.

Kolb, D. A., Rubin, K. M., and McIntyre, J. M. (1971). *Organizational Psychology. An Experiential Approach* (a workbook), Prentice-Hall, Englewood Cliffs, NJ.

Kolb, D. A., Rubin, I. M., and McIntyre, J. M. (1971, 1974). *Organizational Psychology. A Book of Reading*, Prentice-Hall, Englewood Cliffs, NJ.

Kolb, D. A., and Wolfe, D. M. (1977). 'Professional education and career development in social work and engineering: A cross-sectional study of adaptive competencies in experiential learning', National Institute of Education, New York.

Kuhn, T. S. (1962, 1970). *The Structure of Scientific Revolutions*, University of Chicago Press.

Laurence, P. R., and Lorsch, J. W. (1969). *Developing Organizations*, Harvard University Press.

Lievegoed, B. (1973). *The Developing Organization*, Tavistock, London.

Lievegoed, B. (1979). *Phases, Crises and Development in the Individual*, Rudolf Steiner Press, London.

Lindgren, H. G., and Fisk, L. W. (1976). *Psychology of Personal Development*, Wiley, Chichester.

Lippitt, G. L. (1979). 'Developing life plans', *Training & Development Journal*, June, 102–8.

Loevinger, J. (1978). 'Ego states', in Pfeiffer, J. W., and Jones, J. E. *The 1978 Annual Handbook for Group Facilitators*, University Associates, La Jolla, California, pp.192–204.

Mangham, I. L. (1978). *Interactions and Inventions in Organizations*, Wiley, Chichester.

Manpower Services Commission (no date) 'Training of Trainers. Voluntary Registration Scheme', DTT, London.

Margerison, C. J., Lewis, R., and Hilbert, C. (1978). 'Training implications of work preferences', *JEIT*, **2**, no. 3, 2–5.

Marshall, J., and Cooper, C. L. *Coping with Stress at Work*, Gower Publishing Comp., Aldershot, U.K.

Maslow, A. H. (1972). *The Further Reaches of Human Nature*, Viking Press, New York.

Midgley, M. (1978). *Beast and Man*, Harvester Press, Brighton.

Morris, D. (1967). *The Naked Ape*, Jonathan Cape, London.

Morris, D. (1978). *Manwatching*, Triad/Panther Books, London.

Morris, J. (1980). 'Joint development activities: from practice to theory', in Beck, J., and Cox, C. (eds), *Advances in Management Education*, Wiley, Chichester, pp.92–121.

Muller, H. (1970). 'The search for the qualities essential to advancement in a large industrial group', Dissertation, University of Utrecht, Holland.

Muller, H. (1971). 'The search for the qualities essential to advancement in Shell', unpublished internal Shell paper.

Murphy, A. (1977). 'Management training and personal construct theory', Paper of 2nd International Congress on Personal Construct Psychology, Oxford, July.

Ornstein, R. E. (1972). *The Psychology of Consciousness*, Penguin, Harmondsworth.

Osgood, C. E., Suci, G. J., and Tannenbaum, P. (1957, 1965). *The Measurement of Meaning*. (semantic differentiation), University of Illinois Press.

Pedler, M., and Boydell, T. (1980). 'Is all management development self-development?', in Beck, J., and Cox, C. (eds), *Advances in Management Education*, Wiley, Chichester, pp.165–96.

Pedler, M., Burgoyne, J., and Boydell, T. (1978). *A Manager's Guide to Self-development*, McGraw-Hill, New York.

Pfeiffer, J. W., and Jones, J. E. (1974). *Handbook, of Structured Experiences for Human Relations Training*, vol. 1 revised, University Associates, La Jolla, California.

Pfeiffer, J. W., and Jones, J. E. (1978). *The 1978 Annual Handbook for Group Facilitators*, University Associates, La Jolla, California.

Phillips, D. L. (1973). *Abandoning Method*, Jossey-Bass, London.

Pirsig, R. M. (1974). *Zen and the Art of Motorcycle Maintenance*, Bantam Books, London.

Postle, D. (1980). *Catastrophe Theory. Predict and Avoid Personal Disasters*, Fontana, London.

Rackham, N., Honey, P., and Colbert, M. (1971). *Developing Interactive Skills*, Wellens Publishing, England.

240

Ramsden, P. (1976). *Top-team Planning. A Study of the Power of Individual Motivation in Management*, Wiley, Chichester.

Reason, P. (1977). 'Human interaction as exchange and as encounter: a dialectical exploration', WP 77/07 CSOCD, University of Bath.

Reason, P. (1978). 'Exploration in the development of social praxis: ideas for a programme of research', WP 78/06 CSOCD, University of Bath.

Restak, R. M. (1979). *The Brain. The Last Frontier*, Warner Books, New York.

Revans, R. W. (1971). *Developing Effective Managers*, Praeger, New York.

Robinson, A. D. (1980). 'How can intuition help trainers?' *Training and Development Journal*, **34**, no.2, February.

Rogers, C. (1969). *Freedom to Learn*, Merrill Publishing, Columbus, Ohio.

Rogers, C. R. (1970). *Encounter Groups*, Pelican, Harmondsworth.

Rose, S. (1976). *The Conscious Brain*, Penguin, Harmondsworth.

Sagan, C. (1977). *The Dragons of Eden. Speculations on the Evolution of Human Intelligence*, Hodder & Stoughton, London.

Schultz, D. (1977) *Growth Psychology. Models of the Healthy Personality*, Van Nostrand, New York.

Schumacher, E. G. (1978). *A Guide for the Perplexed*, Abacus edition, Sphere Books, London.

Scientific American (1979). Special Brain Issue, **241**, no. 3, September.

Sheehy, G. (1974, 1976). *Passages. Predictable Crises of Adult Life*, Dutton, New York.

Skinner, B. G. (1971). *Beyond Freedom and Dignity*, Pelican, Harmondsworth.

Stewart, R. (1978). *Frameworks for analysing the opportunities for choice in managerial jobs*, MRP 78/4 and 78/15, Oxford Centre for Management studies, Oxford, UK.

Thom, R. (1975). *Structural Stability and Morphogenesis*, Benjamin, Mass., USA.

Thomas, L. F. (1977). *A Personal Construct Approach to Learning in Education, Training and Therapy*, Brunel University, London.

Toffler, A. (1980). *The Third Wave*, Collins, London.

Torbert, W. R. (1977). 'Why educational research has been so uneducational', APA Symposium: Reconceptualization of Research.

Torbert, W. R. (1978). 'Educating towards shared purpose, self-direction and quality work. The theory and practice of liberating structure', *Journal of Higher Education*, **49**, no. 2, 109–35.

Vaillant, G. E. (1977). *Adaptation to life*. Little, Brown, Boston.

Valk, J. M. M. de (1977). 'Tegenstrijdigheden in de samenleving', Informatief no. 16 SMO, Scheveningen, Holland.

Watzlawick, P., Beavin, J. H., and Jackson, D. D. (1967, 1974). *Pragmatics of Human Communications*, Norton, New York. (Dutch version was used, published by Van Loghum Slaterus, Deventer, Holland.)

Watzlawick, P. (1978). *Wie Weet is het ook Anders*, Van Loghum Slaterus, Deventer, Holland.

Zijderveld, A. C. (1975). *De Theorie van het Symbolisch Interactionisme*, Boom, Meppel, Holland.

Name Index

Subject Index

244